More Praise for Jonathan Abrams's

"Lovers of HBO's *The Wire* rejoice: journalist Abrams delivers a comprehensive study of what goes into creating an acclaimed TV show. Abrams indisputably has created a thorough examination of *The Wire*'s conception, production, and lingering cultural afterlife."

—*Publishers Weekly*

"*The Wire* has thoroughly saturated popular culture in a way few television dramas ever have. In their own words, the people involved have given Jonathan Abrams a look at how it happened. You come at a show like this, you best not miss. Abrams doesn't."

—Charles P. Pierce, author of *Idiot America*

"Meticulous. Relentless. Occasionally hilarious. The same adjectives you'd use to describe *The Wire* can also be applied to Jonathan Abrams's essential oral history of the series. As it turns out, the most humanistic drama in television history was itself rife with compelling characters, complex politics, and an excess of whiskey. Abrams tracks down the stories behind every beloved episode with the tenacity of Omar shopping for breakfast cereal."

—Andy Greenwald, host of *The Watch* and *Talk the Thrones*

"Delves deep into the show's creation and enduring legacy through interviews with the actors, writers, and producers who brought the show to life. Whether it's Dominic West reflecting on the allure of his character Detective James McNulty or actor Michael B. Jordan discussing the lasting impression of being in an ensemble cast of primarily black actors, Abrams underscores the indelible mark the show has left on actors and audience alike. Weaving all the interviews together is the enduring connection between the city of Baltimore and the creators of the show."

—*Library Journal*

"*All the Pieces Matter* will enrich first watches of *The Wire*, re-watches of *The Wire*, and even occasional watches of key scenes from *The Wire* on YouTube. It's an amazing companion to the series, no matter your level of familiarity."

—Todd VanDerWerff, critic at large for *Vox*

"Filled with revealing information from the participants, intriguing tidbits, and show trivia, this compendium will have fans scurrying back to their DVD sets."

—*Kirkus Reviews*

"Excellent . . . renders the making of *The Wire* in enough rich detail to please even its most ardent fans."

—*Paste*

CH

ALL THE PIECES MATTER

THE INSIDE STORY OF

THE WIRE®

JONATHAN ABRAMS

THREE RIVERS PRESS

NEW YORK

MAR 19

For Danielle and Michelle,

big sisters who unfortunately knew how to put their

little brother in his place

Originally published in hardcover in the United States by
Crown Archetype, an imprint of the Crown Publishing Group,
a division of Penguin Random House LLC, New York, in 2018.

Library of Congress Cataloging-in-Publication Data is available upon request.

ISBN 978-0-451-49815-1
Ebook ISBN 978-0-451-49816-8

Printed in the United States of America

10 9 8 7 6 5 4 3 2 1

First Paperback Edition

Author's Note

This book is not an episode-by-episode companion of *The Wire*—though the pages *are* filled with spoilers—but, rather, an oral history that hopefully provides an illuminating retrospective from the creators, actors, and others involved in its making. No one anticipated that the show would experience the enduring afterlife it has, but many at the time realized they were working on a project of precision and purpose.

I tried interviewing as many people involved with the show as possible for this book because—what's the saying?—all the pieces matter. Thankfully, nearly everyone happily obliged.

In the interest of streamlining memories and anecdotes, I've removed many of the hitches that we all use in speech ("you know," "um," and "like"). Those occasions are rare, though, and I believe the spirit and meaning of every conversation is preserved. Each quote from an actor is offered with his or her character's name and occupation. Some of the characters' job titles changed as the show advanced; for example, Councilman Tommy Carcetti became Mayor Carcetti. In those instances, the characters are introduced with the job titles for which they are most well known.

The positions of those behind the camera are also listed with their quotes. Some people held multiple roles, moved up ranks, or changed jobs as the show aged. For example, Anthony Hemingway began as an assistant director before directing episodes in the show's later run. In the case of those behind the scenes, the person is listed with his or her most prominent job title.

Contents

Preface

Wendell Pierce addressed an expectant audience at Columbia University. The eager crowd had filed inside Cowin Auditorium in April 2016, ignoring a bitter New York City day that stubbornly refused to recognize winter's end. Pierce sat inside, surrounded by some of his contemporaries from *The Wire*, including Jamie Hector (Marlo Stanfield), Sonja Sohn (Det. Kima Greggs), and Felicia "Snoop" Pearson. The background of the actors reflected the sizable range of those who appeared in the trailblazing HBO show. Pierce is New Orleans through and through. Yet he was no stranger to New York, having attended the Juilliard School's Drama Division. In *The Wire*, he depicted William "Bunk" Moreland, a dedicated, competent detective who struggled to balance his work and his personal life. Pierce discussed his experience of sharing scenes with Pearson, who played an androgynous killer and had never acted prior to *The Wire*. "The first night Snoop came onto the set, Snoop sat in the director's chair with David [Simon] on one side, Ed [Burns] on the other," Pierce recalled. "She's trying to be cool. I'll never forget, there was a shootout scene and she said, 'Motherfuckers don't shoot like that.' I thought it was great, and it shows you how you take your personal experience and bring it to the show. If you're gonna be authentic, you've gotta be authentic."

Pearson laughed with a husky rasp, relaying another story from one of her nascent days on set, when an assistant director cautioned that she shot the prop guns with too much accuracy. "Snoop is an amazing woman," Pierce continued. "You hear that profile and then you engage with this charming, talented, incredible person, and it's this cautionary tale that she's allowed herself to be onstage. Understand that you may never look at any kid who may be going down that wrong path as anything other than a full, loving human being and if you want to change that course, embrace that before you embrace any idea of ignorance or negativity. Understand that there's that humanity there, and she's a living example of why the show tapped into people's psyches and why the show has created an examination of policy, an examination of the influence of art changing people's lives in a practical way at universities across the nation. You didn't see no damn show about Gilligan. These are people's lives and the examination of the dysfunction in our American culture that was on display in *The Wire* has changed people's lives."

From its deliberate pacing to its desolate portrayal of Baltimore's blight and all points in between, *The Wire* strove for realism. Those earnest efforts confused many during the show's sixty-episode life span from 2002 to 2008. HBO had produced groundbreaking, original television prior to *The Wire*, with shows such as *Oz* and *The Sopranos*. *The Wire* was something different, though. Its creator, David Simon, originally frowned upon the entertainment business. He envisioned the television show as a novel, with the postmodern institutions of Baltimore representative of Greek gods. The show plopped the viewer into the middle of a vast universe without an explanatory guide. The plot was complicated, and the dialogue may as well have been in another language. The series shifted focus each season. Too many characters lived in its space, and Simon brought forth no obvious heroes. Few watched the show when it aired. Award voters mostly ignored it. *The Wire* faced cancellation almost annually. "First, we thought it was a silo, because people weren't watching the show when it was on," Pierce told the crowd. "We thought we were doing a good show. But it was really in a silo and it wasn't until maybe the third year when we were coming back and noticed, 'Hey, people are starting to check on the show.'"

No show has aged as gracefully. *The Wire* stood the test of time after only intermittently being acknowledged while on air. "How many shows are being taught?" said Darrell Britt-Gibson, who played Darius "O-Dog" Hill. "That's its impact. It's left a lasting impression on the culture, and hopefully it continues to do so with the next generation and the generation after that. It's a timeless piece of art." The panel at Columbia University took place as part of a weekend conference on *The Wire*. Academics and professors convened, hosting panels that discussed the fictional show's various real-life intersections of subjects such as mass incarceration, narrative journalism, and religion and politics in the inner city. Columbia University is not the only college to host discussions on the show—or even the lone Ivy League school, for that matter. Yale and Harvard are among the many universities that have featured conferences or classes that examine the show's enduring impact. "I actually went to a university to speak about *The Wire* in Utah," said Seth Gilliam, who portrayed Sgt. Ellis Carver. "I talked to kids who were excited to be discussing the subject matter that *The Wire* brought up. I don't know a lot of cop shows that have this far-reaching impact almost a generation later." *The Wire* simultaneously exposed America's sores and, somewhat accidentally, evolved television.

AN ARGUMENT OF DISSENT

Who the fuck is this guy? Ed Burns thought after David Simon introduced himself in the winter of 1984. The moment would mark the beginning of a collaboration neither could have foreseen, one that would mature into a groundbreaking book and culminate in a revolutionary television show. But first impressions? Burns joked—well, partly anyway—that he hoped to arrest Simon. Somehow, Simon had finagled his way beyond security and into the Drug Enforcement Administration offices as Burns readied material for a grand jury preparing to bring an indictment against Melvin "Little" Williams, a disciplined drug trafficker who had successfully flummoxed Baltimore law enforcement for years. Simon told Burns that he was a reporter for The Baltimore Sun and had permission to follow the case. Burns and his partner, Harry Edgerton, both Baltimore police detectives, had finally pinned the elusive Williams through the use of a wiretap. Simon expressed interest in being able to listen in on the wire. "I'd love to take you in there, but if I do, that's a ten-year offense and I'd love to lock you up," Burns said. He stiff-armed Simon's request, but agreed to meet with him later to discuss the case.

Who the fuck is this guy? David Simon thought after meeting Burns a second time. Not much time had passed when they greeted one another at the Baltimore County Public Library branch in Towson. Simon had already surmised that Burns did not behave like any typical detective he had come across. He now eyeballed the book titles Burns prepared to check out, Bob Woodward's Veil: Secret Wars of the CIA and The Magus, by John Fowles, among them. "I read all the time, and it impressed him," Burns recalled. "I don't think David reads anywhere near as much as I do, but a cop reads? My God. I know a lot of cops who read. It was no big deal, but David was a good guy and he had a passion."

That passion unfurled into the canvassing five-part series that Simon wrote on the making and inner workings of Williams as a Baltimore drug trafficker kingpin. For Simon, his life's purpose had been achieved by working at a newspaper. His father, Bernard, had once been a journalist who devoted the bulk of his working days as a public relations director for B'nai B'rith, the oldest Jewish service organization in the world. His mother, Dorothy, spent time working for an organization that aided students from underachieving public schools to find better education. Simon attended the University of Maryland, where he wrote for the student newspaper, The Diamondback. He joined the Sun after graduating, reporting on crime. To him, being a newspaperman and bringing accountability to influencers meant something. "I grew up in a house where we argued politics," Simon recounted. "We argued sociology. We argued culture. We argued. It was not personal. Arguing was how you got attention in my family." One of Simon's enduring memories is debating politics with his two uncles as a boy, the moment climaxing with him flatly telling his uncle Hank that he was in the wrong. "Who knew he had a brain?" Uncle Hank retorted.

Reading Simon's 1987 Sun series, entitled " 'Easy Money': Anatomy of a Drug Empire," is akin to viewing the organs of The Wire's first-season wiretap investigation. Williams was a self-made entrepreneur who imported the bulk of Baltimore's heroin influx as the city's honest economic opportunities shifted and dwindled. "An imperious, intelligent man who chooses words with care," Simon described "Melvin Williams refuses to be stereotyped. Street sales of narcotics were routinely punctuated by murderous violence, but Williams was a family man, devoted to an eleven-year marriage and two young daughters."

Williams conducted most of his business through his number two, a consigliere named Lamont "Chin" Farmer. Farmer orchestrated both a simple and intricate communication system involving the use of beepers. He also headed a print shop and took business courses at a community college, à la Idris Elba's Stringer Bell.

Simon's series meticulously captured Williams's life and downfall—not only as a drug kingpin, but also as a respected figure in the community, where, as Simon wrote, "he was hailed as Little Melvin, the Citizen, speaking at the request of National Guard officials during the 1968 riots, urging a restless crowd to go home." Burns appreciated that Simon showed all facets of the case and offered a depiction of Williams that was beyond a caricature. "When the case came down, he wrote a very good article because he went out and saw some of the gangsters and it was a most balanced article," Burns said. "I liked that."

Simon spent Christmas Eve 1986 on an overnight shift with the Baltimore Police Department Homicide Unit for another story shortly before the series on Williams debuted. During that night, a detective mentioned that someone could write a damn good book if they documented the department's happenings for a year. With the permission of Police Commissioner Edward Tilghman, Simon gained complete access to be a fly on the wall with the unit, despite the objections of some of the department's personnel. "A captain had a vote," said Jay Landsman, then a homicide detective sergeant, who also lent his name and acting abilities to The Wire. "He took a poll of who wanted to do it and who didn't. Twenty-eight out of thirty of us, including myself, voted against it. We worked murders in the ghetto. You lived in a gray area with that. It doesn't always look pretty. Everything we did was legal, but it was kind of how were they going to interpret it? So, naturally, since they had a democratic election and we all voted against it, they gave him the go-ahead."

Simon took a leave from The Baltimore Sun, becoming a "police intern" in January 1988. Members of the department playfully hazed him until he proved game for the task. He gained enough insight into the minds of the squad members that some later acknowledged that he had accurately captured words and feelings they had never verbally expressed. Houghton Mifflin published Homicide: A Year on the Killing Streets in June 1991. The book, like the series on Williams, is peppered with scenes later extracted for The Wire. In it, Simon provides a penetrating portrait of how the detectives attempted to unravel murder cases and the humanistic toll it took on them. "It was daily that we told him if he printed anything we didn't like, we would kill him," Landsman said. "But he grinned at everything. As it turns out, we weren't as bad as we thought we would be portrayed by David."

Ed Burns, working another prolonged investigation, scarcely figured into the book. He was already grappling with the limits of how little one outside-the-box thinker could influence a lurching institution. "We were like family," Landsman said. "But [Burns] was the biggest pain in the ass in the world. He once said everybody in police should have a bachelor's or master's degree. I said, 'Then we'd all be like you. That would be hell, because you're an asshole.' It was all in fun, but he played to his own drummer. When you really needed something done, you had to just put your foot down on it. But he was tenacious as hell, a little bit gullible. Like that informant Bubbles that he had. I wouldn't believe Bubbles as far as I could throw him. A broken clock is right at least twice a day, and I guess that's the two times he gave Burns good information."

Burns left the police force, having knocked his head against his superiors for much of his two decades as a patrolman, plainclothesman, and detective. He was about to start his new life as a middle school teacher when Simon proposed a collaboration. Simon's book editor, John Sterling, suggested that the proper follow-up to Homicide would be observing a drug corner in Baltimore for a year and depicting the story's previously undocumented other side of addicts. Burns agreed to contribute, and the two settled on the intersection of West Baltimore's Fayette and Monroe. For weeks, Burns spent his days gaining the confidence of dealers and users, while Simon worked at the newspaper before taking a second leave. "The badge can get you under that yellow tape, but it can't get you into their shooting galleries and places like that," Burns said. "I could sit down on the third floor of a shooting gallery with five or six guys pumping all around me, a prostitute working out in the bed over there, and have a conversation. Every once in a while, they take the syringe off [from behind] their ear, get a little hit, put it back on, and it would be a conversation where you knew that these people were aware of what was going on and how they had been sucked into this trap." As he had in Homicide, Simon displayed a perceptive ear in deciphering the corner's dialogue. He had to learn the appropriate jokes to laugh at, when to show concern, when to blend in, or when to pop up with a question. Homicide was heavily saturated with cop jargon—a red ball, a whodunit, dunkers. The Corner: A Year in the Life of an Inner-City Neighborhood was published in 1997 and introduced the reader to a new vocabulary, with words such as testers, the snake, and speedballs. The piercing narrative focused on the McCullough family and their efforts to function as a unit even as they dealt with the toll drugs extracted from them. Gary McCullough, the father, had been a businessman who fell into the throes of addiction once his marriage to Fran Boyd crumbled. Boyd, also addicted to drugs at the time, still tried mapping a better life for her sons. They included DeAndre McCullough, who, at the age of fifteen, had already begun peddling drugs. (DeAndre would go on to work on the set of The Wire and portray Lamar, Brother Mouzone's dim associate, before his death at the age of thirty-five in 2012.) Some, including a few inside The Baltimore Sun, accused Simon of ennobling and romanticizing drug dealers and users. In truth, the book offered a voice to those who had been left behind as forgotten casualties of the war on drugs.

Simon originally did not think much of the deal when the Baltimore-born director Barry Levinson bought the rights to Homicide and plotted to develop it into a TV show for NBC. Simon passed on an offer to write the show's pilot—he just hoped that a television show would help sell a few more copies of the book. He accepted a subsequent offer from showrunner Tom Fontana to write another episode and teamed with his college friend David Mills to author an episode that would premiere the show's second season in 1994. The episode, titled "Bop Gun," guest-starred Robin Williams and won a Writers Guild of America Award for Best Screenplay of an Episodic Drama. The experience left Simon unsated. Only half of what he and Mills had written, Simon estimated, prevailed in the final script. While Mills departed for Hollywood soon after, Simon returned to the newspaper, satisfied to spend the rest of his working days arguing with his feet up and bumming cigarettes off younger reporters. But the paper, his paper, started feeling more unfamiliar. It had been purchased in 1986 by the Times Mirror Company. Buyouts cut into the depth and experience of the newsroom. Simon felt that the new top editors placed an unwarranted emphasis on claiming journalism prizes rather than covering the mundane issues plaguing Baltimore.

Simon accepted a buyout, jumping full time to the staff of Homicide. Under Fontana and producer/writer James Yoshimura, he learned how to transfer his journalistic skills into writing for television. It was Fontana who mentored Simon, telling him that a writer becomes a producer in order to protect his words. Some of the cast and crew dreaded whenever Simon arrived on set. They knew they would be pelted with questions, and they tried avoiding eye contact with him. "It was questions with wardrobe," said Jeffrey Pratt Gordon, who worked in the art department of Homicide before acting as Johnny "Fifty" Spamanto in The Wire's Season 2. "It was questions with the cinematographer. He was asking everybody questions, and a lot of the times that he asked the questions is right when we're sort of in the middle of doing stuff. What's this guy poking around for? What's this guy always asking questions about?" It was only years later that he surmised Simon had been educating himself in every aspect of filmmaking. Still, television did not entirely appeal to Simon. He had left the newspaper but remained an arguer, one ready to rail against the status quo. The Washington Post tried hiring him, and he mulled over the offer. It was not until Fontana showed him something else that he had been working on, a pilot for a prison drama shot for HBO named Oz, that Simon visualized television as a worthwhile megaphone. Oz painted a grim world where the initial concerns would not consist of who won and who lost or cleanly separate the bad guys from the good guys. Simon contemplated whether something like The Corner could be adapted for television. Through Fontana, he gained an audience with HBO. He pitched them on what would have been The Wire, telling

Burns, "If HBO's interested in this world, we could write a fictional show." The HBO executives Chris Albrecht, Anne Thomopoulos, and Kary Antholis looked at one another. "Just do the book," Antholis said. "Just do the characters in the book. You have six hours. It's a miniseries." HBO, Simon thought, would need a black writer associated with the project. He floated the possibility of attaching David Mills. The name appealed to the executives but left no place for Burns. Instead, Simon asked Burns to begin outlining the fictionalized world. "I didn't like what happened because David was not forthcoming," Burns said. "He believed he needed a black writer on the show. They wanted me to do another script as if there was going to be seven episodes instead of the six, which was totally not going to happen. They took me out to a restaurant and they fumbled through this, 'We were thinking about this and that,' and I'm thinking to myself, You guys, there would be no Corner, because David wasn't going to go out there by himself. I was more than happy to go out because I liked the experience. I liked to do things like that. David waited until it was safe to go out."

The decision to commit to The Corner, recalled Chris Albrecht, HBO's chairman and CEO, came down to a choice between Simon's project or an adaptation of Taylor Branch's work on the civil rights movement. He took scripts from both on a cross-country plane ride. Albrecht opened The Corner first. Oh man, that's so depressing, he thought. No one is going to want to watch this. He picked up Branch's scripts. He found them entertaining, but his mind wandered back to The Corner, wondering what would happen next. He picked it up again and sifted through the next few pages. This is too intense, he thought. It's just so intense and so raw. The same scenario played out a few more times. As worthwhile as the Taylor Branch project was, anybody could do that, he finally decided. Only HBO could do The Corner.

The gamble paid off. With Charles "Roc" Dutton directing the six episodes, the miniseries aired in 2000 and received critical acclaim, four Emmy nominations, and a Peabody Award. "Assuming the perspective of its characters, the series avoids clichés and condescension; the performances are remarkably free of the cheap mannerisms actors *often resort to when playing addicts," a* New York Times *review of the miniseries stated. "But the insiders' view is still undermined by the tone of a cautionary tale. The fact that the series makes a plea to understand the characters' humanity, rather than a judgment about them, doesn't make it less didactic." Seeds had been planted. Simon possessed juice with HBO. He pivoted to pitching his next project. "I couldn't bring Ed [Burns] on* The Corner," *Simon explained. "I had to bring Dave Mills, and I was happy to work with Dave Mills, but I felt bad for Ed. I said to Ed, 'This is what* The Corner's *going to be. Maybe we'll have a shot doing something bigger if* The Corner *turns out okay.' And sure enough, after* The Corner *was completed, but not yet broadcast, they turned to me and said, 'That turned out really good. Do you have anything more?'"*

"As a matter of fact . . ." Simon replied.

It still took convincing for The Wire *to get off the ground, though. HBO had started making its mark with original programming through shows such as* Oz, The Sopranos, *and* Sex and the City. *HBO had wisely left cop shows that opened and closed cases within the confines of an hour for the networks. "The journey through this one case will ultimately bring viewers from wondering, in cop-show expectation, whether the bad guys will get caught, to wondering instead who the bad guys are and whether catching them means anything at all," Simon wrote in a memo to Albrecht and Carolyn Strauss, the president of HBO's entertainment division, in June 2001. Strauss purchased the pilot and asked for the scripts of two additional episodes before finally greenlighting the project.*

DAVID SIMON (CREATOR): I covered [the Williams case], so I had it in my head, and I did those articles, and that's how I met Ed Burns. We had it in our heads. There was something unsatisfying about the case, because once they got Melvin [Williams] a lot of years, the two prosecutors who were on that case, actually in real life, they both were promoted off. They were the two guys who were going to bring the wiretap case into court.

The wiretap case never went forward. They did the raids. They made them push up the raids, so they could put some dope on the table. They weren't similar in scope or history or anything, but Melvin was similar as an avatar to Avon [Barksdale]. And Stringer [Bell] was Lamont "Chin" Farmer. Chin only got seven years federal back when there was parole. So, Chin went and did two or three years and was out and Chin was really the mastermind. Chin was like command central and [Williams's lieutenant Louis] "Cookie" Savage got like twenty. They all got it over separate charges, but they never did the overall conspiracy case because the prosecutors had been promoted out of it.

So, the whole elaborate case Ed had, really elaborate—it involved the codes and beepers and all that—it never got presented properly. Ed knew more about it than had ever been explained or that I could even do in the articles. It was a lot of fun to construct that, and at the same time, also using the sense that Ed had at the end of that case, which was, *we did not give Chin enough time.* Chin's coming back, man. Seven years. Ed looked upon who was responsible for moving that level of drugs, with that much scope, and Melvin got plenty of time and Cookie got a significant sentence, but Chin was the guy who they just sort of glanced at. That's sort of written into the ending [of Season One], where they leave Stringer on the street.

That seemed the right tonality for the show, the idea that for all of the elaborate police work, it just doesn't matter. The critique of the drug war was everything can be replaced. Everything is endless. The dysfunction of this thing goes on.

ED BURNS (CO-CREATOR): I said I'd help him. I was teaching then, and I stayed teaching for the first year. I would just come in and work on the story with him. Then, I thought, *You've been a cop and a teacher. I wrote* The Corner *and I got twelve dollars and ten cents in the bank. It's about time to cash this in.* So, I did.

CHRIS ALBRECHT (CHAIRMAN AND CEO, HBO): David [Simon] came in and said that he wanted to do the most detailed, most realistic look at a police wiretap investigation that's ever been done. When I read the first script, it was really hard to know how that was going to play itself out, because, obviously, you're not looking at the whole breakdown, the whole investigation. Since the pitch was that, then it's like, "Well, is this really what we're going to get?"

CAROLYN STRAUSS (PRESIDENT, HBO ENTERTAINMENT): This is a relationship business. You start your relationship with David [Simon] on one and then it keeps. You realize that, "Oh, this is real special." Yeah, you can watch *The Corner* and *Homicide* and go, "Oh, yeah. I like this," but then, when you start to talk to him and listen to him, you go, "This is a special guy."

ED BURNS (CO-CREATOR): We wrote together sometimes. Sometimes we did it on the phone. It wasn't difficult to create the story. The story was easy to create. The characters were composites of a lot of cops that I knew and that David knows, so that was pretty easy to make the story.

DAVID SIMON (CREATOR): Everybody has an expectation that much of American television is about redemption and about affirmation. We were trying to make a show that was basically an argument of dissent. It was political dissent. It was saying our systems are not functioning. Our policies are incorrect. We're not going to find a way out of this unless we stand back and take stock and turn one hundred eighty degrees from what we've been doing, particularly in regard to the drug war and inequality that we were depicting.

ED BURNS (CO-CREATOR): The first season was all about how difficult it was to get a wire. We used the retrograde idea of using pagers. It flowed very easily. There were a few glitches along the way, but it flowed really easily storywise. That doesn't mean it flowed easily in the writers' room, but it certainly flowed easily in the storyline.

CAROLYN STRAUSS (PRESIDENT, HBO ENTERTAINMENT): When we read the story, the document that outlined the first season, that's when we knew that it would be great. David's very capable of that kind of story with *The Corner* and *Homicide*. Here, this was just taking all that and really taking that story out.

DAVID SIMON (CREATOR): The one thing you weren't able to pull through a keyhole in *The Corner*—*The Corner* becomes six hours about this broken nuclear family and the culture of addiction, what it's like to try to live in a drug-saturated neighborhood when the drug problem is involving your family. It's a very microcosmic view of the drug culture, the drug war. You can see a straining to get anything about policy, about why this is so fucked up. Whatever little bit we could was in the interviews in the beginning and the end that [director Charles] "Roc" Dutton did. That was the only place where anybody would stand back and be asked a question about anything macro. And that was really us trying to take the arguments against the drug war that were in *The Corner* and squeeze them into a format that really didn't have any place for it.

ED BURNS (CO-CREATOR): It was set up that Baltimore would become a character. The first season, you saw two institutions, the drug institution and the police department. The same problems from mayor all the way down. I like that sort of way of looking at things.

Alexa L. Fogel originally stumbled into becoming a casting director. She knew little about casting when she worked as an assistant to the artistic director of an Off-Broadway play when the casting director abruptly left. Fogel assumed that person's duties and eventually rose to the peak of the profession, showing an adept skill for blending actors with scripts, and casting Oz for Tom Fontana. She worked with television producer Nina Noble prior to The Wire and joked, "I was probably the only casting director they knew." Yet, David Simon knew the show would be in capable hands with Fogel sifting through actors for roles. Fogel worked in conjunction with award-winning casting director Pat Moran, whom Simon has described as a "mad genius" in deftly handling Baltimore casting. Indeed, The Wire became known for its dynamic range of actors, while avoiding Hollywood's better-known stars. Many actors were recycled from recognizable series such as The Corner (Clarke Peters, Maria Broom, and Delaney Williams), Oz (J. D. Williams, Seth Gilliam, and Lance Reddick), and Homicide (Peter Gerety, Robert Chew, and Jim True-Frost). Fogel also successfully pushed for two relatively unknown British actors, Dominic West and Idris Elba, to land prominent roles in The Wire.

The characters were composites drawn from real-life inspirations and often consigned names recognizable in Baltimore lore. To muddle things up further, Jay Landsman read for the role of Jay Landsman, but did not land the part, which went to Delaney Williams. Instead, Simon eventually awarded the real Jay Landsman the role of Lt. Dennis Mello, a figure who, in real life, was the first black man to reach the rank of captain in the Baltimore Police Department. "I was honored to play Dennis Mello, the real Dennis Mello," Landsman said. "Tell me that's not acting. I'm a white guy playing a black guy. That was real acting." The casting largely split the actors into opposing groups: the Barksdale organization, headlined by Avon Barksdale (Wood Harris), Elba's Stringer Bell, D'Angelo Barksdale (Lawrence Gilliard Jr.), and Wee-Bey Brice (Hassan Johnson), versus the wayward police unit charged with building a case against it, which featured West's Jimmy McNulty, Reddick's Cedric Daniels, Clarke Peters's Lester Freamon, Kima Greggs (Sonja Sohn), and Bunk Moreland (Wendell Pierce).

Many of the show's actors remained blissfully unaware for some time that their roles had been sourced from real figures. It was months before Williams, for example, realized that a real Landsman existed. Simon preferred that the doppelgängers not meet their inspirations. "They were going to be who they were going to be and it can sometimes fuck an actor up," Simon explained. "They start embracing things that you're not writing. Better to have them be rock solid in who they think that character should be and chase that."

To solidify the show's production, Simon solicited the addition of two trusted figures in Nina Noble and Robert "Bob" Colesberry. Both had proven themselves while working with Simon on The Corner. Noble was no frills, having developed a reputation of landing a show under budget, an enviable trait in any producer. While she came recommended to Simon for The Corner, Colesberry originally arrived forcefully from HBO's Kary Antholis, who wanted to add a visual producer. Simon immediately distrusted the quiet Colesberry, concerned that he would be more meddler than anything. His opinion changed once he watched the first cuts of The Corner. Colesberry would advance to play the small recurring role of Det. Ray Cole and also to direct an episode of The Wire. "I thought back to that first meeting with Bob Colesberry and realized I did not want to put anything to film ever again without him," Simon later wrote in Rafael Alvarez's The Wire: Truth Be Told. "For something that began as a shotgun wedding, it was turning out to be quite a marriage."

DAVID SIMON (CREATOR): [Wendell Pierce] came in and just nailed [his audition]. He was really pissed off. He had gotten in an argument with a cab driver. It was one of those sort of trying-to-hail-a-cab-while-black moments in New York, and he came in and he was steaming. He was harried, like a bear who'd hit the hornet's nest. He had to focus on the scene, and he was apologizing for what he thought was a bad read, but it had that air of Baltimore—put-upon workaday—homicide detective. As soon as he came in and read, it was like, "That's our Bunk."

WENDELL PIERCE (DET. WILLIAM "BUNK" MORELAND): It was weeks later, maybe even a year later, while we were shooting, that David said, "You know, when you came in, it was not your reading that got you the part. You just came in and you were bitching and complaining about this taxi driver and that was the thing that got you the gig, because you're so much like Bunk." I was kind of indignant about it all, but in my own way, I guess. The fact that I would bring it up in the middle of a major audition shows some gumption on my part.

DAVID SIMON (CREATOR): We talked to Ray Winstone [about playing the role of Det. Jimmy McNulty]. I was not convinced, but he was very hot at the moment, and HBO wanted us just to consider Ray Winstone. So, we went to the Toronto [International] Film Festival, where he was. This was September 2001. We showed him the script, and I was concerned about the accent, that he would not be able to turn the corner. It's so East End. But I'd seen *Sexy Beast*, the movie, and I thought, *Well, the camera loves him, and he's gruff.* We left Toronto, and he was thinking about it. Then 9/11 happened, and he couldn't get home for like two weeks. The planes were all grounded. He just went straight back. He was like, "I am not." There was something traumatic about that, and we never heard from him again.

I thought John C. Reilly could be a different McNulty, certainly not the same, but I thought he could carry all of the excesses and vices of McNulty in a different way. I've loved his work in a lot of stuff. I was on the phone with him. It was three weeks before Halloween, because I was in a corn maze with my kid, Ethan, who would have been like seven, six. So, I'm trying to keep up with my kid, who's running around like a madman in this maze, and that's when John C. Reilly called me back. I really couldn't take the call. I talked to him for maybe five minutes, and I said, "Hey, listen, can I call you back? I'm in a corn maze with my kid." And he said, "Yeah, yeah. Call me back." In the time between when he called me and when I called him back, he stopped taking calls. He later told Dom [West] that his wife was like, "We are not moving to Baltimore." I never actually talked to him more than those five minutes to even talk to him about the role.

Later on, Dom was working with him on *Chicago* and they're looking at each other. They're so different, and Dom's like, "What were they going for?"

That's kind of how casting is sometimes. You go in one direction. You find out you're on the wrong track or circumstance thwarts you, and you end up going in a different direction.

DOMINIC WEST (DET. JIMMY MCNULTY): To read, I was given one scene from the pilot and nothing else, and I put myself on tape. I didn't think much of it, but it got too late in the night, and they wanted it the next day, so I got my girlfriend to read the dialogue. It was a scene between McNulty and Bunk, and she read the Bunk part and I held the camera and I did McNulty. She couldn't stop laughing at my accent, so I sent her out of the room and I had no one else and it was late, so I just left a gap for when Bunk spoke and reacted to whatever he was supposed to be saying and sent it off to them.

David Simon said he found that it was so funny, this fool reacting to complete silence, that he thought we'd better get him over and have a laugh.

DAVID SIMON (CREATOR): I had never seen an audition tape like it. The camera was on him, and he was reading and then he was leaving the pauses for the other actors, who didn't exist, and he was reacting to the lines. A lot of acting is reacting, and to see somebody doing it to nothingness is a pretty unusual audition tape.

We fell around the room laughing, like, "What the . . . ?" Then, we sat down and watched the tape, and the accent was slipping. It was his first time trying an American accent, and it seemed to be there were shades of sort of New York De Niro-isms. But it was really good acting. He was a good actor, and the reacting to nothing was a tell. Of course, we knew that McNulty would probably be sort of a guy with unrelenting vices, sort of his own worst enemy. Dom had that. You could see that even in the audition tape.

ALEXA L. FOGEL (CASTING DIRECTOR): He was too young. He was too attractive. I'm not sure that anyone else knew this at the time, but he was really well educated. I didn't let everyone know where he had gone to school, because it wasn't important. He understood the guy.

DOMINIC WEST (DET. JIMMY MCNULTY): I went to New York and I met Wendell Pierce, who was the first person to be cast, and we hit it off pretty well. So, I think that's what kicked it all into start.

WENDELL PIERCE (DET. WILLIAM "BUNK" MORELAND): I'm from New Orleans, and we have a laissez-faire sort of approach to everything. It's a cultural thing in New Orleans. Dominic is very much that. We had so much fun. It started from the beginning. I remember reading with him, and I was like, *Oh my God, this guy is prepared, and I don't have this shit memorized.* He was on point and prepared, and he maybe dropped one line and went on and was like, "You were so prepared and I was awful." I was like, "Wow, I was thinking the opposite, man. You were prepared and I was awful." Our chemistry—it's been a great friendship from the bat. He has a great curiosity about things. He's very well read, loves to go out and have a good time. I think we share that approach to life.

ALEXA L. FOGEL (CASTING DIRECTOR): I did have to sell the head of HBO at the time, Chris Albrecht. I flew out with Dom, and then he and I worked at it at the hotel, and then we all went into HBO and he and I read together for a couple of the executives. I stepped in because I felt like we needed to explain to Chris what it was about, this guy who looked so different than what was written about this character, that he had this kind of darkness and [this] lost quality and a sense of cynicism about everything about him that he really managed to embody.

At the end of my little monologue, Chris turned to me and he pointed and said, "You better be right." For three weeks, I would wake up every three hours and all I could see was the end of that finger pointing at me, saying, "You better be right."

CHRIS ALBRECHT (CHAIRMAN AND CEO, HBO): Dominic is British. That was before people were casting a lot of Brits as American.

DOMINIC WEST (DET. JIMMY MCNULTY): Ed [Burns] always thought that he was, and rightfully so, the smartest guy in the room. Not on *The Wire*, but when he was a cop. To a lot of the frustration with the bosses, a lot of the sort of maverick disobedience and thinking everyone else is an idiot, and he's the only one that knows how to solve the case, a lot of that in McNulty was from Ed.

I think that's what struck a chord most with the cops that used to watch the show. They'd go, "This is exactly what cops think about all the time." It's, I suppose, what everyone thinks about all the time—is what an asshole their bosses are and how they could do the job so much better if only they didn't have to answer to these idiots who are their superiors. I think Ed brought that very much, the sort of experience of being a cop, to the show, which is what made it so different and so real. A lot of McNulty was based on Ed, particularly the intelligence and the intellectual arrogance, I think.

ED BURNS (CO-CREATOR): That's what I did. I went to my captain first and said, "This doesn't work against gangs. It just doesn't work." Of course, in Baltimore, we pretended we didn't have gangs. That was something. It took many, many years to acknowledge the fact that we had gangs, but that was just the brass being stupid. Then I went up to the State's Attorney's Office and got Howard Gersh, and he basically put pressure on the police commissioner. I got sprung loose from the Homicide office, much to the chagrin of the major, and was able to go after all the gangs, which got me away from Homicide and also got me away from the Narcotics Unit, sort of carved my own little niche. I did that almost up until the day I retired.

But McNulty is more of an expression of David, with the divorce and that kind of stuff. What McNulty did, as far as pressuring the police department to establish a unit to go after gangsters, was what I did. His personal life and stuff like that—that wasn't my personal life. I'm sort of a homebody.

ALEXA L. FOGEL (CASTING DIRECTOR): Idris [Elba] was up for a Fox movie that I was casting right before I did *The Wire*. He didn't get it, which was really frustrating for me. I thought he had tremendous presence. His American accent was perfect. But he was an unknown face, and for a studio, that was tricky. He was very much on the forefront of my mind when I started on *The Wire*. Because of the experience that I had with the feature, I told him to just use an American accent. I've never done that before, and I've never done it since. But I was sort of coming off of this frustrating experience where he didn't get a role and I was trying to kind of create an environment in which everything was going his way.

IDRIS ELBA (STRINGER BELL): I couldn't afford to stay anymore. This was literally the last audition that I was up for that could change my life. It was in December when I was auditioning. In January, my lease was up, my daughter was about to be born. It was a really troubling time. It was like, *Get this job and you stay. Don't get this job and you won't be able to afford to stay and you'll go back* [to England]. Also, my visa was running out next year as well, so it was really the last hurrah for me, to be honest. Then eventually, the day my daughter was born was the day I got the job.

WOOD HARRIS (AVON BARKSDALE): Me and Idris were two of the first people cast. Alexa was talking to me at the time about how she loved us working out. She said, "Oh my God, you two are going to work really well together."

MICHAEL B. JORDAN (WALLACE): I remember feeling so bummed the first time I went in there and I didn't get the job. I originally went in there for Bodie, and I was too young for it and I didn't get it, and I was just super sad, and I remember [pilot director] Clark [Johnson] and Alexa calling me back in. They brought me back in for Wallace, and I ended up getting that character. That was cool. That was the silver lining.

ALEXA L. FOGEL (CASTING DIRECTOR): We had to do all these extra things, because [Michael B. Jordan] couldn't go to Baltimore by himself. He had to have a guardian because he was underage. Every time we did the deal, it was sort of for two people.

ANDRE ROYO (REGINALD "BUBBLES" COUSINS): I had just finished doing a play and got mad love from all these actors that I looked up to. I was on cloud nine. My manager called me and was like, "HBO has a new show." At that point, because of *Oz* and *Six Feet Under* and all that stuff, it still was the biggest. That's what every actor wanted. You had *Law & Order* and you had HBO. That's what every actor in New York wanted to be on.

When she said, "HBO is doing a new show called *The Wire* and I got you an audition for this junkie character named Bubbles," I was mad. I was like, "I'm not doing that. I'm not playing a junkie." I didn't know anything about the kind of addiction Bubbles was in. I just felt like it was one of those roles we always heard would be either that typecast guy or ridiculed because you never get it right. Only a few. You had Sam[uel L.] Jackson as Gator and you have Chris Rock in *New Jack City*. I couldn't see myself doing better than that. If you can't see yourself doing better with the role, then why take it? I was a little like, "I don't want to go." My manager, being the great manager she was at that time, was like, "You're broke, motherfucker. You ain't got no money. They didn't offer you the role. You got to go audition. How about you go there, so people in the television world can see if you can act? If you book it, then you can turn it down, if you want to."

She made it in a tone where it was a challenge, like, "You ain't booked it yet." I was like, "I'll book it." I was high on myself at that time. I was like, "All right. Let me go in." I went in. It's New York. You see the same black actors in all the auditions. It's a small circle. I see all my boys, and everybody's auditioning for this guy. His name is Bubbles. Someone's chewing bubble gum. I was like, "That's so fucking juvenile." I spat my gum out.

LANCE REDDICK (LT. CEDRIC DANIELS): I originally was called in for Bunk. I read for Bunk three times. The last time I went and read for Bunk, it was the only time that David, Ed, and Bob Colesberry were in the room. David asked me to read for Bubbles on the spot. I went outside and looked at the words, came back, and I read for Bubbles. I'm sure that was because he'd just seen me play two drug addicts in a row. I worked with David and Bob on *The Corner*, where I played a crackhead. Then I was cast in *Oz* in March of 2000, where I'm an undercover cop who gets addicted to heroin. He saw me play two skinny drug addicts in a row. It's funny, because I even remember, toward the end of my run on that season of *Oz*, David was stopping by to say hello to [*Oz* creator] Tom [Fontana]. I remember him saying to me, "I'm working on a new project. I'll keep you in mind." I was grateful for him saying that, but people say that stuff all the time. I didn't expect it to go anywhere.

ALEXA L. FOGEL (CASTING DIRECTOR): That's just the way it goes until you get deeper into the process. The beginning of the process is a total crapshoot. You're just trying everything out, and then it starts to makes sense, because the quality of the actor starts to adhere more closely and strongly to specific qualities in the role. But in the beginning, you just don't know.

ROBERT WISDOM (HOWARD "BUNNY" COLVIN): Alexa Fogel is one of the great casting directors around. Alexa nailed this one. She's really an unsung hero of the show. She just had her finger on the pulse of a broader array of talent than our industry is given credit for.

PAT MORAN (CASTING: BALTIMORE): I knew right off the bat that this was not any Cosby kids here. That wasn't going to fly. In order for that to translate, even though the words were great, you needed to match it up with the eyes. I also feel that there's a role for everybody. After a period of seeing a lot of people, perhaps they couldn't carry a show, but there's a one-liner waiting for them somewhere.

I was always happy to be a part of it. I believed in it. There wasn't one rotten script that came, and that's what you really love. The characters were so specific, and you saw what it looked like in your head. Until it looked like that, I wasn't happy.

JAY LANDSMAN SR. (LT. DENNIS MELLO): I actually read for the part of Landsman, but I'm still working now. I'd have to take off three days of work, whenever they want. I said, "I can't do that all the time." All of a sudden, they had Delaney Williams read for it. Delaney Williams wasn't anything like me. David Simon said, "You did fine on that reading, but you're just no 'Jay Landsman.'" Asshole. He thought it was the funniest thing in the world when it happened. We met all these people, and he had this big, fat guy. I was one of the thinnest guys there at the time and never ate.

DAVID SIMON (CREATOR): Jay is not heavyset. Jay had, at that time, probably put on more weight than he had normally had. When I was in the Homicide unit, Jay was and still probably is the worst practical joker in the history of the Baltimore Police Department. There were so many practical jokes he played on me. It was so hilariously humiliating when I was the intern there. So, I finally got him back. Delaney is a great actor, and I loved working with him. We didn't cast him because he was heavyset. We cast him because he was great in the read. Once we did cast him and I'd realized what I'd done, then it was like, "Jay, you're good, but I got a guy who's much better at being Jay Landsman than you."

When he saw Delaney walk on, Jay immediately went on a diet. The real Jay. Jay dropped like thirty pounds. He'd put on some weight. I'm not saying he was heavy. He was heavier than he'd been. He saw Delaney walk on-screen, I think Jay didn't have a doughnut for the next two to three years. Next I saw, he was thirty pounds lighter. Jay was like, "You motherfucker."

DELANEY WILLIAMS (SGT. JAY LANDSMAN): I didn't know I was going to be on a lot, and they didn't tell me anything about the character. I had no idea there was even a real Landsman until the end of the first season, when I met Jay. That's how little I was told about what was going on or what it was about. I think they kind of said, "Well, this is the person we need." As an actor, I chose things to play, and they were happy with it. Then they wrote toward those things. As far as that goes, he was functioning as the guy between the bureaucracy of the city government and a police department. I really wasn't told anything about it, but it turned out that, looking back on it, it was a comic relief device of sorts.

LAWRENCE GILLIARD JR. (D'ANGELO BARKSDALE): When I booked the role, I was living in New York, and my agent called me and he told me that there was a script, new HBO show, and it was going to be about Baltimore. He knew I grew up in Baltimore. He sent me the script, and I read it. Instantly, I just had a connection with it. I knew the neighborhood. I knew the streets. I'm reading it and I'm just thinking to myself, *I know these corners. I know these streets, and I know these characters. I know these people.* It was very personal to me, having had the experience living, growing up in Baltimore. I just felt like, *I really need to get this part.*

Doing the show, playing D'Angelo, I knew cats who were in that situation. I knew cats on the street. I was fortunate. My mother sheltered me from a lot of that stuff. I was lucky that way. I grew up right in West Baltimore. As a matter of fact, I played football for the Lexington Terrace football squad, which is where the high-rises where the Barksdales were operating and all that stuff was going down. That was my hood.

When I was like thirteen, fourteen, I got into high school and I went to a school that pretty much took me away from all that. I knew cats who weren't taken out of it, were still in it, weren't as lucky and fortunate as me. When I was playing that part, I was just thinking about some of those cats and thinking to myself, *The person that I'm playing is a real person somewhere in the world. I want to do that character justice.* And because it was personal to me, I wanted to do the story some justice. I wanted it to be as true as I could and do some justice to the stories for them.

DEIRDRE "DEDE" LOVEJOY (ASST. STATE'S ATTY. RHONDA PEARLMAN):
I was shocked when I got cast, because when I got the call, my agent said, "This is an HBO show and there are two female parts in it." I was like, "Right. I am sure that I am going to be cast as sort of the kind of on-again, off-again interest to the main character." I was like, "That's not me. I am not that girl. I am not." As a result of that, I just thought there was not a chance in hell that I would ever get cast. I walked in the waiting room and every award-winning actress that you could name was there, and lots of my colleagues were Tony Award winners and much more beautiful than I am. I would consider myself always a character person. I'm a leading lady, but on the theater generally. I was so relaxed. I just visited with all of my friends. I didn't think twice about the audition, because I knew there wasn't a chance in hell.

I did my audition, and a couple days later, I got a call that there was interest, and I went for my callback and I still knew that there wasn't a chance in hell. I did my reading, and David was there and Robert Colesberry, and Clark [Johnson]. I was trying to quit smoking for the ninetieth time back then, but I had my little nicotine patch on my chest. I went to put my microphone on and the nicotine patch was showing. I was like, "Oops. Sorry. That's my patch. I'm a little spacey today, but it's because I've got my patch on." I don't know if that made me more relaxed or whatever, and I booked it and I didn't have to screen-test.

I can't remember if I had this conversation with David Simon or if I sort of gleaned it from several conversations with him, but they auditioned a lot of people for that role. They just didn't quite know what they were looking for. They knew they were looking for something, but they didn't know what it was. That is why there were really beautiful people and people like me. They said that when I walked in the audition, they were like, "That's her." That just happens once every million years, and the stars align for an actor. It wasn't anything I did better or worse than I usually do in a thousand other auditions, but I am eternally grateful that it happened to align for me to be part of a project that wound up being sort of historically significant.

JIM TRUE-FROST (DET. ROLAND "PREZ" PRYZBYLEWSKI): For all I knew, it was just another cop show. I had worked a single episode of *Homicide*, and Clark and David and Bob all remembered me from that.

UTA BRIESEWITZ (CINEMATOGRAPHER): When Bob Colesberry called, I had just moved to Los Angeles from New York and also had changed agencies. At one point, I got a call saying I had an interview for *The Wire*, this HBO pilot. I seem to remember my agent saying, "We got the in, but don't get your hopes up." When I had my meeting with Bob, Bob told me that he was the producer that [had] brought Michael Ballhaus to America and then kind of hooked him up with Martin Scorsese. Of course, I was very impressed by that story, because Michael Ballhaus was the cinematographer that German cinematographers looked up to. Everybody was aware of who Michael Ballhaus was. Just taking that away from the meeting, I felt like, "Oh, cool. I met the producer who brought Michael Ballhaus to the States."

At the same time, Bob Colesberry also kind of let me know that he considers himself somebody who can find new talent and bring people up. At that point, I didn't really apply that too much to myself. I really thought I was just getting a meeting as a courtesy to somebody at my agency and that's all. I had no expectations. The entire time, Bob passionately was talking about the show. He asked almost nothing, no information from me. I didn't get to say anything, but I remember walking out of the meeting, calling my agent, like, "I think this was the worst meeting I ever had, because I didn't really get to say anything." In retrospect, I learned that when a producer passionately talks about the show, it kind of indicates that they already made up their mind about you and what they are doing right now is trying to sell the show to you.

ANDRE ROYO (REGINALD "BUBBLES" COUSINS): I was off to Baltimore. We wasn't going to start shooting for three weeks or so. I had time to really get on top of this and doing this character justice. Not knowing about that addiction, that's when I started doing my homework. I started doing what I thought would best serve me understanding what this character's going through and why he's making the certain choices that he makes. That was exciting. That's when all your acting classes and all your teachers—all that stuff you can put into practice. You can go, *What's my objective? How do I get into this person's head?*

You start doing your homework. It was awesome. It was exciting to find different ways. I found out just talking to people. I talked to a ton of people. This woman named Fran Boyd was out there in Baltimore and she helped me out a lot. She was a recovered addict. She was the one they based the character on in *The Corner,* the miniseries. She was dope. We really hit it off. She had no apologies and took me around all over Baltimore talking to people in the midst of their addiction or coming out of their addiction or fighting their addiction. I was looking for a gimmick. I was just trying to find little movements that I can do that would just automatically go, "Oh, he's a junkie." I didn't find it. Everybody was different. It got me a little scared. They were talking to me like, "Please don't fuck it up. This is heroin. We're not crackheads. There's a difference between a crackhead and a meth head. There's a difference between a meth head and a heroin addict." I was like, "Are you fucking kidding me? I watch movies. They all act the same to me."

I got deeper into understanding not about the addiction, but about the person. I started looking at myself like, *What do I do?* One day, I was in New York and I was going somewhere and I saw these people standing outside smoking cigarettes. I think it was one of those zero-degree days. I was like, "What the fuck would make somebody come outside and smoke a cigarette outside in the cold?" I started going, *Wait, you know what? They do whatever it takes to get that fucking nicotine. That's the same thing as Bubbles getting his heroin fix.*

What do I do every day? I found out. I started studying myself. When I come in the house, no matter what back then, I would turn on the TV. That's the first thing I would do. I would drop my keys, turn on the TV, then go about my business. I was like, *Why? Why do I turn on the TV?* Then I made a list of things I do every day. I always drink Coca-Cola. I was a Coca-Cola fiend. I didn't like water. I was horny. I was trying to make love to my wife, or my lady at the time, every day. For about thirty days, I didn't do any of that.

When you go in your house like day seven and you don't turn on that TV, you start fiending. You're like, *Damn, I just want to see a commercial. I just want to see who won the game, the Knicks or something.* I couldn't turn on the TV. I'd be pacing around the living room trying to think about, *What if I turned on the TV just once and turn it off real quick?* I started building this need and writing down how I act when I'm agitated, or I'd be mad at myself when I couldn't have Coca-Cola. I started writing all that stuff down, and that helped me build the desire that I thought Bubbles would have every time he woke up. You start by getting high.

There was a couple of movies—there was two movies that I saw. I never subscribed to watching other actors, but I was in New York and I just wanted to see certain ideas and feelings. I watched *The Panic in Needle Park*, with Al Pacino. With him, with that character, you just saw him. Every day, he was trying to get high. His character would be looking on the floor because he might find cigarettes or something. *Lady Sings the Blues* was the other one. I remember watching that with my mom and dad. Richard Pryor had this small part. He was such a cool dude, funny. He was a junkie. He got high, but he was functional, played the piano. When he died, it was heartbreaking. It was awesome that he wasn't in the movie that much and he was a cool guy, a nice guy, just a down-to-earth guy. He just had an addiction. I fell in love with him. I was like, *That's what I want Bubbles to be. I want Bubbles to be a human first, addict second.* I wasn't trying to play the addiction. I was going to play the person.

LANCE REDDICK (LT. CEDRIC DANIELS): We all had an opportunity, at least the cops, to spend time with other cops. I had to spend a day with a narcotics lieutenant. At the time, he was also going back to school at night, at Johns Hopkins, to get his MBA. I later found out from David that that's a fairly common thing for cops to move up the promotion ladder: to get advanced degrees.

Two things that I remember most about that guy were how he talked about leadership. I remember him saying, "In a lot of ways, you have to treat people like your children. You have to be firm with them, but you have to be compassionate." He also said that whenever he would go in [to arrest people] with waves of his people, go in front, so that they knew that he was doing it from the front.

The other story that he told was telling, because that was when I started to understand the mentality of what it is to be a cop. They had figured out that there was a dirty cop on the force. They raided the guy's house. He was the first person on the guy. Apparently, the guy went to reach in his dresser, and he thought it was for a gun, and he said, "Please, reach for it, because I would love nothing more than to blow you away, because I fucking hate dirty cops." That stuck with me, because not being a kid from the streets and not having grown up around law enforcement, I realized just how much there has to be underneath the surface, because that's the world that you're dealing with. You have to have that level of savagery and ferocity that you have to be able to call up in an instant and be able to tame and put away in an instant.

SETH GILLIAM (SGT. ELLIS CARVER): The ride-along was terrifying for me. It started off with him giving us bulletproof vests. And I thought, *Well, this can't be good.* And then, at one point, Dom [Lombardozzi] and I were sitting in the backseat. This is after he had already jumped out a couple of times, the officer—his name was Super Boy—and Parker, his partner, was still behind the wheel. But at one point, we're driving along and the car suddenly stops and the doors slide open and they all jump out and start running to some people who they were trying to corner. We're just sitting in the back of the car, both doors open, and I'm thinking, *My head is going to explode at any moment. My head is going to explode at any moment.* I'm sitting there protecting my head. I was sure that I was going to get shot in the head from behind. It was a bit of a rush at first. Aside from that end, it was pretty uneventful.

Those guys went from zero to one hundred miles an hour in a moment's notice. They'd be joking with each other and joking with each other, and in two seconds, the entire energy would change and shift among them. Then they had each other's backs. It was very much working like a fine-tuned machine, in terms of being able to turn it on and turn it off. Also, the interactions that I saw them having with the people in the neighborhood—everybody knew Super Boy, and he would be jumping out and he would have his hand on his gun behind his side. Then things would just stop at one point, and it was like, "This guy's pretty serious, because he knows who's dangerous and who's not at this point."

SONJA SOHN (DET. SHAKIMA "KIMA" GREGGS): Like most black folks who grew up in underserved areas, I did not have a positive view of the police. For me, that was my main obstacle to playing a cop at the time. I had to get over my own sort of early traumatic interactions with the police and what I had experienced. My early interactions with the police in my childhood were never positive, and that had affected me more deeply than I had imagined going into the show. I realized for me to play this character, I had to have some understanding of the motivations of good cops and what the motivation was for a good cop to become a cop. Kima was the good cop. She's the moral compass of the police. For me to embody that, truthfully, as an actor, I have to be willing to understand that that kind of cop existed and how that kind of cop came into being.

MELANIE NICHOLLS-KING (CHERYL): In my audition for the show, they had told me, the executive producers, not to be too upset that I wasn't getting the chance to continue to read for Kima, because she was going to die. When I met Sonja and we were hanging out, I said, "I think it's really horrible that they're killing Kima off." Then Sonja was like, "What? What are you talking about?" I was like, "Oh shit. That's what they told me. I totally told them that it was a bad idea and how could you do that? You finally have two lesbian characters on a national show. How are you going to kill off one of those characters?" I would like to believe that it was because of me fighting for it that they didn't kill her off.

SONJA SOHN (DET. SHAKIMA "KIMA" GREGGS): She revealed that to me during the pilot, when I met her, thinking I already knew the information. It was a shock for me to learn that the character was actually slated to be killed off. For the first, I'd say, solid ten years of my acting career, I was always questioning the profession itself. I did not have a lot of respect for it. I had people coming to me during my poetry years, thinking that I was an actor because of the delivery of my poetry. For me, it was very offensive that you would think I could be involved in such a shallow business as the entertainment business and [that] I would even want to endeavor to choose a career that, at the time, I thought was so vain. It sent me into a questioning of the integrity of the producers, because I felt that if that was the case, then why not just tell me off the bat, just so I know? People get these jobs and you assume that you at least are going to have a year's worth of work. You're going to be a part of the full show, if you book a job as a series regular.

This was the first show that I had booked, so I didn't really understand the business side of these contracts at the time. I didn't know at the time that, even though I was a series regular and I [had] signed the contract for five years, that they could actually kill me off at any time. That would be fully within their rights. Because I didn't know that and had an expectation that I would be a part of the show as a series regular for the duration of the show, when it was introduced to me during the actual pilot that I'd be killed off, that ends up being a one-season recurring role. It's not a series regular. I'll have some episodes, and then I'm gone. Why not just present that to me from the beginning? Because I had come from a place of really struggling and meeting my bills at the time, I had felt some level of relief having booked a job. That's why it came as such a shock. It was just like, *Why not just be up front and tell me about it?* For me, that signified to me the kind of bullshit about the corporate business world. I've always been a bit of the anti-establishment side of things. I had very radical opinions about capitalism and the corporate structure.

For me, having people not being transparent, upfront about it, my anger really was based in that. My anger really came out of that, and then, because I felt like if these producers who were presenting the business side of things for me at this time, based on my limited knowledge of how the business worked, were of high integrity, then they would have been transparent with me about the information right off the bat. What means something to the people who are putting the show together is the show. They have a show and a vision that they're trying to execute. For me, in not being transparent about that, it meant that there was no care or concern for the people involved, for the human aspect of what an actor who is booking a job and raising a family and making plans on how they need to move.

DAVID SIMON (CREATOR): Carolyn [Strauss] was the one who said, "That character has legs. Don't kill that character so quick." She was wounded and not killed at the end of Season One, and Carolyn made compelling arguments about the show going forward and the need for a strong female lead on the cop side, that we were short on female leads and that it was a perspective that could allow us things that we otherwise would not have.

Carolyn came back to Ed and I, and I remember saying, "Man, Carolyn really wants Kima to go on. What does that do to the show?" We trotted it out a little bit and said, "You know what? Okay. It doesn't allow McNulty's darkness to go as deep that he got her killed rather than wounded. It closes some doors to us dramatically and it opens others."

CAROLYN STRAUSS (PRESIDENT, HBO ENTERTAINMENT): I just thought she was a great character. Yeah, she was supposed to have an untimely demise. I think it boiled simply down to, I thought she could be really good for the rest of the storytelling. She could be really useful to him. It was just a different stripe. Number one, different from anybody else in the show, and number two, [different from] anything that we've seen before.

2

LIKE A NOVEL

The pilot's complexity alarmed a number of the show's actors, and they openly wondered among themselves who would watch it. Several figured that HBO would pass on picking the show up, and they expressed surprise when the network signed off on it relatively quickly—surprising especially when one thinks of the later impassioned pleas needed from David Simon to secure future seasons. David Simon and Bob Colesberry deliberated opening theme songs for weeks before Tom Waits's "Way Down in the Hole" beat out John Hammond's iteration of "Get Behind the Mule." The show used a different version of the song each season, with the Blind Boys of Alabama recording the initial rendering. The Wire—beyond a hiccup involving the iconic orange couch following the filming of the pilot—was off, and premiered on June 2, 2002.

The Wire's first season hemmed loosely to the antiquated real-life wiretap investigation of Melvin Williams. It bypassed television's traditional redemptive narrative for a thirteen-episode exposition on the futility of the war on drugs. The audience gained perspectives on characters ranging from high-ranking police officials, such as Dep. Commissioner Ervin Burrell (Frankie Faison) and Maj. William Rawls (John Doman), to low-level drug dealers such as Wallace (Michael B. Jordan) and Preston "Bodie" Broadus (J. D. Williams), to drug-addicts-turned-informants such as Reginald "Bubbles" Cousins (Andre Royo). Det. Jimmy McNulty (Dominic West) watches as D'Angelo Barksdale (Lawrence Gilliard Jr.) escapes a murder conviction through witness intimidation orchestrated by Stringer Bell (Idris Elba). McNulty's complaints to a judge infuriate his police superiors, who initiate a haphazard detail that is designed to superficially appease the judge. (In real life, Ed Burns said he had told the state's attorney, who went to a judge, that the police department should be more proactive in its investigations. "He called up the deputy commissioner, who in turn called my captain, who in turn screamed at me as I was walking out the door to go to work on that case," Burns said. "Sure enough, at the end of the case we brought back, he was very, very happy, and then they tried to get rid of me.") Largely through McNulty's stubbornness and disregard for his future in the police department, the ragtag detail infiltrates the drug ring by using a wiretap and pager clones, as D'Angelo begins pondering the morality of a life spent dealing drugs. The case's tentacles spread into the political spectrum, an area the police chain of command refuses to visit. The police command prematurely reels in the case once a cop is nearly killed in an undercover operation gone wrong, with elusive kingpin Avon Barksdale (Wood Harris) sentenced to a light charge and Stringer left free.

Critical reception initially varied. Those who viewed The Wire's singular episodes as chapters in a novel appreciated the show. "The Wire is compelling in its complexity, heart-rending in its humanity, and surprising in the ways it finds to spin the conventions of cop drama," wrote Steve Johnson of the Chicago Tribune. After reviewing five episodes for the New York Daily News, David Bianculli described the show as interesting but slow. "But without characters to care for, much less root for, I'm not exactly burning with curiosity—the way I am with most of HBO's other series," he wrote. The New York Post's Adam Buckman ventured further: "If I were from there, I'd really be offended," he declared. "As it is, I'm not from Baltimore, so I'm put off only by [Simon's] new show, which demonstrates, if nothing else, that even the vaunted HBO can cough up a dud once in a while."

UTA BRIESEWITZ (CINEMATOGRAPHER): I read the pilot several times because I felt like there was a lot going on. Many characters are being introduced. I felt like, "This is something really complex we're setting up here." Even I sometimes felt confused shooting the pilot.

LAURA SCHWEIGMAN (SCRIPT SUPERVISOR): I was there for the scene with a shooting where Snot Boogie was killed and lying in the street. That was my first really long overnight shoot I had ever done. Everything was just very real. If you looked away from the movie cameras, I just thought to myself, *Wow. I see this. I see this when I drive around in Baltimore.* It was sad, but it was, at the same time, amazing, how real it felt, how real it looked.

BENJAMIN BUSCH (OFF. ANTHONY COLICCHIO): That first scene with Dominic West and Snot Boogie, you already knew the show got the street right. It was beautiful in its depiction of that space. The ugly alleys were fascinating. It was a strange combination in *The Wire* of both cinematic beauty and that play with the line between that and photojournalism, documentary filmmaking. Those two are combined almost like [William] Friedkin and *The French Connection*. I was a visual artist. My father was a writer. *The Wire* combined the two for me. I enjoyed it visually, and it was just so smart, the way it went after a story. *The Wire* didn't allow you to predict anything, much like your life. It didn't allow you to guess who would succeed or how and who would fall, with any accuracy.

The Wire was a show of shit happening and it happens to you. Over and over again. You either bring it on yourself or you're a collateral casualty or you feel for someone else who falls. You talk about how drama intersects. I was on the set when my father died. He died of a heart attack in New York City, while I was finishing a scene I knew he would love. I, being a particular bastard, I was pouring out some beer on a guy we were arresting, that scene where we're just busting people for anything, open alcohol laws, etcetera. I went to

Dominic West's trailer to have him sign copies of *Rock Star*, which had come out. I have a number of friends who are musicians. We all love that movie. Dominic West plays the guitarist. I went from his trailer, home to my wife with the phone. I turned right around and raced right to New York, right through Baltimore, where I had just been. So, I was actually on set thinking, *My dad's going to love this scene*. He loved *The Wire*. That's as far as he made it with that season. He never saw all that work.

KAREN THORSON (PRODUCER): We had to fight to keep the epigraph because the Directors Guild does not like anything between the director's name and the show. The director must get the last credit, and their claim was, "Well, you can't have the title of the show after the director's name. The director has to come after the title of the show." We said, "But this is not the title of the show. This is an epigraph. It is part of the show. It is the first frame of the show, so the director's name is coming before the first frame of the show." Getting that layout needed to be approved by the guild. Nowhere in the episode does the title of the show ever appear. Episode One is "The Target," but the epigraph is ". . . when it's not your turn," by McNulty.

VINCENT PERANIO (PRODUCTION DESIGNER): The first season takes place in Section Eight high-rise housing. Six months before, Baltimore tore the last high-rises down. So, we didn't have any high-rises. We were scouting around looking and found some Section Eight housing that were low-rises next to a high-rise for senior citizens. So, every week, I had to take the bottom three floors of that building and put cages up and make it look like Section Eight housing.

We were walking through the low-rises in that neighborhood, and there, by a Dumpster, was that orange couch. It was from the seventies, Mediterranean, crushed orange velvet and torn and soiled, but it seemed perfect for the script. I asked the people in charge of the housing development if I could just put this in a vacant house or something, just until we start doing the film. They did, and a month later, when we started working on the film, we put it in the middle of the court, and it surprisingly became a main part of the script. It was the hangout.

Well, we did our pilot. It came out nice, and then the show was over until HBO decided whether to pick it up, which usually is months of waiting. Within three weeks, they decided to pick it up. I was talking to my decorator. I said, "Well, at least we have the orange couch." He went mute. I said, "Oh no. You didn't do it. You didn't do it." He said, "Yes, we threw it out."

NINA K. NOBLE (EXECUTIVE PRODUCER): I had to go back to Vince Peranio and say, "You know that couch that we got rid of? We need to get it back." Of course, we couldn't get it back, so we found a couch that was very similar, and Vince found a fabric that was somewhat similar, and we got it reupholstered and hoped that David wouldn't notice.

VINCENT PERANIO (PRODUCTION DESIGNER): We just started designing the couch all over again. We had it built. We had to go to England to get orange crushed velvet, which was not particularly in in the 2000s. Then, when it was finally, totally finished, we aged it, cut it up, pulled the stuffing out. And it looked pretty close to the real thing. We just set it up there in all its glory the first day of shooting, and nothing was mentioned about it again.

DAVID SIMON (CREATOR): I didn't know it at the time, no. He told me later in the season, once we'd established. He said, "We had a little bit of an emergency with the couch." They sold the second couch as the first.

NINA K. NOBLE (EXECUTIVE PRODUCER): That was the irony of it. That was a cheap thrift shop couch, which we then had to custom-upholster at great expense in order to duplicate.

VINCENT PERANIO (PRODUCTION DESIGNER): It really kind of became an icon, the orange couch. A year into filming, I was reading a *New York Times Magazine* and the cover of the magazine was about new urban fashion, and it was an orange couch in the middle of a Manhattan street. So, I know somebody had seen the film that year.

UTA BRIESEWITZ (CINEMATOGRAPHER): In the pilot, we established, "When we go to the projects, we go handheld." After a couple of episodes, I approached Bob Colesberry and I said, "What these drug dealers are doing is so well-thought-out, I just don't see like it deserves any less control, visual style, or elegance, than we are trying to apply outside the projects. If anything at all, we should portray them the same way." That's where I think we changed things, and we were all shooting the projects from dolly instead of just going handheld there. He agreed and he went with it, and that was the great thing and the wonderful thing with me and my collaboration with Bob. Bob just really liked what I did, and he gave me freedom. He was just supportive. He was the guy behind the monitor, and he was nodding his head and giving the thumbs-up. It was a great way of working. I experienced unbelievable freedom while I was working on *The Wire*.

KAREN THORSON (PRODUCER): Uta and Bob really collaborated well. I see a lot of homages to certain setups that Bob particularly liked. He liked the work of Gordon Willis. In Rawls's office, Rawls is standing against the window, emerging out of the darkness, when he has that encounter with McNulty, flipping the two birds when he's really angry with him for having stirred up business with the judge.

DEBI YOUNG (MAKEUP DEPARTMENT HEAD): I used to work for the police department when David would come in to get the stats from the things that had happened. I worked in the nine-one-one center. This is way before *The Wire*. Because I knew that Ed was a homicide detective and that David was a journalist, I had to make sure that everything was on point, because they would know if it wasn't, as far as how the person looked when they died. My key makeup artist, Sandy [Linn Koepper], had found this pathology book, and we had it in the makeup chair as one of our reference books. Because it had real dead people in it, I couldn't look at it. It just bothered me so much to see these dead people and how they had died. The photographs were very vivid.

We had a consultant from the medical examiner's office when we started. What I did to get around that, when I would read something in the script and they would have it so vividly described in the writing, I would call the medical examiner's office to speak to the consultant, and I would say something like, "So, if I had a body that's been floating in the harbor for thirty days and it's in the middle of February, how would he look?" The medical examiner would then describe it to me, and then I would jot down his description and then I could translate it into makeup. It was the easiest way for me.

BRUCE LITECKY (SOUND MIXER): They were convinced in some ways that the wiretap had to be really sort of dirty and hard to hear, but we also had to give the audience something to listen to, so there was always a back-and-forth about that. A ground was found where there was enough information for people to follow along, but not so much that it didn't leave a sense of mystery to the whole procedure.

It being called *The Wire* and being about wiretapping, it was about the eavesdropping and listening in. That was a really important thing on that show. You really had to listen.

KAREN THORSON (PRODUCER): [Tom Waits] wanted to see what we were up to, visually, and how the story was coming, and he wanted to see a cut of the show, which made sense. When we were producing *The Wire* the first couple of years, we were still using VHS for screeners. We had a timeline, and so we FedEx him a VHS player and a tape, and he said, "Well, I got the tape, but I don't know how to work the machine. I have to set it up, and my wife's the only one that can do that, so that'll be tomorrow." That made David Simon chuckle. There was nothing we could do. We had to wait for the machine to get set up so he could watch it, and he called fairly quickly after seeing it and said he would participate.

What was interesting is changing the performer from season to season. That wasn't clear to me right away that that's what was going on in David's mind, and I'm not sure that he had that fully formed, either. He wanted the voice of the vocals to reflect the main theme of the content of the season. That's why we have kids doing it, for example, on Season Four, when the focus of the storyline is what happens to the kids and how they get into the drug trade or how do they avoid it.

BLAKE LEYH (MUSIC SUPERVISOR): While we were working on the pilot, I wrote the tune that became the end credit music for the show. Still, from seeing the pilot episode, I didn't have a very high opinion of the show. It just seemed to me like a slightly more glitzy cop show. I didn't understand HBO. To me, they seemed like a functionally inexperienced kid. Then, a couple months later, I remember also having an exchange with Nina Noble, where we were watching the finished mix, and there was a scene with Wallace in it, and I remember saying to Nina, "Maybe someday someone will make a TV show where they star that character. I'd like to see that. That would be much more interesting to me than this copsy-joke stuff."

She said, "Well, if we get to really make the show, maybe we'll go there and you'll stick around to see that." I was like, "Yeah, right." That was my beginning on the show. Then the show got picked up, and they asked me to come back and work on the sound, but also on the music. Honestly, I still wasn't very excited about it.

ED BIANCHI (DIRECTOR): I do like the idea that there was no scored music for the show. It went to the realness. It was so raw. I think that was part of it. Nothing was sweetened. Nothing told you what to feel in terms of music, where music usually pushes you. Just words and pictures are telling you.

ANDRE ROYO (REGINALD "BUBBLES" COUSINS): When they said "Action," first day we started shooting, I pretty much stayed in character as much as I could, because I didn't want to fuck up. I knew that I'm a people person. I like talking to people. I like being around people. I said, "I don't want to be going back and forth, because I don't know if I have the discipline to jump in and out of character at that time." It was my first show. I was like, "Let me stay in character as much as I can." I stayed in character. I stayed by myself a little bit. I stayed in the trailer until the last minute. They put me in my wardrobe. I wore it as much as I could, just to feel the dirt and the grime of somebody being out in the street all the time.

The first scene we shot was me and Johnny, going to just cop something, easy fiend. It wasn't that much dialogue. It wasn't a wordy scene. We just go to the corner, go into the pit, and buy something and walk away. I remember doing the scene. It was the first take. I did it, and [director] Clark Johnson came up to me, and he's like, "That was great. That was good. We're going to come in closer now. That was a wide shot. You guys are doing good." He pulled me to the side, and he was like, "Are you going to be you or are you going to be Ratso Rizzo?" I was like, "What are you talking about?" He was like, "Nothing. I was just saying, I see a little too much Ratso Rizzo." I was like, "What the fuck does that mean?"

I walked away and I started thinking about it. I remember seeing *Midnight Cowboy* with Dustin Hoffman as Ratso Rizzo. He had this little walk. He had this little shuffle. I guess, unbeknownst to me, I was doing that little shuffle. I didn't know I was doing it, but when he said that, what happened was this whole internal challenge in my mind was like, *I'm no fucking copycat. I'm not doing that. I'm doing Bubbles. I'm not doing Ratso Rizzo.* I really had to trust myself and concentrate even more. In my mind, it felt like one of them Jay-Z songs.

Allow me to reintroduce myself. My name is Dre. This is my character. It worked, because all of a sudden, I just really started having blackout moments. When the director yelled, "Cut," I didn't know what I just did. I was just in the moment. I was in the zone. Bubbles was doing what Bubbles would do.

It really forced me to be more Method without being in the danger of actually taking drugs. You always heard that in acting class, acting is not doing, it's being, or some shit. I think I really just became Bubs. Bubbles became me, so to speak. After that, that whole first season, I couldn't tell you what I did in the scenes. I had to rewatch it. I don't remember some of the stuff I did. I was really immersed in it. It was probably the most transcending, best time of my life as far as an artist, because it's when everything clicked. Everything clicked, and I think it was helpful that we were in Baltimore. It felt like a big stage. Everything was saturated to help all of us as artists. Everybody on that set, in my mind, all the actors, all we had to do was look to the left or look to the right and we were inspired by the city of Baltimore, by the people in Baltimore, of how these characters were supposed to live and be portrayed.

Baltimore being the place that it was, there was really not much to do out there unless you wanted to get in trouble. We weren't trying to get in trouble. Everybody wanted to do a good job. Everybody stayed together. We would be in the hotel. We would be talking to each other, talking about the scenes, arguing about certain things. We really held each other accountable. If I wasn't shooting that day and Sonja was shooting, I could either be at the bar, I could be spending my per diem, or I could be on set. Why not be on set watching my fellow actor? I would be there, and we would be looking at each other. That's never really done, as far as I know, at any other show, where I can look at a fellow actor and go, "That was whack." We were just really, really looking out for each other. We really brought into the situation. It was about the story and not about the egos.

LEO FITZPATRICK (JOHNNY WEEKS): I know a lot of junkies. I always wanted to bring a little bit of a human element to it, because junkies are always shown in such a bad light. But they're fuckin' somebody's kid or somebody's girlfriend. They're fuckin' people, too. They're just caught up in some bad shit. I think makeup was just sort of embellishing my bad genes. There wasn't anything too over the top. It was just like, "All right, let's just make him look yellow." It wasn't anything too extreme. Then, strangely, outside of that, I'd never shot heroin or done heroin. But the guy that worked the props department, who showed me how to shoot heroin, ended up being one of my best friends.

ANDRE ROYO (REGINALD "BUBBLES" COUSINS): While we were doing the pilot, I had a conversation with Ed Burns. He came to me, and Ed Burns wasn't really a talkative guy, but he fucks your head up. You ask Ed Burns, "You watch the football game? I want to know who won." He'll be like, "Is that what you do with your life? You want to watch a game? The world is being destroyed and you just want to watch a football game?" He just breaks it down.

Ed Burns, he came to me one day, like, "You're doing a good job. You're really doing good. Bubbles was my snitch. He was my informant." At that point, with the whole audition process, I didn't know Bubbles was a real character. I was like, "What?" He was like, "Bubbles is my informant." I was like, "Why didn't you tell me? I would have been asking you for research. I would have been asking you questions." He was like, "Because you were doing a good job. Why muck it up?" Then he told me, "If we were going on the look of Bubbles, Lance Reddick would have gotten the job. He was number two. We heard you might have had some trepidation playing the character. If you said no, we'd [have given] it to Lance Reddick, because Lance Reddick looks like the real Bubbles."

I was like, "Lance is six-two, big. Why the fuck did you cast me, then, if Bubbles looks like that?" He said, "Because you had more of the essence of what Bubbles was about, the human spirit of who he was. He's a nice guy. This dude had a habit. He still wanted to be functional in society. He still cared. You had more of that essence of who Bubbles was." I was honored by that. Of course, my mother was like, "What the fuck you mean my son's got the essence of a junkie? What the fuck you talking about?"

PETER GERETY (JUDGE DANIEL PHELAN): Bubbles just drove me nuts. I just thought, *Where did they get this heroin addict?* And then, the next week, there was a cast party in some bar in New York, and there was Andre Royo, who plays Bubbles, and he's the sweetest guy. He's just a really good actor, that's all.

DEBI YOUNG (MAKEUP DEPARTMENT HEAD): When we first started, he went to the craft services table. We were working in downtown Baltimore, and he went to get something to eat, and the security people stopped him because they didn't know who he was. They thought he was somebody off the street.

ANDRE ROYO (REGINALD "BUBBLES" COUSINS): I was shuffling around and mumbling to myself and grabbing at the food, and Security chased me. They thought I was a junkie trying to steal stuff from craft service. This boy was ready to fuck me up. One of the other guys came like, "No, no. That's one of our actors." They were like, "You about to get knocked out. You look for real." It was certain things like that that would happen that really kept me feeling like I was doing a good job or going in the right direction.

STEVE EARLE (WAYLON): My scenes were meetings, and it was relatively early in my own recovery, so that part of it was really cool, because when you see those places in *The Wire*, they are places where meetings actually take place, and a lot of the extras are members of those home groups. Anonymity, you don't tell anybody which one. There's other people in there that are just extras. I have people in recovery come up to me all the time and say, "Those meetings are so real." Usually, twelve-step meetings on television, you can tell that they aren't that great and that's why. It was funny. With the exception of one director that I worked with, we were always encouraged to say when something didn't ring true. We were encouraged to speak up on those things, and the writers put it in.

ANDRE ROYO (REGINALD "BUBBLES" COUSINS): I call it my street Oscar. We were shooting a scene. I think it was that one time where I sat on a bench and I had no lines. I was planning whether I was going to stay clean and waiting for Sonja's character to call me. I was walking back to my trailer. This junkie came, and he was just walking by me. He saw me and he said, "Yo, they giving out testers over there. You need this." I guess my makeup was exceptionally beautiful that day.

He gave me a handshake. At first, I didn't know what he was doing. He's just like, "They're giving out testers." Gave me a handshake and kept moving. When I looked at my hand, I had a little vial of some drugs. I was like, "Oh, shit. This is awesome." I kid you not, walked in my trailer and sat there and pondered a little bit. This is one of the moments where I'm like this, *If I really want to know how this feels, if I really want to be awesome in this role, maybe I should take this. See what it feels.* I did; I thought about taking it. Then I was like, *Motherfucker, you'll be good for one take and one take only. It will be over. You might fuck yourself up.* Then it was like, *If they find out you're trying it, it might be all the love you got for your acting, that you're not an actor. You copped out. You became a junkie.* I didn't take it, but I kept it for a little while.

SETH GILLIAM (SGT. ELLIS CARVER): I had to watch the show with the subtitles on, even though I had the script, to understand what was happening on it. I seem to recall the first episode that Dom Lombardozzi and I were watching, and figuring, *Wow, this show is really slow and boring. I don't know how long this is gonna last.*

LAWRENCE GILLIARD JR. (D'ANGELO BARKSDALE): I didn't think that it would get picked up. I'd never read anything like it before. When you're reading scripts, there's a formula. Anything that deviates from that formula, you think, *Okay, this is an issue. There's a problem. This isn't going to work.* You read a show like that, it's kind of taking its time. It's developing. It's not trying to spoon-feed you the information too fast. It's just taking its time. I'm reading it and I'm thinking, *Who's gonna watch this?* We all want our entertainment quick, fast.

ANDRE ROYO (REGINALD "BUBBLES" COUSINS): The first reviews we got was from the *Daily News,* and they gave us half a star. Said we were too slow, a TV show that wants to be a book or a book trying to be a TV show. There's too many characters. HBO's under the wire with this new show.

DOMINIC WEST (DET. JIMMY MCNULTY): Initially, it was, "Don't worry, they won't get past the pilot." And then it got past the pilot, and they said, "Don't worry, they won't do more than one season." And then it was, "They won't do more than two seasons."

In fact, David Simon had to fight for every season. It would have been canceled every season had David Simon not been so tenacious, so it wasn't until Season Four or Five that we realized certain people enjoyed it, lawyers and gangbangers, but no one else. It was more obvious in America, but in the UK, I'd just come home after each shoot, and no one had ever heard of it. It was only in the fifth season, I walked into my local store and someone recognized me and I thought, *Oh God, people are watching it.*

It was not like any show that had come before. I was aware of that and aware of also how special the writing was, but I was so, so scared of it and so sort of concerned to get it right, to get the action right. I suppose that was my main consideration. I didn't really care how special it was as long as I didn't fuck up, but, really, in terms of it being popular or watched by anyone, that wasn't apparent for years. I remember for the first two or three years, I wasn't aware that anyone was watching it. Not many people were watching it, and whenever I went home, people back in England said, "What are you doing at the moment?" I said, "I'm doing this little show that you wouldn't have heard of," and sure enough, they hadn't.

JOE CHAPPELLE (DIRECTOR/CO-EXECUTIVE PRODUCER): We had a cast meeting, when all the cast members come and you sit at the table and everybody reads their part and you go through it. David and Bob were there, but they had left the room, and so then the cast turned to me. They hadn't seen anything yet. It was Episode Six, so they'd been shooting, and the pilot hadn't aired yet. But I had seen rough cuts of like the first two or three episodes, and the cast was like, "Is this show working?" They had no idea if this whole concept would work, because it was so dense and it was so layered. Nobody had really seen anything like this in television. The cast was questioning whether it was all working. I said, "Guys, it's working. Stick with it. You're going to be fine."

WENDELL PIERCE (DET. WILLIAM "BUNK" MORELAND): I definitely thought it was done. I was like, "Oh man. Damn. This shit." Because you weren't accustomed to it. We're accustomed to it now. Now everyone's like, "Oh, an anthology show that goes on? Okay, I understand it now. A show that changes every season? Oh, okay. A different case every season?" They understand it now.

ANDRE ROYO (REGINALD "BUBBLES" COUSINS): Nobody wanted to let HBO down. We wanted to be a hit show. We wanted to be big. We assumed we were going to be big because it was HBO. Everything they do is big. We were happy and even shocked that this is a big fucking cast. It's a lot of black people. We haven't seen this many black people on-screen since *A Different World*. This is awesome. We also were like, "This is really slow." When we saw the pilot, we only had that little pilot testing. We thought that show wasn't getting picked up, because it's too slow. TV doesn't move like this. Everybody in TV world, in La La Land, they know *Law & Order*. You catch the bad guy at the end. It's all wrapped up. This is some slow-talking shit. They're going to hate this shit.

At the same time, we're watching shit like *The Shield*. That shit is a hundred miles an hour. There's action every five minutes on *The Shield*. We're like, "This show is going to suck. They're not going to pick it up. Hope everybody didn't spend that money, because it's over. It's a one-episode job. Now back to the grind." A lot of us felt that way. When the show got picked up, we were shocked. Truly. We believe this show got picked up—or *I* believe this show got picked up—because I just thought HBO is making so much money. *Sex and the City* taking in money. *Six Feet Under* is nominated all the fucking time. HBO was like, "We're not going to be a network where we're going to have all these shows with white people. We need a show with some black people in it, so that people don't buzz us and say, 'What about diversity?' We got a show with all these black people. Fuck it. Let's do it. Let's just pick it up and see how it does. In the meantime, we're paying attention to *The Sopranos* and all this shit." We got picked up, and it was off and running. It always felt like we weren't the show that HBO was thinking about. We always felt like we were about to get canned.

CHRIS ALBRECHT (CHAIRMAN AND CEO, HBO): We were trying to distinguish ourselves from what else was on television. We were a paid channel. It had to be worth paying for [and] needed to be something different. Certainly, on the comedy side, with stand-up comics and with stand-up comedians, having black artists on the channel was always something that was well received. I always thought there was a real valuable voice in that, that it was important to include in whatever we were doing. Honestly, to me, it was just the quality of the work, the quality of what was on the page, and the fact that I thought, *We're the only place that could do this. No one else will ever do* *this.* When you got something that's good and that no one else would ever do, I think you just take the leap.

BRIAN ANTHONY WILSON (DET. VERNON HOLLEY): It was so urban and so dark, physically, literally, and figuratively. I remember the first day I shot. You normally have set decorations, but we shot in an alley that had actual crack vials there. They weren't put there by Props. It was an alley that had crack vials in it. You didn't have to dress it. I was, "Wow, isn't that deep? Life imitating art, and vice versa."

VINCENT PERANIO (PRODUCTION DESIGNER): I picked the right neighborhoods. I know Baltimore. I've lived here all my life. I'm not afraid of any neighborhoods. I've been down every alley in this city. So, pretty much, when David talks about places, I know what he's talking about. The story is about more West Baltimore than East Baltimore. East Baltimore is different than West Baltimore, even though there's a lot of crime in both. East Baltimore is the typical row houses. There are blocks and blocks of these row house façades. It's very graphic. And it's even more graphic in that there's no trees in that part of the city. It's just cement, asphalt, and brick. That's all you see, and when you walk in the alleys, it's jungle. I love that contrast, and I love the bleakness of it.

Also, I like the lighting. In so many vacant houses where we were filming, we're filming in a natural light or making it look like natural light, because it didn't have electricity. Actually, some of the lighting to me was almost like a painting from the past, like from the seventeenth century, a Rembrandt look about it, the darkness of the house and the sunlight searing through the boarded-up windows. I think the show was bleak and beautiful in the way that looking at ruins in a ruined civilization are.

DOMINIC WEST (DET. JIMMY MCNULTY): I'm from Sheffield, which is quite similar to Baltimore in a way in that it was a formerly industrial powerhouse, but it lost its industry, which happened to Baltimore as well. I grew up in the seventies and eighties, when Sheffield was in economic depression. All the steelworks were closed down, and there was no new industry replacing it. There was a lot of unemployment. It was quite similar to Baltimore, but the difference was that Baltimore was hot and sunny, and so anywhere that was sunny, when you come from England or certainly from Northern England, seems to be incredibly affluent and well off.

When I got to Baltimore and we went down the beautiful row houses and those streets in the hot, bright sunshine and blue skies, David Simon even—lots of people—kept saying, "Isn't it terrible?" There's shooting galleries and there was empty houses and a bit of derelict buildings, and I thought, *No, I think it's great. You should see Sheffield.* I told that story in Sheffield, and it didn't go down very well.

MICHAEL KOSTROFF (MAURICE "MAURY" LEVY): *The Wire* gets you on Episode Three, because David Simon is a very artful and gradual storyteller. He tells stories the way a novel unfolds, and so it's very easy to watch the first episode and go, "Okay, and . . . ?"

ERNEST DICKERSON (DIRECTOR): The show really plays like a novel. You can't just tune in any time and know what's going on. You have to pretty much watch it from the beginning. It is like reading a book. I like that. I wasn't too crazy with the way American television was going, where you had the hour-long series and the conflict happens and it's totally resolved within an hour. I like the idea that this was a serial, that it was stretched out over time and it gave the characters a lot of time to develop. It felt more like life. That's one of the things I loved about it. Plus, I love the fact that it was shot on the streets of Baltimore and that it was very, very gritty.

CAROLYN STRAUSS (PRESIDENT, HBO ENTERTAINMENT): If you go back and you look at that pilot, there's a lot in that pilot that's obscure. There's a lot of things yet to be revealed. Things that aren't stated out loud. Things that aren't shouted. *The Wire*, about the fourth show, you're like, "Oh, yeah. I'm in this." You give it a couple episodes, and I would say, for most of the shows that I did that were really good shows, the pilot's good but there's a couple episodes and then you really lock down. It's a slow unfolding of complicated people, and it takes a while.

DEIRDRE "DEDE" LOVEJOY (ASST. STATE'S ATTY. RHONDA PEARLMAN): My first day of shooting on the series—after the pilot had been done and the show had been picked up—happened to be the scene at Rhonda Pearlman's house, where McNulty shows up and they wind up having sex. We were filming that sex scene in a house that had been picked to be Rhonda Pearlman's home location. It was Season One, so nobody had certainly seen the show, and we were on the second floor, in the bedroom of this house that these people had rented to this HBO TV show. Unfortunately, the people were still there on the third floor, with their little child. They had just decided to stay on the top floor and let the crew have their bottom two floors. We were shooting the scene, and we had a Hungarian director who was very, very vocal and screaming things like, "Louder! Louder!" Then, he, many times, screamed really loud, "Climax, now!" Then, you have to wait a little after he is done talking to actually do it, so that they can actually cut the sound in. Anyway, this went on, and these people were listening to this. Apparently, they decided that night that their house was no longer available as a location for this trash show because they thought we were shooting porn. Everybody got such a kick out of it that the crew, as a wrap gift, made tee shirts that said, "*The Wire*, Season One: Climax Now! Louder!"

DOMINIC WEST (DET. JIMMY MCNULTY): The camera was coming around the bed behind us. We couldn't see where it was. He said, "When the camera gets to your left shoulder, will you climax?" I said, "Look, I can't see the camera. I don't know when it's coming, and I'm concentrating on Dede." He said, "All right. I'll shout." We'd get into it, and the camera would be coming around, and he's Hungarian and he shouted, "Climax now!" We all fell about laughing. Yeah, that was the funniest sex scene I think we did. That was bloody funny.

PETER MEDAK (DIRECTOR): That love scene was great. It was very sexy and very clean. When I do love scenes in movies, to take the curse off the nudity, I always shoot it in a circular way, around the bed, so the duvet kind of semi-hides what is going on. It's always so much better with love scenes to be very suggestive and beg everybody not to cover themselves up, because it's better to be completely naked when you make a love scene, and I can avoid showing both of the people very easily, but if they're strapped up, the ladies, with all kinds of padding and things on the nipples, it always shows and it restricts you. It's much better just [to] hide it with the movement of the camera, and then it becomes very sexy. That really is one of my best memories of that episode.

DEIRDRE "DEDE" LOVEJOY (ASST. STATE'S ATTY. RHONDA PEARLMAN): I had done one day on the pilot, and Dominic is literally lying on top of me; we're completely naked. He's got the little bag that covers the male parts, and I've got the pasties on; they're covering the female parts. He is lying on top of me, and he says, "Oh, this is weird. Last week, I was on top of Renée Zellweger." He had just shot the movie *Chicago*. I was like, "Oh, thanks for that. That was really helpful to me."

DOMINIC WEST (DET. JIMMY MCNULTY): What an asshole. Did I say that? Dear, oh dear. What a jerk. It was actually true. In *Chicago*, that's all I did. I came on, had sex with Renée, and then she shot me. Then *Chicago* starts. That was a hilarious scene.

DAVID SIMON (CREATOR): He has that kind of personality where he can say things and you just sort of go, "How did you get away with that?" I once stood behind him on an elevator—this was back in the early days, before he was married. We had a beautiful day player in the scene, and she was only there for the day, then she was taking the train back to New York. I stood behind him. He didn't know I was behind him. It was a crowded elevator, and he's only got this moment. She's headed for the teamster van. He just worked a scene with her, but there was no time while they were working. You know what his pickup line was? She turned toward him and she said, "You know, I just broke up with my boyfriend." And he looked at her and he went, "Really?" And so, later on, when she missed her train back to New York, I was like, "That's all you needed? 'Really?'" I think for the next two years I just kept going up to him whenever he was talking bullshit, "Really?" That was my code for "Fuck you."

ED BURNS (CO-CREATOR): That guy, they just flocked, and it's the most incredible thing you've ever seen. It's like, the PAs [Production Assistants] would bump into telephone poles, that kind of thing.

DOMINIC WEST (DET. JIMMY MCNULTY): I do think Americans are particularly forgiving with people's accents. I mean, if you listen to Mel Gibson in any of his heyday films, his American accent is terrible, but he got away with it.

ED BURNS (CO-CREATOR): David and Dominic spent a lot of time: "Now, say it like *po*-lice." "Police." "No, *po*-lice."

PETER GERETY (JUDGE DANIEL PHELAN): Dominic had a trailer as his dressing room, and he said, "Pete, come here. Come on in my dressing room, my trailer, all right?" I said, "Yeah, what's up?" He said, "I need you to listen to me. I've got to get this Baltimore accent down," because, of course, he's British. He actually does a really good American accent, but I sort of sat with him, and he just worked through stuff for a couple of days, just to get his Baltimore American accent closer. Not that I was all that great with it, but I think I helped him a little bit.

DOMINIC WEST (DET. JIMMY MCNULTY): It never got any easier for me. It was a real problem for me, actually. I worked pretty hard on it. I think the producers felt that, eventually, perhaps I wouldn't need the coach anymore, but I did. I needed it right up until we wrapped the whole series, and it was a constant effort particularly anytime he got emotional or you started shouting. That's when you lose the accent and start going into your own accent. I always dreaded those scenes, and it was a pain in the ass.

It would have been so much easier to have done it in my own accent, but I suppose that wouldn't have necessarily sounded right. I do remember meeting Idris for the first time, and he's got a London accent, and I was saying to him, "Fuck, what about this accent?" Actually, I didn't realize he was English initially, because he was talking the whole time in American and he was living in New York at the time. I was chatting to him, and eventually he said, "Look, you've got to stop talking in that English accent because you're fucking me up." He was trying to do American the whole time, as a proper actor should, so we had to keep clear of each other for the first few weeks because we'd fuck each other up.

IDRIS ELBA (STRINGER BELL): We would laugh about it. There was only one scene where we actually worked together, and as soon as he walks in, he was talking in his English accent, and I started talking in my English accent, and I said, "Mate, we're never going to be able to pull this off." He was laughing about it. I never really said to him, "Don't do it." It was more of a joke. It was really hard working with an English actor and you're both playing Americans. It feels a bit fake.

ANDRE ROYO (REGINALD "BUBBLES" COUSINS): They were battling over who would lose their accent first. Idris won that bet. Dom would go in and out all over the place. Maybe he's Irish. Maybe he's from Baltimore. Keep him drinking. Get some Jameson in him and cover up his accent.

Early on, HBO executives asked David Simon to cut a seemingly pointless scene featuring a shadowy figure named Omar, who robbed drug dealers. His presence did not seem relevant to them in moving the story along. Simon asked them to wait. The introduction of Omar, he said, would serve as a placeholder for the character when he was reestablished later in the inaugural season.

The request paid off. Television had never seen a character as full of multitudes as Omar Little, depicted brilliantly by Michael K. Williams. The role was the first major gig for Williams, a native of Brooklyn's East Flatbush, who had dropped out of school to pursue a dancing career. Omar wore a duster and a bulletproof vest, carried a .44 Magnum, and whistled "The Farmer in the Dell" as he stalked the streets, ringing fear in the neighborhood. Yet, he nurtured out-of-luck mothers, refrained from cursing, attended church with his grandmother, and showed a caring, tender touch with his gay lovers. As inconceivable as it sounds, Omar, too, was sourced from real-life inspirations. During his days on the force, Ed Burns found that stick-up artists roamed independently and often maintained their own set of rules, while providing accurate information. He cultivated several into his best sources. Donnie Andrews, one of the primary inspirations for Omar, positively transformed his later life, becoming a consultant on The Wire.

"The guys that I knew, the Anthony Hollies, Shorty Boyd, those type of guys, they all had a code," Burns said. "They all lived by something, and they hunted drug dealers. That's what they hunted. Donnie [Andrews], he was ferocious. Ferdinand [Harvin], this guy was amazing. He gave me a call one time, and says, 'You want to hit this house.' We got a search warrant, hit the house. It's three guys who are in their fifties. You don't see many guys in their fifties with shoulder holsters, with .45s in the

shoulder holsters, at a table. It was a substantial amount of drugs on the table, but we didn't find all Ferdinand said was in there.

"I went outside, and I called him up. I said, 'We can't find it.' He says, 'I don't understand you. Every time I been at their house, I find everything.' I said, 'Ferdinand, I can't put a gun down a guy's mouth. I mean, I'm willing to talk to the guy, but I can't do that.'"

ALEXA L. FOGEL (CASTING DIRECTOR): Michael K. had auditioned for me for *Oz.* You keep very good records for all your auditions. I had to figure out which character it was that he had auditioned for, and I had to go back every season and go through every page until I could find him. I knew I had wrote in my notes that he had this scar, so that's how I refound him to have him in for *The Wire.* He made an impression. I knew I wanted to see him again.

MICHAEL K. WILLIAMS (OMAR LITTLE): I mean, it was odd. How many people walk around with a scar in the middle of their face? It's a very odd thing to see. When you really think about it, on my face, you know? My face got mauled over. It's jarring.

ED BURNS (CO-CREATOR): We picked Omar, primarily, because of the scar. His first scene was him and his partner, getting ready to go do a robbery, and the guy comes and gives him a sawed-off shotgun. He takes the shotgun and—Mike was the name of the guy who gave it to him—he starts walking away, and Michael K. says, "Excuse me." "Yes?" "How do you open this?" "It's a fucking shotgun, Michael." I'm standing right next to him going, "Oh God, this is going to be so bad," And then he goes out there and it looked like when he was in his crib, his mother gave him a shotgun.

MICHAEL K. WILLIAMS (OMAR LITTLE): My contract was for seven episodes. It was guaranteed seven, and then after that, we'll see. The direction and the development of the character happened as the character in the show went along. It served the storyline and the authenticity of the story that David was telling to take Omar out at any given time. It was clear to me that that would be the case. No one knew when Omar was going to go. No one knew. He didn't have a trajectory for Omar. I was told that Omar would meet his demise at one point or another. I remember me being told that early on. When, how—that was up in the air. I went into every season like, *Now this could be it.* His trajectory wasn't as thought out, in my belief, as maybe a Barksdale storyline or the Stringer Bell storyline.

DAVID SIMON (CREATOR): He was only supposed to be in seven [episodes] of the first season. He misapprehended the idea of "And then you're dead." We basically only contracted for seven, and we didn't have a pickup for another season, so I knew we weren't going to bring him back every episode, and I think he only comes on in [Episode] Three. I don't think he's lying, but I've since seen his interviews and I've joked with him about it.

MICHAEL K. WILLIAMS (OMAR LITTLE): I was a deer in the headlights, full-on in Season One.

ED BURNS (CO-CREATOR): Omar is a composite of five or six guys that were my informants who were gun slingers. Each one brought a little something to the Omar character, and it became the present character.

This guy, Anthony Hollie, he was extremely soft-spoken, very gentle, and a ferocious gunslinger. I mean, ferocious. He had a buddy that he always hung around with, who was a younger guy. That might have been in the back of my head. His buddy was beaten to death by the drug dealers, and Anthony retaliated. That scene of the body slung across the car—that's probably how David and I came up with that, just by going over his story. Anthony and Donnie [Andrews], when they were on your side, it was a one hundred percent. It was no games. They didn't play games. They trusted you implicitly, and I trusted them implicitly. They were solid. A lot of the other guys you would never turn your back on, but that's how that happened.

Anthony never cursed, never raised his voice. He came out of his house one Sunday morning and there must have been six or seven guys waiting for him. If you go down the street, you can still see the pock marks, the bullet holes, where they shot, and that was a true violation, because he went to visit his mother. That was Sunday; he was supposed to have a break. Didn't happen. They wanted him real bad, so I got him into witness protection and got him out of the city.

DAVID SIMON (CREATOR): [Avon and Stringer] are not Melvin [Williams] and Chin [Farmer]. They start from that starting point, but then you're grafting into all these different guys that you knew or heard stories about. There's elements of [Maurice] "Peanut" King. There's elements of Will Franklin. The characters become ten different guys, and then the actors become themselves. They become totally somebody else. There's no one-to-one ratio for anybody.

Omar's six different guys.

MICHAEL KEVIN DARNALL (BRANDON WRIGHT): I worked my first day on *The Wire*. It was awesome. I met Michael K. Williams and Lance Williams, who played Omar and [John] Bailey. We got along really well. I met Dominic, Sonja, and Andre, and it was really great. It was awesome, but it was really hard. Because, after that first day of work, I went home to my day job, because we had wraps so early in the day. I was telling my coworkers about this great day on set. They were asking me a million questions, and then something said, *Check your voicemail.* I was having this aching suspicion. I called my voicemail, and one of my close friends, actress Amanda Fields, she had left me a message. I called, and she told me that my girlfriend had passed away. So, it was like, "Holy shit." The best day of my life was suddenly the worst day of my life.

I, of course, was frantic, and my boss said, "Go home. Take care of yourself." I did, and the next day, I was up at five in the morning to go back to *The Wire*. So, that next day was not as great. I was really kind of in a daze. We filmed well into the night. We did the scene where we robbed the stash house, where Omar takes the shotgun and blows the guy's legs away. I just remember Peter Medak, the director—he was so frustrated with me. Uta, the cinematographer, she was like, "Michael, you got to slow down." I was moving so fast, and I didn't tell anyone but my cast members and the makeup people, Debi [Young]. So, they didn't really know what was going on with me, but, yeah, I was completely out of it that day.

MICHAEL K. WILLIAMS (OMAR LITTLE): I think it was about two or three days on set that I had been working before I even met David. He ran up on me one night when I was wrapping, going to get my ride to go back to base camp to change, and he ran up on me and he introduced himself and he said, "Man," his exact words, "if I'd known you guys, the three of you"—and it was Omar, Michael, the guy who played his love interest, and Lance Williams, who played Bailey—and he goes, "Man, you guys know how to make it work." He goes, "Man, I wish I would have known in the beginning that you were going to bring it to where you were, because I would have made you kind of like my *Wild Bunch*." I was like, "What do you mean *Wild Bunch*?" He looked at me and said, "You never watched the Western *The Wild Bunch*?" I was like, "No." That was probably the first and only homework that David gave me. He told me I was to go watch *The Wild Bunch* and another Western because he wrote Omar's duster, the Wild, Wild West, and the standoff with Brother Mouzone and Omar in the alleyway—those are an old-school Western thing.

DAVID SIMON (CREATOR): There were some of these guys who robbed drug dealers I knew all about. Some of them I didn't. Obviously, Donnie [Andrews] I knew. There was a duo that always worked together. Ed told me many stories about Cadillac and his partner. He told me the story, and somehow, in one of the stories he told, I assumed that they were gay, that they were lovers. They were inseparable. They worked together robbing drug dealers for years and years and years. They lived together. I thought they were gay. So, I looked around our universe and said, "Can anybody in this world be gay? Somebody ought to be." I knew lots of openly lesbian cops. I didn't know any openly gay male police. But I knew plenty of lesbian cops, proud ones, so Kima was an obvious choice. And then I looked around in the structured drug trade and—I could be wrong; I'm sure there are exceptions, but it seemed to me a very homophobic culture. But a guy on his own robbing drug dealers? That feels right. And hey, we have the example of Cadillac.

It was, like, a year later when somebody was asking me a question in an interview and I started to bring up that there was a duo in Baltimore, and Ed looked at me and said, "They weren't gay." In my mind, I'd used them as ballast to justify it, but I just got it wrong.

MICHAEL K. WILLIAMS (OMAR LITTLE): They kept writing. I knew that the dude was gay. All they kept doing: *Omar rubs the boy's lips. Omar rubs the boy's hair. Omar holds the boy's hand.* I'm like, "Don't gay people fuck? You know what I mean? Don't they kiss? Don't they grab each other?" I was like, "Listen, we've got to step it up." [Michael Kevin Darnall] was with it, and I'll never forget, he made me laugh. He said, "When do you think it should happen?" I went to tell him. I wanted to tell him right after I cut that barrel, that double-barrel shotgun and say, "Let's go hunting." But he was like, "Don't tell me. Don't tell me, because if I know when it's coming, I might freeze up. Just go for it."

[Director Clark Johnson] looked at me. He gagged. That dude, he was like, "Whoa, whoa, whoa. Hold on. Stop the work. Run that back."

MICHAEL KEVIN DARNALL (BRANDON WRIGHT): Michael and I were sitting in that van once, waiting to shoot another couple of lines of dialogue. He was just sort of sitting there quietly, looking out in the distance. He said, "You know, Michael, when this thing finally airs, we're going to get a lot of phone calls." He, more so than I ever could imagine, knew how big this Omar character was going to be. He was just prescient in that way. Just in the bottom of his heart, pit of his stomach, he just really had a feeling that this was going to be big. And it was. Look at what Omar became, and look what it did for Michael's career. Pretty amazing stuff. I really think that we were, perhaps, the first two men of color to have a kiss on national television.

[After Brandon is killed], to see the amount of vitriol and ignorance coming from the viewing audience, by making the mistake back then of reading comments on message boards and YouTube. As an artist, I was not afraid. I guess that's my ignorance as a young, eager artist. Then reality hit. It was like, *There's a lot of ugliness in this world, and I don't think you were really ready for it.* That's not to say that that's the overwhelming response. Because the overwhelming response, of course, has been absolutely positive to this show, and to Omar and his relationships. Yeah, I think that was the big surprise for me. That there is a world of hate out there.

There were things like, "I'm glad that faggot is dead." People who will be like, "Omar's a real man or Omar's my nigga, but that little faggot bitch . . . His little, red, dick-riding bitch." Things like that, that kind of make you laugh, but then you're like, "Oh, that's pretty terrible." I think what hurt the most was the idea that a quote-unquote hypermasculine gay person was okay, but a fair-skinned, soft-spoken, light-haired gay guy who people couldn't tell if I was black, white, mixed, Latino—they called me everything under the book. That somehow that kind of gay person didn't deserve to live or that he was unworthy of any sort of admiration or love—that hurt. Even though, look at what Brandon did, he went to bat, and he didn't give up Omar's name. He sat and—of course, this is all off-screen—he sat and got tortured and got his life taken because he didn't give up Omar's name. That's not as macho or impressive as toting around a sawed-off shotgun and whistling "The Farmer in the Dell." People, not everyone, but some people forget about that aspect of Brandon, that he went out rather valiantly.

MICHAEL K. WILLIAMS (OMAR LITTLE): It was the first time I ever got an extreme close-up; it was on *The Wire*. My knucklehead up in the full screen—it was on *The Wire*. It was the scene where Omar says, "Omar don't scare." That scene where he's being interrogated in the police department about who killed his lover, played by Michael? The director was Ed Bianchi, right? Ed wanted me to play it like no emotion, like cold, all bravado. It's like Omar the Terror.

Uta was the DP [director of photography]. She stood up. She has such a strong feeling while she was looking up through the camera. It was so intense. She said, "I think that he should have a little bit of softness, like a little more emotion, to show that he has a little softer side. This man has lost his lover viciously. There should be something else there. Not just all rage and terror." They started to argue. It became a thing. I have never seen it before or since in my career, when the DP felt that strongly about something that they argued with the fucking director, but she did.

If you know Ed, you know that Ed don't take no shit. You ain't going to work. No, Ed don't take no shit. She had to bow down and play her position, but when it was all said and done, before them cameras rolled, she came up behind me and patted my shoulder. She said, "Find a way to give us both what we want." No pressure. No fucking pressure at all. All I know is when you go back and look at that scene where Omar says, "Omar don't scare," and you look in his eyes, whatever you see there, that is me trying to give them both what they felt they needed to see. I'll never forget that.

UTA BRIESEWITZ (CINEMATOGRAPHER): I would never, ever go behind a director's back and give opposite directions to what he or she has given the actor prior. That would be completely undermining the director. It's not my position as a DP to do that. And I know in my heart I would have never done such a thing.

Yes, I have strong opinions, but I also tried never to argue with directors, but respect their word as the final direction, especially speaking performances. It's absolutely not my place to make my opinion heard in any way.

It happened to me often, though, that sometimes actors would come up to me with a question regarding their performance. My answer to them always was, "Sorry, but I can't speak to this. You have to ask the director." And this is the absolute truth about how I carried myself as a DP on set.

I am not sure what triggered Michael to have such a memory of that scene. I would never argue with directors, especially not with Ed Bianchi, who always was one of my favorites and who I respected very much. Michael and I had a great relationship. Maybe he is trying to give me credit here for something that just shouldn't be given.

The Wire *allowed its audience space to interpret. It would not fully explain scenes, instead leaving viewers pondering the meaning of them for episodes, and sometimes seasons, at a time. One early moment hammered that methodology home. In real life, Ed Burns and Harry Edgerton had worked the murder of Dessera Press, who had been dumped by one of Williams's lieutenants, Louis "Cookie" Savage. In retaliation, she had threatened to turn Savage into the state's attorney. A gunman killed her, firing from outside a glass window. Through that case, Burns and Edgerton unearthed Savage's connection to Melvin Williams. In a storyline that recalled Press's killing, Jimmy McNulty and Bunk Moreland visit the apartment of a murdered young woman in Episode 4. They quickly discover that the previous detective bungled the investigation, and they slowly and methodically retrace the murder and link it to Avon Barksdale's conspirators. Television had never seen anything quite like it. McNulty and Bunk conversed in the nearly five-minute scene by using only iterations of the word fuck. Simon credits the scene as an ode to Terry McLarney, a detective sergeant and a fixture in* Homicide: A Year on the Killing Streets.

DAVID SIMON (CREATOR): We're standing at a crime scene. We're staring, and cops are just cursing left and right. Somebody said something that was so profanity laden that Terry McLarney just started giggling and saying, "One day we're going to get to the point where we're all going to be able to just use the word *fuck* to communicate." And it was just a throwaway line for Terry, but I remembered it. So, I came to Ed with it, and then Ed wrote that scene.

ED BURNS (CO-CREATOR): Terry is an amazing guy. He might even still be on the force. He was telling David, basically, these homicide things are so matter-of-fact, it just becomes a matter of grunts. I wrote it, and I used four variations of the word *fuck*: "What the fuck? Oh, fuck. Fucked up." But just four, and the actors were uncomfortable with the four lines, so then he was like, "Fuck, fuck, fuck, fuck, fuck," and I asked the director, "Just give me the one. Get them to do the fucking job that they're being paid for," and I went to them and I said, "We need the one." It turns out that David used the "Fuck, fuck, fuck, fuck, fuck," which, to me, is like, wait a minute, the scene is about this harmony of doing an investigation and they're so used to it. But we ended up with the "Fuck, fuck, fuck" because it was a little bit, apparently, more fun. I didn't particularly see it that way, but it was fine.

WENDELL PIERCE (DET. WILLIAM "BUNK" MORELAND): David comes up to us and describes a scene. He says, "You're going to go to the scene. You're going to realize that [the previous] detective, he did a bad job. Wendell, you're going to see the photos of the girl. Dominic, you're going to start getting the stats, looking at what the report was. Going back over, you're going to realize it's impossible to have gone down the way it was reported, because the guy would have to be like eight feet tall to get that trajectory. If he did, then something must be left in here, and you're looking for any evidence that may be around, and Wendell, you discover that there's a shot through the window. The glass is on the inside. It means it came from the outside. That means whoever the perpetrator was wasn't inside, like the person they say in the report. The bullet came from outside. From there, let's see the trajectory. It would be right here, in the refrigerator. Let's see, not the wall. In the refrigerator, we find the bullet here. Let's go outside, make a new discovery." He explained the whole scene to us. He said, "Now you guys are going to do that whole thing, but they're going to be on me about the profanity and language that we use." So, I said, "Let's just come out the box with it." He said, "You're going to do that whole scene, but the only word you can say is '*fuck*.'" I said, "What?"

CLEMENT VIRGO (DIRECTOR): I wanted to really let the audience in and know exactly what was happening visually. It took a long time to shoot that scene, but I wanted to get it right. I wanted it to be kind of like the shower scene in *Psycho*, where it was a lot of setups. The story was told visually, and so I was very detailed in shooting that scene. I remember our cinematographer, Uta, shot the whole thing—we shot the whole thing handheld—and I remember looking over at her, and she was wiped out from holding the camera for a long time. I really wanted to get all the kind of little details, and I wanted the audience to not have any mystery about what was happening in the story.

WENDELL PIERCE (DET. WILLIAM "BUNK" MORELAND): I think it's an example of one of the best displays of my acting in the whole series. I tell folks, "Study that if you want to study what intent is," because everyone understood exactly what we were doing at every moment, even though we were using just that one word or [a] variation thereof. That was one of the best-acted scenes that I did on the show. The one thing they cut out that I regret is we said, "Fuck. Fuck me. Mother fuck. Fuckity fuck," all of that. Then we were [being] watched the whole time by the super. "Fuck. Motherfucker. Fuck." We go outside and we find the casing, and the super says, "Well, I'll be fucked." They cut that out, though. I was like, "Oh, man, they should have left that in."

DOMINIC WEST (DET. JIMMY MCNULTY): Every time someone said, "Cut," we were crying with laughter, Wendell and me, because it was really fun to do. It would get outrageous, sort of go, "Fuckkk," and "Fuuuckkk," most of which hit the cutting room floor, thank goodness, but it was just the most ludicrous varieties of saying "fuck" that we could think of.

Throughout The Wire's *run, David Simon fielded one question often: How could a white man adequately tell a story so intimately linked to the experience of blacks? He would grow weary of the question, and tried allowing his work to speak for itself. The fact is he would have failed as a reporter covering the crime beat had he not learned to listen and interpret the demographic of the city he reported on. Behind the scenes, Simon attempted to groom young black writers and directors. He was a fan of Spike Lee, and hoped Lee would direct an episode of* The Wire, *although talks over this collapsed. Simon has conceded that he probably missed aspects that black creative minds could have spoken to more capably. Often, he would be tested with his cast on his intentions. It started with Sonja Sohn in the first season.*

WENDELL PIERCE (DET. WILLIAM "BUNK" MORELAND): The first year, Sonja and David bumped heads. David Simon said, "It's a show with no hope." Sonja went off.

DAVID SIMON (CREATOR): What I was saying to her is effectively what the show said, which is: "This is going to be a cruel world and nothing's going to get fixed that matters systemically." Systemic. I was going to promote all the wrong people, and the same policies were going to go on. Regardless of any conversation I had with her, that's how the show ended.

But she's right, the characters themselves, as individuals, were entitled to a certain figure of dignity at points. Some of them, anyway.

As it should be. Even in a rigged game, people don't cease to be human, and the human heart doesn't stop beating. But at the time that I said it, I think we were arguing past each other. She was talking about characters, her character, other characters, and I was talking about the systems that we were depicting. I think the system part of the show was more in my head, and Ed Burns's head, than in the people who were being asked to depict the world. Because it has to be. You're asking them to be in the moment, and human beings in the moment, we all live as we live. We're not constantly standing back and going, "Let me have my omniscient moment of seeing the whole."

Actors are particularly susceptible to seeing the world powerfully from the point of view of their characters. It's what their job is. You never tell an actor who's about to do a bad thing, "You're a bad guy." I'm always telling my actors when they're about to do something bad or something morally transgressive, "You're a good guy. This is a bad moment, but you're a good guy." Because unless you're a total sociopath, which very few people are, the people doing bad things are still people, and the people having noble moments are still people, and the next moment they'll do a bad thing. I think, in some ways, we weren't even applying the terms in the same way. But I do remember butting heads with her. Because she's a progressive, optimistic person, and I'm a progressive, pessimistic person.

SONJA SOHN (DET. SHAKIMA "KIMA" GREGGS): It's really important [to know] that the context of my understanding of the business, my knowledge of who David was, is very different now than it was then. My perspective now has adjusted a little bit from what it was at the time. Because of David's experience, twenty years on the streets of Baltimore, and now that I have been on the streets of Baltimore, I fucking get it. I thought that he was losing it in that blanket statement.

Today, I understand the truth of that statement, where he was coming from, because he really was talking about the systemic, struc tural, racist policies that inevitably are going to keep a large number, if not the majority, of people struggling to survive in the hood. I didn't understand structural, institutional racism at the time the way I understand it now, so David was really making that statement more from that perspective. For me, I was someone who had spent a lot of my childhood, a lot of my life, making sure that I was not going to be one of the people that was going to stay oppressed and suppressed by my environment.

I found that statement appalling because I knew that even though I didn't grow up in Baltimore, I did grow up in a comparable environment. I grew up in an underserved community that was dealing with a lot of those poor issues. Even though it was a generation earlier, and it looks different in the seventies, the core issues were the same. I had worked my way out of having to live in survival mode. I had worked my way into a place where some people call it the beginning of life's success. All I had was my own hopes and dreams and the knowledge that I was going to escape the traps. When David said that, it just struck me as a real sour note. I also knew there were some guys who were actors who had all transcended those environmental obstacles to be on the show, to get to a place in life where they could have a successful acting career.

We were the hope. We were evidence that it's possible. All of us, not just actors, but all of us who have come from those backgrounds, have acquired some level of success in the world. We are the hope for those who are struggling.

LANCE REDDICK (LT. CEDRIC DANIELS): Somehow, I was alone with David, and we just got to talking. I asked him something. I remember him saying organizations can't be reformed, but people can. I remember being struck by it when he said it, because I knew that I had never thought of it that way, and I knew that there was something profound in the insight. Then, over time, particularly when I watched the show, I realized how we see both on the criminal side and on the police side, you see people struggling to live up to the codes of the institutions that they're a part of and seeing how it chips away at their humanity.

DAVID SIMON (CREATOR): I had told him it was much harder to reform a system. The things that reform systems are trauma. Great trauma. Nobody gives up status quo without being pushed to the wall. I believe that politically. The great reformations of society are the result of undue excess and undue cruelty. The reason you have collective bargaining in America and it became powerful is that workers were pushed to the starvation point. The reason that you have the civil rights we do is that people were hanging from trees. That notion of the system [being] self-reforming without incredible outside pressure and without first [bringing] about incredible trauma through inhumanity or indifference—I find that to be really dubious. I'm arguing for reform. It's not like I can say this and say we should throw up our hands and can't try. Every day, you gotta get up. I'm saying this with the clarity of: there's no choice but to try.

Over time, the name of the novelist George Pelecanos kept popping up in conversations David Simon was having. Kary Antholis, the HBO executive, originally recommended that Simon read Pelecanos's book The Sweet Forever. Simon took the suggestion as needling. He owed Antholis late scripts for The Corner and interpreted the earnest recommendation as a prod to him to hurry. Simon and Pelecanos finally talked at the funeral of a mutual friend. The pair, standing next to each other, believed that the friends and family of the deceased bookstore owner would gently place the first layer of dirt on the grave in traditional Jewish burial fashion. Instead, a backhoe jumped to a start and began piling dirt onto the plot. "Is this traditional?" Pelecanos asked, turning to Simon without a trace of a grin on his face. "Is this traditional for you guys?"

"He cracked me up," Simon recalled. "He just slayed me. I was no good for the rest of the day. I was like, Man, not only is he a good writer, he's funny. Dark and funny. I sought him out after that."

Pelecanos became a needed third voice and, in some cases, tie-breaker, for the creative forces of Simon and Burns during the run of the show. Simon entrusted Pelecanos to author many of the show's fine-grained scenes, and he wrote the seasons' penultimate episodes, which often killed off major characters, beginning with the gut-wrenching murder of Michael B. Jordan's Wallace by his friends Bodie (J. D. Williams) and Poot (Tray Chaney) in Season 1. Eventually, actors began flipping to the back of any script Pelecanos had written to make sure their character had survived.

GEORGE PELECANOS (WRITER/PRODUCER): [David Simon's wife, the novelist] Laura [Lippman] and I both knew this woman who passed, and we went to the funeral, and David was there. Laura, unbeknownst to me, had given David one of my books, and it happened to be a book called *The Sweet Forever*, which is one of my deep, sort-of urban novels from that period. It was very close to what he was doing. It was kind of fortuitous that he read that book in particular.

DAVID SIMON (CREATOR): My wife and I [had] just started dating then. My wife's a novelist, and she was a contemporary of George's. She'd been on me to read George. She goes, "You should read Pelecanos. He's interested in the same stuff. His heart is where your heart is." And I'm like, "Yeah, he's from DC." I had that Baltimore [thing], like, "I'm sorry, those are the lawyers who come to the Orioles games and sit there on their cell phones for five innings. Fuck those guys." And I'm from DC originally, so I had sort of like [a] Baltimore chip on my shoulder. So, I hadn't pulled one of his books up.

GEORGE PELECANOS (WRITER/PRODUCER): I didn't have a ride back to the shivah. He says, "Ride with me. I want to talk to you about something." I ride with him, and he says, "I've got this show. Would you want to write an episode? Would you like to try it?" I said, "Sure, I'll try it." I didn't know David at all, even though he grew up just about three or four miles from me and we went to Maryland together. But I didn't know him at Maryland. He's a little bit younger than me, and he was real involved with *The Diamondback*, the school newspaper there. I wasn't involved with anything. When I got out of classes, I went to my job, which was selling women's shoes.

Even when he first approached me to write for the show, he didn't overdo it. He said to me, "Yeah, I've got a show. I just sold the pilot to HBO. It's about drug dealers and cops in Baltimore." That sounds pretty basic, right? I had watched *Homicide* for the whole run, but especially *The Corner*, [which] had been on already. I saw what he had done. *The Corner* is sort of a blueprint for what *The Wire* was going to be. I knew what he was capable of and where his heart was politically and socially. And actually, that's what convinced me to give it a shot. I think, in a very broad sense, he's always had the overarching idea in his head of this show, and what he wanted to do with it. He's a macro guy. If you say to me, go write a book about the drug war's failure, it would probably intimidate me. I'm more of a micro guy. I like to dig into the characters in the individual scenes and dialogue. But David knew what the big picture was.

My first script for *The Wire*, I wrote it and turned it in, and I can't even remember if David gave me any notes. When I got the published script, let's say about thirty percent of what I had written was in the final script. I called David up, and of course I said, "What happened to my script?" If I remember correctly, he had Jim Yoshimura in the room with him for some reason. They were hanging out. He's friends with Jim. They worked together on *Homicide*. They were on speakerphone, and David says, "Hey, Jim, Pelecanos got thirty percent. He's complaining." And David said, "That's pretty good, to get thirty percent your first time."

DAVID SIMON (CREATOR): It's hard to get into the voice of a show that is not your initial creation. You're flying one plane and on the runway. Other people in the control tower are looking at the whole screen. Some things you did perfectly well, but the script came in before you went in a different direction, or the script that's coming after you has to do something and you're not setting it up right. Maybe because the beat you were given was imprecise. Maybe because you veered in a way that was worthy for your script, but doesn't work for the whole. There's all these variables that can conspire against even a perfectly fluid and competent writer when they turn in a script on a continuing series.

ANDRE ROYO (REGINALD "BUBBLES" COUSINS): A long time ago, David was like, "Do you want to be an okay television show or you want to be a classic television show? This is not Walt Disney. People have to die. It doesn't matter if you kill one actor that's in a couple of scenes. If the audience doesn't care about the actor you're killing, then you haven't done your job. They got to care about this person." We knew that was the theme.

MICHAEL B. JORDAN (WALLACE): Once my character started taking drugs a little bit and started sniffing coke, I kind of knew there was a slow decline.

DAVID SIMON (CREATOR): I said it to Michael, "People are going to remember Wallace. Wallace is going to bother them for a long time after the whole show is forgotten. You're going to work. You're going to have a career. You did great with this." They all look at you like, *This is the last job I'll ever get.* You can never convince them enough.

MICHAEL B. JORDAN (WALLACE): I kind of knew it was coming. Especially when you get that knock on your trailer door from David Simon. I'll never forget it. He said, "I love you. The audience loves you. We've got to kill you. We've got to kill you off." I remember telling my mom not to show up on set that day. My mom gets extremely emotional, and this was kind of too much. I didn't want her to see it. It was a long time to shoot that shot. We definitely overshot that for sure. I remember them having to duct-tape the windows, so the light wouldn't go through, because we were going so late into the night, to the morning. But it was really quiet. The crew knew.

Everybody showed up. Even if they weren't working, they kind of showed up on set. I know Andre Royo did, for sure. He was definitely a mentor of mine on that show. He showed up to help me get into the mind-set and really talk me through it. I remember getting the squib under my shirt. They had a tube running down my leg with warm water for when he peed himself, when he got scared and shit. Me and J. D. Williams, who played Bodie, we're both from Newark, New Jersey, and we both spent a lot of time on that show together, and I learned a lot from him over that show. We was just talking to each other, and then [when we started shooting the scene] it was like I didn't even know him.

GEORGE PELECANOS (WRITER/PRODUCER): That was shot as I wrote it. I was very fortunate, because I had these extraordinary actors doing the scene. I heard that it was a very emotional day on set, because everybody loved Michael B. Jordan.

DAVID SIMON (CREATOR): I gave him the Wallace scene because, at that point, I had read three or four of his novels, and his violence was never gratuitous. It was always on a human scale, and it had a narrative tension that was that of a novel. So, I always knew that those things would always have heart. And I thought he was the best person to chase that stuff. That was "use what you have." To have a novelist's sense of tension when it comes to violence is really picture perfect.

ED BURNS (CO-CREATOR): It was Pelecanos who wrote that murder scene, and I didn't like it. We made Bodie a psychopath, and psychopaths don't hesitate. It was great for the character growing. I won't deny that. It was great for the actor—really gave him a stretch. He turned out to be a great actor, but to me, it didn't follow the logic of who the kid was. You create a psychopath, there's no moral sense of having him not pull the trigger.

DAVID SIMON (CREATOR): I was listening to Ed. But I'm also listening to George, and one of them had a better argument. Once you read George's scenes, there was something surprising. Bodie seemed to be heading for this moment the whole time. If somebody goes exactly where they say they're gonna go always, human beings aren't like that. The Chekhovian model of character is people don't say exactly what they mean. They say what they think other people want to hear or what they want to hear themselves. They don't say exactly what they're thinking. They're not blunt. They have a roundabout way of avoiding certain truths. Then they find themselves as contents under pressure. And then there are different outcomes. Sometimes that makes for the best moments in drama and also the most interesting moments in real life. People are contradictory. I felt like I was watching Bodie becoming a much more interesting character. You can see the dividends that got paid on it in Season Four. It's a self-reflection on his life. You couldn't have him just blot-out lawless. I couldn't do anything ever with him ever again. It would've stunted him. That would've been it. There's nowhere to go with that character at that point, other than have him perform various acts and be serviceable to the plot.

J. D. WILLIAMS (PRESTON "BODIE" BROADUS): It wasn't an emotional thing for my character. Bodie, he tries not to step over the line, but once he's over the line, he's committed. That's where he was going with it. Throughout the day, you might have been seeing Bodie's apprehension or him thinking about what he has to do. Then, there is that flash in the room where he's like, he should've stayed away, but at the time, I was feeling it should've been just more resolute. The way I had been playing the character all that season, he was pretty committed to certain things he was doing, whether it's walking out of the juvenile hall or punching out an old man cop. I felt like once he made a decision, he pretty much stuck with it. It worked.

I don't think either one of us is wrong, because the audience loved the fact that Bodie did feel. They could tell that he felt compassion, which I think they would've been able to tell anyway. The audience loved that fact, and the point still got across that Wallace's death was tragic.

TRAY CHANEY (MALIK "POOT" CARR): I had just experienced a loss, a death in my family. This guy that was like a brother to me was abducted and killed, and he was like my best friend. As you could see, the way the scene was set up, it was set up for whatever it was, but I think the emotion for me came from my reality.

MICHAEL B. JORDAN (WALLACE): I don't think there was a dry eye in the house. I think everybody was kind of affected by that one, man. Everybody was fucked up.

LAWRENCE GILLIARD JR. (D'ANGELO BARKSDALE): I think it was his mom, came to me like, "Can you talk to him?" I'm like, "Bro, you're talented. You're young. Don't stress it. It's just a job. You'll move on. You'll move on from this, and you'll get on something else that's great. Just keep doing your thing." That's all we can do as actors. It's hard when you're doing it, but you gotta remember that it is just a job.

J. D. WILLIAMS (PRESTON "BODIE" BROADUS): He was going through it. I had to pull him to the side. I explained to him, I said, "First off, a death scene, this is where that theater training comes in, because that's the main thing you want to do on the stage, is die. You can't do any more acting than that." I tried to explain to him that a death scene is an honor, and it's very important because, once you die, the people are going to start looking for you. They're going to say, "Well, he was great. I loved that character. Who was that guy?" Because you did your job. Now you're going to be embedded in people's emotions, and they're going to be looking for you, and they're going to root for you because of the sympathy. This is going to be good for you. He calmed down some. He got his self together. He shot the scene, and as soon as the director yelled, "Cut," as soon as he hit the floor, he sat up and he started crying.

MICHAEL B. JORDAN (WALLACE): You just get into it and then you just go from there. Yeah, man. Went through it, got shot. Then I remember we did it a couple times. I want to say we did like two takes, three takes. And then I took a break or something and I went out. I just remember my mom bawling, hearing her sob. I remember hearing her crying, and I'm like, "Oh God." The whole emotional thing. That was cool. That was an intense night.

CLARKE PETERS (DET. LESTER FREAMON): I've put it to my agent, "Don't give me jobs where I'm getting killed off all the time. Please don't." It sends the wrong messages to people. There are actors who really like to and will die really good, give real good death scenes. Give the job to that cat. I want to live to play another day.

GEORGE PELECANOS (WRITER/PRODUCER): The tragedy was that [Wallace] couldn't leave. He couldn't leave his environment, and he kept coming back. I think that's what I wrote in that episode: "This is me, yo. Right here." Like, "I'm Baltimore. I'm not going anywhere." He even goes out to the country for a while, and he can't stand it. And he keeps going back.

MICHAEL B. JORDAN (WALLACE): Wallace was the heart of the show. David wanted to rip that heart out and really use Wallace as a harsh example of sometimes being the victim of your circumstances. Good kid, good heart, he had good intentions, and you could see with that environment what those types of circumstances can do to a kid like that. All these guys may be looked at a certain type of way. All aren't what they maybe seem to be. I love that symbolism and what that stood for. And to see that end so viciously with his two boys, his two best friends . . . That death scene is something people always come up to me and talk about and say how they were crying and how much it affected them. Years later. It's just a testament to the writing and that crazy performance. It was awesome.

That's when I fell in love with acting. I fell in love with acting right around the time where Wallace started sniffing coke. That was the first moment when I ever lost myself in a character, where I didn't feel like myself, where I was totally zoned in, and Andre Royo really helped me with that. I really fell in love with acting at that moment. Up until that point, it was a lot of imitating or trying to be in the moment. My mind state was, *Play it, make it as real as possible, and just try to go through it.* At that age, my mind isn't as developed as now. My strategy, my process, wasn't as developed. It was really raw. That was me as raw as you was going to get.

GEORGE PELECANOS (WRITER/PRODUCER): After that, unofficially—we never shook on it or anything like that—David always gave me the penultimate episode of the season. That happened to be the episode where people got killed. By the end of the run, people were wearing tee shirts on set. I don't even know who made them. It said my name, Pelecanos, and it had a pen with blood dripping on it. Even the actors got to the point where they sort of dreaded the script coming out that I was going to write because, by policy, we would never tell the actor that he or she was going to get killed. We didn't want the performances to get telegraphed. If they knew in the beginning of the season that they were going to get killed in a certain episode, we felt like they might telegraph it. Think about it. When your character is killed in a TV show, it's like somebody handing you a pink slip. You're fired. It's not a pleasant thing. But I always got that penultimate episode, and it's because of the Wallace scene in Season One.

LAWRENCE GILLIARD JR. (D'ANGELO BARKSDALE): I'm maybe eighty percent prepared when I get to set, because I like to leave a little room for whatever the director's ideas are, whatever the other actors in the room, whatever their ideas are. It's all about collaborating. I didn't prepare. I wasn't at home in the mirror repeating, "Where's Wallace?" and "I'm gonna look like this. I'm gonna do that."

I remember Clement [Virgo] coming out at one point. There are certain moments when you're working when the director can just give you a certain look. It's really just a look. They don't have to say anything. He came out and he just gave me this look. I guess I took it up another notch after that. It changed something in my performance. Obviously with that scene, it took something up a notch, and that was when it really started cooking, after that. It was a very emotional scene, and I was just in that moment. You could feel it. I remember. Everybody in the room and around me could feel that it was really happening. That's the magic of it all. That's what you're always striving for when you're acting, when you're on set, when you're in front of that camera. You always want that magical moment where it's really happening, until they say, "Cut."

DELANEY WILLIAMS (SGT. JAY LANDSMAN): When Kima gets shot, that first season, we had a scene where we're doing the search in the train yard for the shooters. This was a big helicopter, nighttime scene, closed down all the streets, and then we spent a lot of time in the train yard looking for evidence, where the perpetrators had gone through and got to their getaway car. It was a long, long night, much longer than it should've been, because it was in a train yard and we shot out the scene, and then a train pulls in and stops. And when the train pulls in and stops in a scene that you've already shot, you have a new train, and you can't cut between shots. So, they had to get the train to move, but to get a train to move out of a train yard is quite an operation. At least an hour and a half to get the right people on the phone to get the train to move out of the train yard, so we could finish shooting.

BRIAN ANTHONY WILSON (DET. VERNON HOLLEY): We were shooting a very tense scene where we were in the hospital, and Frankie Faison was cracking jokes, and I had to gain my composure and stop smiling. He's a really funny guy, and he's a very great actor, too, but he keeps it light on the set. There was a lot of tension, because it was a somber thing. We're waiting to see if she survives, when a cop gets shot.

DOMINIC WEST (DET. JIMMY MCNULTY): I was sort of rather hung up about crying, because I thought it was a sign of great acting. It wasn't something I could do very easily. I think a lot of actors, and certainly male actors, are hung up about crying on-screen. But for some reason, I thought it was appropriate that I should cry on-screen at this point. I had to spend the whole day before in a sort of miserable gloom and thinking about dead babies and trying to get myself into the space.

I was hanging around Frankie [Faison]. Fantastic guy and really funny, but I was trying to be deadly serious in between takes, to keep in the zone and try and keep the tears coming, which is impossible to do and a pointless exercise anyway. Frankie kept cracking jokes. I'd made the set really gloomy, and no one felt they could speak. It was tense on set because I was acting so hard. It was some sort of music on some radio, a sort of low rap beat coming out of a speaker somewhere, and Frankie started moving to the beat and going, "Would it be inappropriate if Kima was dying and then we all just started dancing?" It was so funny that I couldn't stop laughing, and I thought, *Fuck, Frankie really fucked me up. I've lost it, you know.* I've come out of the zone. In fact, I think he was trying to lighten things up anyway, because that's the only way you can act it. Then I did the scene, and I tried to cry as much as I could.

STEVE SHILL (DIRECTOR): I was completely taken aback by John Doman [addressing McNulty in that scene]. It's one of the great pleasures of being a director: you can just sit down. I was just watching TV. I didn't need to direct him in that scene. I just sat there, and I was like, *Oh my God, these guys are making me look so good.* I was absolutely completely taken aback by John Doman's power. He later told me he was a captain in the Marine Corps in a previous life and he also worked in advertising on Madison Avenue. He was an alpha type in the real world. He didn't come to acting until he was in his forties. That's where that power comes from. It comes from real-life experience.

JOHN DOMAN (DEP. COMMR. FOR OPERATIONS WILLIAM A. RAWLS): For me, that was probably the best scene that I had. As an actor, you don't want to have a one-dimensional character, and things like that really make it worth doing. When you can show another side of the character, it makes it so much more interesting.

ANTHONY HEMINGWAY (DIRECTOR): There was also a synergy within our production due to the familial nature we like to foster. We love a lot. We laugh a lot. It's the only way to get through the challenging schedules and demands of the job. The first season on most shows are always hard, as you're establishing so many different elements, and *The Wire* was somehow harder than most because of the complexities of the show: so many actors, shooting all on location in the real elements, etcetera. Toward the end of the season, the show started airing while we were still shooting, and it immediately became a hit in Baltimore. We were shooting around the low-rises set when a school bus passed by and all the kids yelled out the window, "Omar, we love you." That was a satisfying moment, knowing that all the blood, sweat, and tears from all was being appreciated.

DONA ADRIAN GIBSON (COSTUME SUPERVISOR): We really became a family, and I think that what helped to develop that was the first Fourth of July. Anthony Hemingway and I had a cookout at my house for the people who weren't going to leave to go home. It was really well attended. I'll say maybe fifty people came. We had a really good time. It was not a big deal. We threw some burgers on the grill. Well, the next year, we decided we would do it again and it just only grew. By the time we were done, it was like three hundred people were coming.

DAVID SIMON (CREATOR): It was like the middle of America was hollowed out. The people who were watching the show were either in West Baltimore or North Philadelphia. They were in the places that the show was about, because they couldn't believe there was a drama about their neighborhood. Or it was people who were like book people or whatever who had found it in a weird way, and that's how it felt after two or three seasons. But, man, it took forever.

3

CHARACTER RESEARCH

Baltimore and The Wire would become eternally linked in an increasingly layered relationship. The show nearly always filmed on location and established more of a documentary template than that of a traditional television show. Critics argued that The Wire exposed only a negative fragment of Charm City, while hurting potential tourism. One city council member proposed a resolution to contradict the bleak image with an upbeat ad campaign. The efforts fell through, but David Simon once wrote in Baltimore magazine that the city's then mayor, Martin O'Malley, threatened to pull permits to shoot for the show's second season. "We want to be out of The Wire business," O'Malley said, according to Simon. And that conversation arrived before the start of a story thread featuring an ambitious white mayor inspired, in part, by O'Malley's political rise. Even responses to the show from inside the city's police department varied sizably throughout the years. The department opened its doors to Simon and often hosted actors and writers for ride-alongs. Ed Norris, the police commissioner handpicked by O'Malley, occasionally played a detective by the same name on The Wire. "Show me the son of a bitch who can fix this department," he once demanded on the show—he might as well have delivered a wink to the camera along with the line—"and I'll give back half my overtime." At an Amplify Baltimore event, Commissioner

Frederick H. Bealefeld III, who arrived five years after Norris, derided
The Wire as a "smear on this city that will take decades to overcome."
Bealefeld complained that crime shows in other cities showcased
models, tough cops, and competent prosecutors. "What Baltimore gets
is this reinforced notion that it's a city full of hopelessness, despair, and
dysfunction," he said.

Nina Noble recalled a rapport that frayed over time. The show's
soundstage was originally hosted in an old Sam's Club, but was forced
to move to Columbia after the third season, when the landlord wanted
the space for a retail tenant. "The unfortunate thing is I think we were
sort of part of the end of show making in Baltimore," Noble said. "In
other words, there were some incentives here, not in Baltimore, but in
Maryland, that ceased to be funded at the end of The Wire. Once
O'Malley then became governor, he was not interested in funding this
industry, and that's really unfortunate because there was a good crew
based here, great locations, and infrastructure."

The show injected millions of dollars into the city and offered sound
to those either without a voice or with a muted one. "By choosing a real
city, we declare that the economic forces, the political dynamic, the class,
cultural, and racial boundaries are all that much more real, that they do
exist in Baltimore and, therefore, they exist elsewhere in urban America,"
Simon wrote in that same Baltimore magazine article. The cast and crew
soon reflected a working-class mentality. Michael Potts (Brother Mouzone)
once stood in the rain during a shoot. An overeager wardrobe assistant
asked to hold an umbrella over him. Potts tried refusing her. He felt odd,
but finally acquiesced after she insisted several times. Soon, Potts spotted
Noble signaling to someone and that person beelining toward him. "Nina
says for you to hold your own umbrella," Potts recalled the crewmember
saying. "We don't do that stuff. That's LA stuff." The show stayed away
from Hollywood. The city adopted the cast and crew and became home
to some of their best, most challenging work. The spotlight also created
a pressure cooker, and the city served as a locale to occasionally blow off
steam.

ANDRE ROYO (REGINALD "BUBBLES" COUSINS): People ask me what was the best character on the show. I always say Baltimore. It helped us all stay really tuned into what we were doing and what we were talking about. It can be any city. What we were talking about happens everywhere. Right now, we're in Baltimore and we're talking about it. The first time I got to Baltimore, coming from the Bronx, I had an idea. In my mind, I'm not scared to go in any hood. I know what a hood looks like. I ask my boys about what Baltimore's like. They were like, "Baltimore is a place where you sell drugs, and you get more bang for your buck if you go to Baltimore." When I went there, it fucked me up. When I got to Baltimore, I took the Amtrak. I got to the neighborhood. I started seeing where we were shooting. I started looking around.

The feeling of Baltimore at that time was so despaired, so, *We're not trying no more. It is what it is. This is where we live and who gives a fuck? People just drive through, people on their way to DC or New York. We're forgotten.* At that time, I don't know what the mayor was doing, but at this point, when we got there in 2001, there was these big billboards that said, "Believe. Keep Trying," weird subliminal messages saying, "Don't Give Up." It looked like something out of *A Clockwork Orange* or some shit. I was like, "What's happening?" I saw this half a building torn up and somebody coming out the building locking the front door. I'm like, "What the fuck are they locking the front door for if the other half of the building is rubble?" In my junkie garb, I would walk by some kids, and they would look at me with a look on their face. I'm talking about nine-year-old and seven-year-old kids looked at me like I was their uncle. Wasn't scared of me, just giving me a dirty look like, "Move on, junkie."

I was like, *This place, they don't care. It is what it is.* That just broke my heart. That just made us feel like you don't want your world to end up like this, where nobody gives a fuck anymore. That's what Baltimore felt like. As we got on telling the stories and when the show started airing, you start feeling different. People start feeling like, *They're talking about Baltimore. We matter. This is our show.* They started taking a little sense of pride. People was like, "I saw the front of my house on your screen. On one of your episodes, I saw the front of my house. Shit, I got to clean it up." We started seeing and feeling that. Even people that didn't like the show. People were complaining about it, but they were talking about it. "We don't like your show because you're showing the bad parts of Baltimore." At least they were talking. Before, they were just not giving a fuck. Now they're fighting for it.

You felt the energy coming back to the city somewhat. It's one of those cities where the architecture is beautiful. It looks different at different angles. It has so many different looks to it. The people are the most honest people. There's no lying in the people. It's just that, at one point or at some time, it was a forgotten city. They got John Waters. You had rich characters coming from Baltimore, Tupac [Shakur], you got one of the greatest performing arts schools there. It didn't feel like it was being talked about. Nobody was giving it a look. Now, all of a sudden, it's starting to get a look because *The Wire* was giving it so much attention that we felt the city was starting to care more. They enriched us with us being a part of that. We would walk around; we became these little heroes of Baltimore. We got mad love. It was awesome. It was awesome to feel like you were a part of some sort of rejuvenation or some sort of pride about a place.

FREDRO STARR (MARQUIS "BIRD" HILTON): Filming in Baltimore, that itself was an experience. Baltimore is one of the, I would say, less financial cities. It's broke out there. Everything is torn down. It's not a lot of businesses. I don't know about now, but when they shot *The Wire*, it was like living in the past. It was kind of like a third world country to me, almost. Just cracks on the sidewalk. When you come out your trailer: bums, crackheads, gangsters, all by your trailer. Me personally, coming from [the hip-hop group] Onyx, the hood knows me from Onyx, too, so it was like, "Yo, what's up, Fredro?" I'm out there mingling with everybody. Being a part of the community, not just in my trailer, because of who I am as far as what I do in hip-hop.

It was an experience in Baltimore. It was an experience just being out there. It was kind of like, *Wow, this is very real out here. They picked an ill place to shoot this shit.* They could have shot on set somewhere that look like the hood and put fake crack vials on the floor and busted glass on the floor, but that was all real. When I got thrown on the floor in one of the scenes—I was coming out of the store—glass was by my face. It was like, "Hold up, let's shoot the glass." It was real. Like, *Oh, this shit is ill.*

STEVE SHILL (DIRECTOR): What would typically happen is you're sitting there at four o'clock in the morning, at some miserable street corner that's either one hundred ten degrees in the middle of the night or it's snowing, but they're saying, "Steve, what line are we picking up from?" My little joke with them—I'd say, "We're going to pick it up from 'I'm going to pop a cap in your bitch ass.' " They'd say, "Picking up from, 'I'm going to pop a cap in your bitch ass.' Where are we going to cut?" I would turn the pages and decide. "I think we're going to cut on 'You're a motherfucker. I'm going to bitch slap you upside your head.' " We had some laughs about that.

JOE CHAPPELLE (DIRECTOR/CO-EXECUTIVE PRODUCER): When David and all the writers, when they would write something and it was on a corner, whatever the street corner was, we would shoot at that corner. It wasn't like we go to a fun location and put up fake signs. We'd go to that specific corner.

UTA BRIESEWITZ (CINEMATOGRAPHER): I remember coming out of a scouting van and the van pulled forward a little bit and pulled over an empty plastic bottle. The plastic bottle made a pop and, instinctively, Robert Colesberry went for cover. I remember finding that incredibly amusing. Not so much anymore, after I'd been involved more and worked on *The Wire* for a while and witnessed and experienced what, obviously, Bob already knew. If you hear a pop and you are not quite sure whether it is a shot or not, you had better duck for cover. Later on, we lost locations because row houses simply would burn down. It was just all very, very real. You really immersed yourself into the culture. It was not always a very pleasant environment to be in. The houses that we would shoot in, where characters would shoot up in, you would step on syringes and vials and everything. It was there. Everything was just real.

LEO FITZPATRICK (JOHNNY WEEKS): Walking from set to the trailer, I don't think we ever had any kind of security. We just blended in with the other people in the neighborhood. When I was in Baltimore, it was fine. But sometimes I would have to run to get the train back to New York at night, still kind of, not in wardrobe but in makeup. That's when you noticed the difference of how people looked at you. In Baltimore, in those particular streets, it was fine.

But if you were on an Amtrak looking like that, you noticed people changed seats and kind of separated themselves from you. At the end of a shooting day, I would have a beer. I would walk into a deli or a liquor store and buy a beer. Nobody batted a lash. Nobody looked at me crazy. They just assumed, "All right, here's just another white kid junkie." I think the white thing threw them off more than being a junkie. They were like, "What are you doing in this neighborhood, kid?"

KWAME PATTERSON ("MONK" METCALF): Season One, they said they were shooting a scene with the cops, and somebody had just robbed somebody. He was being chased by the police, and he had pretty much got away, and he turned a corner and he was on *The Wire* set. He saw all these "police officers," and he just lay down on the ground and gave himself up, and he didn't realize until the other cops caught up that those ["police officers"] were actors. I know he felt so stupid when he was in jail, because they say he had gotten away. The real cops were so far behind him that he was gone.

UTA BRIESEWITZ (CINEMATOGRAPHER): I remember going up to the location where we were shooting, and we were held back a couple of blocks away from where we were supposed to shoot. Two things happened. One, I couldn't get closer because there was a sniper somewhere on a roof and they were trying to get the sniper off the roof. Another time, they were clearing out a dead body. Those are two things that happened.

DOMENICK LOMBARDOZZI (DET. THOMAS "HERC" HAUK): We were shooting once, and two blocks over, you see cop cars flying and gunshots, kind of simulating what we were doing. It was just happening two blocks over for real.

J. D. WILLIAMS (PRESTON "BODIE" BROADUS): I'm from Newark, New Jersey, so we have a certain level of harshness or brutality, exposure to those types of things. Anywhere I go, most places are easier to adapt to than Newark. Most places I go just might be missing something, like maybe the store closes too early or you can't buy this or find that. As far as the trouble and danger and things you get to see, you kind of get used to certain things. Baltimore just reminded me of home basically, and then it took me that first year to get used to Baltimore.

MICHAEL B. JORDAN (WALLACE): Growing up in Newark gave me those layers. Being able to see real shit on a daily basis made it something that I was comfortable with. That was normal. So, being in Baltimore and in that environment, it wasn't something that was strange. It wasn't foreign. The dialect, being around it a little bit more, they might move a little different, talk a little different. You've been in one hood, you've kind of sort of been in them all. Some are different than others, but for the most part, poverty is poverty.

J. D. WILLIAMS (PRESTON "BODIE" BROADUS): Baltimore closed down two o'clock sharp, and I mean sharp. So, I came outside of the club one night, not moving fast enough for the police or just not being where I was supposed to be. The police, they grabbed me, slammed me down into the gutter. I was dressed up. It was a nice suit, and they slammed me down into the gutter, put the ties on me, and threw me in the truck, and they held me there. That was two o'clock when they took me in, and I didn't get out until about ten o'clock in the morning. I had to walk home.

My point in that story was about how the police, particularly Baltimore police, at that time, how they just respond without thinking and with force. It could've turned really ugly and really dangerous really quickly. Thank God it didn't. I'm sure that type of occurrence was common, if it's not still common now. That was my first year down here, so I had to learn Baltimore quick.

VINCENT PERANIO (PRODUCTION DESIGNER): The strip club [filmed in Season One], I have to say is a real strip club about two blocks from my house, but I never really frequented. We scouted for that. We found the most urban one, on Eastern Avenue, what is called the Ritz in reality, and we really liked it. They were really game to let us film there, and the thing is, we knew we would be filming there several times. So, it's different than just a one-time thing. They really have to want to put up with you. And part of it was we were going to spiff it up a little, add some lights and decorate it a little. So, we filmed at the strip club. While we were filming at the strip club, the owner got charged federally with money laundering and was put in jail, and the FBI took over the strip club. So, for the next six months—because of course we weren't finished with the season—we had to deal with the FBI as our landlords.

WOOD HARRIS (AVON BARKSDALE): It's funny, because we didn't really use the strip club as much. We never saw actual dancers in there, just actors whenever there was any [dancers]. We used the upstairs area of the strip club. It ended up being like any other set. The only thing is, because that was a popular place, sometimes people would show up for us, the actors, and wait outside for hours and hours and hours until we came out. We started seeing some fanfare occur every so often. You get the PA come up to you. "Wood, Idris, there's people waiting outside." "Oh yeah, okay." We don't think anything of it. Then, six hours later, they're still outside.

IDRIS ELBA (STRINGER BELL): Eventually, Wood and I would hang out and we were like buddies and friends. Even though our characters were best friends and were going through stuff, Wood and I spent time outside of the set hanging out. He was into music, and I was into music. We used to write songs, a couple of songs. I don't even know where those songs are. We had a couple of songs that we'd get together when he was rapping and I was rapping. Overall, it was a really good relationship and good chemistry.

DOMINIC WEST (DET. JIMMY MCNULTY): There was quite a strip club culture, Chubbies.

MICHAEL B. JORDAN (WALLACE): I'm grown now. I can say that shit. I went. They took me out, man. They took me out. They let me see the strip clubs and be in that environment. We called it character development, character research. We would go down to some of the strip joints and have a good time.

ANDRE ROYO (REGINALD "BUBBLES" COUSINS): Mm-hmm. That's right. We're playing these characters that you know were out and about in the streets and talking shit. It's all part of the Method acting. We all logged it into research. We're just doing research.

DOMINIC WEST (DET. JIMMY MCNULTY): Wendell and I had to judge a pretty pussy competition there once, I remember that. We took it really seriously and were very technical about it. Six girls bend over. It's brilliant.

WENDELL PIERCE (DET. WILLIAM "BUNK" MORELAND): We looked forward to Baltimore because we knew we would have a good time. "Let's paint the town red. Let's go for it." It was a boys' weekend that lasted for six months.

DOMINIC WEST (DET. JIMMY MCNULTY): It really was a bit tricky. I wasn't with the mother of my daughter, but my daughter, she was only three or four, so I really missed her. Three weeks was the maximum I could be away without going mad. I had a lot of jet-lagged weekends, just come back for a day or two, just to see her. That was pretty tough, and then I'd be spending most of my time fighting off sleep and jet lag and trying to brave it out. Then she came out whenever there was school holidays. That wasn't great, but I was single, I hasten to add. The only drawback was that I did miss a lot of her years of a two-, three-, and four-year-old. That was pretty tough.

ANDRE ROYO (REGINALD "BUBBLES" COUSINS): We used to get hammered. You do some positive stuff and you also let go of some steam. We got fucked up. J.D., he challenged Idris to a drinking contest. Somehow or another, it was Idris and J.D. and they were arguing about some shit, either about [John] Madden or about hip-hop. They start talking about drinking. I believe J.D. started having visions or some shit. He started having visions and went under the table fearing for his life, like Pokémon was coming to get him or some shit. He got fucked up. It was a lot of fun. There was a lot of moments that we just got tore up and we got to pushing the envelope in so many aspects.

J. D. WILLIAMS (PRESTON "BODIE" BROADUS): Me and Idris, we have a million stories. With the drinking contest, Idris is like two hundred and something pounds. At the time, I might have been one forty, one fifty at the most, maybe, but I was a drinker. So, I told him, "Let's go." So, we went in. We downed a pint each, but then, after that first pint of Hennessy, I got probably through another quarter bottle, and he was still going. It was over. I was literally under a glass table looking through it at him, and a couple of other cats came in. Andre came in. I think Larry [Gilliard] was there. Hassan [Johnson] might have been there.

I'm looking at all of these guys from under the table, through the glass, and they're all cracking up at me. I woke up the next morning in the middle of my floor in my underwear. It looked like my clothes exploded off of me or something, and I had to make some phone calls that morning, asking the guys what happened the rest of the night. The last thing I remember was being under the table. I had a little cut on my forehead.

IDRIS ELBA (STRINGER BELL): J.D. was my guy, man. We used to hang out a lot. He just liked being with the old actors and talking shit and whatnot. He used to rag on me for being English, and said, "You guys can't drink." I think we poured a couple of bottles of Henny and started doing shots and seeing who would last. He didn't last, just put it that way. I don't remember how he got under the table. I just know that he was three sheets to the wind.

DOMINIC WEST (DET. JIMMY MCNULTY): Idris is a big man, yeah. Yeah, he can drink his drink. No, there was quite a lot of that. I mean, everyone was away from home. In my case, I was really missing home. I was really missing my daughter, so you tend to go out at night, and there were some titanic drinks and boozers among the cast and the crew, the crew particularly, and then, of course, once the show was a bit better known, every bar Wendell and I went into, we'd be bought whiskey constantly. People would be constantly sending over Jameson, and I still get that now, so it was hard to stay sober.

ANDRE ROYO (REGINALD "BUBBLES" COUSINS): When Seth got in, he was like Rage Against the Machine. You couldn't fuck with him. When Seth got drinking, he loved you so much he'll punch you in the face. "I'll punch you in the face, and you punch me back, because we love each other." He was one of those dudes.

SETH GILLIAM (SGT. ELLIS CARVER): One time, we were out with Wendell and Sonja and Andre and a few other people. I wasn't paying attention, but I went over, and Wendell was weeping. I was like, *What did Andre say?* And he was weeping because he had offended Andre and he didn't realize it. And he was feeling very badly about it, and he was apologizing to him. And Andre was looking at him like, *You fat fucker.* And I looked at Andre and said, "Where is your compassion?"

DOUG OLEAR (FBI SPEC. AGENT TERRANCE "FITZ" FITZHUGH): For the most part, I was hanging out with the cop side [of the actors], but they were all partiers. As soon as they cut or Friday night came, we were partying till six in the morning, and then you get a couple hours sleep and go on set. It was a party atmosphere.

I had [actual friends in the FBI], and I'd invite them all the time, like on Friday night, and they would always get so pissed off at me. Dom and some of those guys were paranoid, too, because they were much more in the limelight than I was. Going out and getting hammered, doing the fun stuff we'd do, a lot of it was illegal. You don't bring an FBI agent. I had to stop doing that after a while. Although, I've got to tell you. The FBI agents were just as rowdy. It was crazy. Behind the scenes, they're humans.

FREDRO STARR (MARQUIS "BIRD" HILTON): My niggas, Hassan, J.D., and I went down to Baltimore, and I hadn't seen them in a while. We all blazed in my room. The whole floor smelled like weed, and HBO told me to move hotels. I did, and they blazed up the room again. I think that's why I got wrote off the show real quick.

I do think they probably thought I was a handful or maybe too much to handle. Maybe. I only did two episodes. Then they was like, "You're going to jail," or whatever. The writers wrote that because they were writing it every week, so they could have wrote that in: "All right, let's just send him up to jail forever. He'll come out of jail when Jesus comes home." Something like that. I think maybe that might have played a part. Or maybe that was just the way they wanted Bird to be, a hit man, in and out.

Back in the days—I'm not going to lie—I was just doing a whole lot of other stuff. It was on my part, not even thinking. Whatever. Fuck it. We're going to blaze the hotel up. In corporate America, you can't do that.

SETH GILLIAM (SGT. ELLIS CARVER): [Lombardozzi and I] both ended up talking to a couple of different police officers that said, because of the amount of time they spent together and because of how much they had come to rely on each other, that they could basically finish each other's sentences, that they were more like married couples in terms of how much they knew about each other and how familiar they were with each other. Dom and I wanted to have that sense on-screen, that we knew each other real well. And to do that, living together seemed to be the best way. And also, we didn't figure the show would go on very long, and it was cheaper to do so.

DOMENICK LOMBARDOZZI (DET. THOMAS "HERC" HAUK): It was Season One, so we both rent an apartment together. Seth is really heavy into [the football video game] *Madden*. I kind of played. He turned me into a maniac with it. We kind of left our door open for whoever wanted to come and play, so Corey [Parker Robinson] would come. Michael K., Andre, and Hassan Johnson. There were two types of groups. The other one was with Clarke Peters. They were very bohemian, which we enjoyed. Clarke Peters, I love him. I used to love his house. It was just a different vibe there.

CLARKE PETERS (DET. LESTER FREAMON): We were given a stipend for each year, and it just seemed to make sense that, if the amount of money that you're spending on rent is equal to the amount of money that you could be spending on a mortgage, what would you do? I am, after all, Lester Freamon. Follow the money, buddy.

NEAL HUFF (CHIEF OF STAFF MICHAEL STEINTORF): I was living with Clarke Peters and Reg E. Cathey on North Calvert. I basically took over Jim True-Frost's room after he was gone. Reg E. would always get recognized in Baltimore when we were walking. They would kind of say, "Oh my God. I love you." They would then turn to me and do a double take and go, "I hate you. I hated you." If I'm ever recognized for *The Wire*, that's generally the second sentence. "I fucking hated you, man."

CLARKE PETERS (DET. LESTER FREAMON): It was a five-bedroom house. I myself don't need five bedrooms, despite the fact that my son and wife were coming out. That still left three bedrooms that were just there. People were coming in and out. Some of them were there for weeks on end, sometimes just for a couple days. Anytime someone came on in, like John Doman or Jim [True-Frost], they'd hole up at the Tremont. I said, "Look, whatever you're paying at Tremont, pay me half of that. Come stay with me." The one who took it up first of all was Reg E. Cathey, in the fourth season. Reg E. and I was pretty much the mainstay of that house for those last two seasons. That helped.

I wasn't looking to make money. I was just looking to make sure that we all had a place to stay, and that was that. The good thing about it is that for those first two years that we had it, we didn't have a television. All we had was a radio, guitar, some painting, a couple of bottles of wine, a fireplace, and conversation. What had happened was that we wound up finding ourselves organically creating this little salon kind of society, where we would read books and sit down and talk. We spent our time like that. It was really very edifying. I really miss that.

NEAL HUFF (CHIEF OF STAFF MICHAEL STEINTORF): Like the first night I was there, like ten a.m. one morning, the sound of an alto saxophone was coming out of Reg E.'s bedroom. I came out of my room, and the door was open. There was Reg E. playing his saxophone in his underwear, ten a.m. in the morning, just loving life.

REG E. CATHEY (NORMAN WILSON): We would paint. Clarke's an amazing painter, and he would make everyone do a painting before the year was up. We painted. I played the sax and the guitar. Clarke plays the piano and the guitar, and he was learning the bass. We grew grapes and made wine. We came up with five different film ideas, because there was no TV. We would just talk, with lots of wine drinking, lots of music.

JOHN DOMAN (DEP. COMMR. FOR OPERATIONS WILLIAM A. RAWLS): He's quite an artist. In the basement of the house, he had an art studio, and we'd all go down there. We'd all have our own paintings going.

CLARKE PETERS (DET. LESTER FREAMON): The only TV that came up was actually [Dominic West's]. That's because he needed someplace to store his from one season to the other, and that stayed downstairs in the cellar. I think maybe somewhere in the fifth season, we put a DVD, used it as a monitor.

NEAL HUFF (CHIEF OF STAFF MICHAEL STEINTORF): With Clarke, we had a lot of really, really great meals.

CLARKE PETERS (DET. LESTER FREAMON): A healthy body. *Mens sana in corpore sano.* A healthy mind is a healthy body.

4

BUILD A CITY

The Wire's second season proved disorienting for the few viewers who had previously tuned in. Prior storylines were nudged to the background. David Simon had pledged from the beginning to take The Wire beyond the norms of a typical cop show and planned to deliver on that promise. With Season 2, the series' focus largely shifted, a dynamic that persisted in subsequent seasons. The diminished camera time rattled the show's established actors who had enjoyed their first taste of mild success, including Andre Royo and Michael K. Williams. They noticed, as did the tiny loyal audience, that their time had mostly been bequeathed to white actors and characters. Simon preached patience to the original cast. The second season would be the most watched of the series, although its ratings still lagged severely behind HBO mainstays such as Sex and the City.

Season 2 highlighted the choking death of America's blue-collar working class and how a son could no longer necessarily trail in his father's footsteps in a postindustrial world. The series told the story through the decaying Baltimore waterfront, its unions, and the Sobotka family. In order to increase lobbying funds for a port expansion, Frank Sobotka (Chris Bauer), the leader of the dockers' union, begins smuggling goods for a shadowy figure known as "the Greek." His erratic son, Chester "Ziggy" Sobotka (James Ransone), and his nephew Nick Sobotka (Pablo

Schreiber) turn to drug slinging as their opportunities to earn money legitimately dry up. Lester Freamon's line of "All the pieces matter" became apparent as the show progressed. Maj. Stanislaus Valchek (Al Brown) appears sparingly in the show's inaugural season but becomes a central figure in Season 2. His petty argument with Frank Sobotka drives the plot and reestablishes the Major Crimes detail. McNulty, reassigned to a harbor boat, finds a floating body and links it to the deaths of thirteen more young women found in a can meant to be smuggled off Sobotka's dock. The season ends in the tragic dismantling of the Sobotkas, with Ziggy charged with murder and Frank killed after he agrees to become an informant and betray the Greek.

The season hit home for Rafael Alvarez, who came up with Simon as a young reporter at The Baltimore Sun. Alvarez's father had worked as a tugboat engineer, his grandfather as a shipyard worker. The expectation had been that he would always have a job at Bethlehem Steel if all else failed. Alvarez opted for a buyout from the paper in 2001. Shortly after, Simon asked if he wanted to collaborate on a book about the docks and the death of the working class. Alvarez passed, as he was already planning to write a book on his family's maritime history, and Simon sold the show to HBO. Alvarez spent two years on the ships after leaving the paper, then joined The Wire as a staff writer. He saw his grandfather and father as Frank Sobotkas, people who worked their tails off so that he did not have to work with his hands. "I knew that this had been on David's mind for a long time," Alvarez said. "I knew that he wanted to somehow document the death of organized labor in a city like Baltimore, and I was thrilled when he decided to use the docks as the vehicle to tell that story."

DAVID SIMON (CREATOR): To be honest, I thought, *if they give me thirteen episodes and I get to tell a singular story about the drug war in Season One and they cancel me, at least it'll be a single season.* Until they came back to me somewhere in the middle of the first season, after they'd seen five, six episodes, and said, "We're picking you up for another season," that was when I was like, *Okay, now I'm going to build a city.* I didn't know I was going to get more than the one. And then I remember going back to HBO and saying, "We're going to go away from this. We're going to go to the port." That was after I talked to Ed, and I remember Chris Albrecht saying, "Was that the plan?" to Carolyn Strauss, and she was just like, "It is now."

CHRIS ALBRECHT (CHAIRMAN AND CEO, HBO): Then, at the end of the first season, we went back and told David, "Hey, you got to keep some of these characters alive and let's see if we can do a totally different thing, but we can't just drop this story." He then went off and figured out a way to have them both be parallel, with a slight interweaving of them.

DAVID SIMON (CREATOR): I think Ed will confess he didn't want to do the second season. He was like, "We just built this universe. We can do more with it." And I'm like, "Yeah, and we will. But if we stay tight on the Barksdales second season, then the show is only going to be about the drug thing, and it's going to veer into that us-against-them soap opera of a cop show." I said, "We have a chance to build a city."

To credit Ed, he fought and he fought and he fought. Then, the first moment that we started touring the port and talking to people and meeting the union guys, he was like, "This is great and I have ideas." That's Ed. You've got to lead him sometimes and go, "We're doing this, Ed. I'm taking you by your shoulders. This is what we're doing. I already sold it to HBO. Let's make the best of it." Then he goes in, and you turn around and he's in the middle of its guts, chewing. That's who he is.

ED BURNS (CO-CREATOR): We were wondering where McNulty would end up. I said he would end up on the boat, and the reason I said that was my dad bought a twenty-two-foot old wooden boat. I'm surprised it even stayed afloat. He would take us out when we were kids, to go fishing in the Chesapeake Bay. By about one o'clock, the water stops rocking. It just bakes. It's hotter than hell. That damn engine wouldn't start most of the time. We had to have someone tow us in.

There's a diesel smell. I hate boats. I said, "That's where they're send-ing him, to the boats." And that gave us the docks. It was pretty easy after.

DAVID SIMON (CREATOR): Season Two, I knew I wanted to go to the death of work. Because where do these drug corners come from? They come from deindustrialization. Our economy no longer needs mass employment. The only factory in town that's still hiring and is always hiring are the corners. You can see the need for it, to show the economy shrugging people off. But did I know they were going to be port workers? No. In fact, the first thing I thought of was, *I wonder if they'll let us do an assembly line.* Because I had in my mind the *Blue Col-lar* movie with Harvey Keitel and Yaphet Kotto and Richard Pryor. As it happened, the place that let us in to do a working-class movie was the port. It was state-run, and they were for the film industry and they wouldn't let us into other factories, so it ends up being a port. Did I have an idea that we were going to do a working-class story? Yeah. And that we were going to have a guy as the local union president? Yeah. But did I think it was going to be the United Auto Workers at first? My first thought about it? That's the adaptation that happens.

NINA K. NOBLE (EXECUTIVE PRODUCER): We initially were turned down by the port. They had concerns about safety. It's not that long after 9/11, and they had a lot of different Homeland Security mea-sures changing all their guidelines every day, so that was a nuisance for them, and they didn't want to be involved. The way we got permis-sion was we rented a section of the port, an unused part of the port in Locust Point, and built a set there. By doing that, we became tenants, and I was able to start attending meetings of the private-sector ports association as a tenant. By attending those meetings, I learned that a lot of the concerns that we have about making our days work and staying on budget were concerns that they also had, so I was able to forge some relationships there that made it possible for us to film.

RAFAEL ALVAREZ (STAFF WRITER): My dad was a tugboat engineer in Baltimore Harbor for thirty years. A lot of it, I was reliving my childhood.

ED BURNS (CO-CREATOR): We had a young assistant who had an in at the docks. He took us down there.

NORMAN KNOERLEIN (RESEARCHER): There are checkers and then there are longshoremen. They are two different things, completely two different roles, and we really focused on the checkers, but we couldn't get the checkers to talk to us. Finally, we set up a meeting where it was all the producers, all the writers, everybody was in the room: Simon, Burns, everybody. I was literally the last person in the line, just jotting down notes. The head of the union came down, shook everybody's hands. Then he looks at me and he goes, "Are you Phyllis's son?" I said, "Yeah." He's like, "You can have whatever you want. You guys have complete access."

This guy's Walt Benewicz. He went to high school with my mom, and my mom is this sweet, sweet person. They ran in the same circles, so when Walt's mom died, my mom wrote a letter saying how much Walt's mom meant to my mom and how friendly they were. Because of that, Walt Benewicz gave us complete access to information.

DAVID INSLEY (DIRECTOR OF PHOTOGRAPHY): Everybody was invested in the show. Most of the crew was there from day one and lasted all the way through. They were all invested in it. They looked forward to it. They did whatever. They went beyond doing whatever was needed to make the story, because we all felt like it was a mission, something important to get across to the viewing populace.

LAURA SCHWEIGMAN (SCRIPT SUPERVISOR): One thing that I loved about working with David is that we work really, really hard. He works just as hard right next to you. He works just as hard, if not harder than you do. When Bob [Colesberry] and David and Ed would be in there in the preliminary meetings, talking and working, just to kind of be a fly on the wall and see how passionate they were was incredible. You're telling this story. You're telling the story of someone's life. You're telling the story of a community, and that's different than "Wouldn't it be cool if that happened?" It's totally different than a lot of other things, like, "Oh, this will be cool. That would be interesting." It's like, "No, this is a story we need to tell," and it always related back to life experiences or things that they knew about or were involved in, which helped made it real.

I remember we're doing this Russian piece once, and we're trying to get this Russian translation. The people that we were talking to for the Russian translation weren't getting what we were saying. I'm like, "Well, I live in Pikesville. Right next to where I live was this Russian neighborhood and Russian bakeries." We needed to know how to call somebody a pussy. The guy couldn't get it. The researcher, initially, he's like thinking, "Oh, it's a cat." "No. That's not what I mean." He couldn't get what we were saying. I took the script and I drove to the bakery. First, I talked to the main manager, and he wouldn't talk to me about it because he was embarrassed. Then, there was an older lady, and she was like, "Oh. Oh." She's going to get whomever; it was like her daughter or her niece in the back.

A woman comes out. She's probably in her early twenties. I explained to her, "I'm doing this TV show. There's this Russian and there's a bunch of strippers, and we have to say these things. I need to know how to say it." She knew it, but she was so embarrassed to tell me. She's like, "Let's just go over here." We went into the corner of the bakery, and she's pronouncing it for me, and I'm writing it phonetically. Sometimes, it was stuff like that that you had to figure out.

NORMAN KNOERLEIN (RESEARCHER): If someone says, "I need a three-legged blue pony," the only two questions you ask are, "When do you need it and how much are you going to spend?" That's it. There's no other questions you need to ask me. One of the more interesting tasks I was given was—Uta Briesewitz, she's a wonderful, sweet, sweet person—and Nina said, "We want to do something special for her birthday, can you get her this cake made out of this German meat product?" I was like, "You want me to get a cake made out of meat?" "Yes." "Okay, when do I need it?" "This afternoon." "Great." Think about that. I can't call a bakery. This is a really interesting request. I called a place and said, "I'm looking for this German kind of meat, do you have it?" They were like, "Yeah we have it. We sell it by the pound." I said, "Great. Can you make it look like a cake?" They were like, "How many pounds of it?" I go, "I don't know how many pounds it is. Just can you make it look square, like a cake?" I literally went to this place, got this meat cake, and took it to set. Everybody goes, "What the hell?"

RAFAEL ALVAREZ (STAFF WRITER): We needed a crime to launch Season Two. You couldn't forget that it was still, in some ways, a story about police and criminals.

ED BURNS (CO-CREATOR): I had one question I needed to answer. I knew the story in my head. We went to the management. After they gave us the whole dog and pony show, I said, "Can you steal one of these things off the docks?" "No way." Fuck. Then we went to the bar that night, where the longshoremen were. Same question, "Can you steal?" The guy says, "Which one do you want?" I said, "There we are." That was the story. It was as simple as that. Everything flowed from that.

DAVID SIMON (CREATOR): I was able to vocalize the rule once we had a writers' room. A real writers' room began in the second season. It was a nicer, new construct of what we tried over the first season. Once we had a full writers' room, I had to sort of express the rules. We had to say, "It either happened or it didn't happen or it is rumored to have happened, but we're not quite sure." With all three cases, it could have happened. The parameters of this universe make all of the outcomes plausible.

Some things *The Wire* made up. Some things absolutely happened. Some things we always heard they happened, but they were part of cop stories or what people said somebody did or why somebody got killed. But it couldn't violate the basic tenet of: This is the world. This is how it works. This is a logical and rational outcome of this.

ED BURNS (CO-CREATOR): You're trying to say, "There's a truth here," and you have to see it. These characters are not the everyday world of the inner city, because the everyday world within the inner city—you wouldn't want to watch that show. It just goes on. It's relentless. I always think of it in terms of human drama, with the emphasis on the *human.* You're staying true to the characters and you're just trying to share what they're going through. They're all composites, but there's an integrity to them that flows. There's no miracles happening. They're on this course, and tragically enough, very little can steer those kids, those people, away from that particular course that they've started out.

You don't get a story unless there's a back-and-forth. David and I provided the wind, and guys like George Pelecanos and Bob Colesberry, if we went off too much in one direction, they would turn the ship back, get closer to reality again. It's like a hop, skip, and a jump. Next thing you know, you're way over here and you don't want to be over here. Yes, we argued all the time. I would say there's two-thirds argue.

DAVID SIMON (CREATOR): The argument was creative, and if somebody stops arguing, it's because they don't give a fuck. Ed gave a fuck, and I expected him to argue and I expected him to be frustrated and I learned it is not always pleasant. We probably finished four to five seasons with Ed feeling like we left stuff on the table that we couldn't get to. Ed is a guy who if you present him with a scenario like, *we're going to have a story arc that goes here,* he'll come up with enough material for thirty-five episodes. Then it's up to the practical choices of what we can get to and what's best. What would be the best choices here? Even when you make those choices, you're leaving thirty elements behind, because that's how fast and how thoroughly Ed turns a Rubik's Cube. "If we do this, then we can speak to that." He does all that. Ed would always finish the seasons incredibly frustrated. He'd be like, "We blew it. We could have done this." Like, "Yeah, well, we did what we did, Ed. We opened some doors, we closed some other ones." He would go, "What's the point?"

He would go into the hibernation of being off for a month, completely disgusted with the whole process and then by the end, the episodes would come out and, not that he was sanguine about everything, but he would come back ready to work the next season. He needed the month off to just take a breath. Everybody in the room would be in agreement. "Okay, this is what we're doing." Ed would come back the next day and say, "It's not right," and he would proceed with the argument. Sometimes he would turn us all around and sometimes we would just have to go, "Ed, we can't. We don't have the characters. We don't have the locations. There's no sensibility in the story that that would happen. We've traveled a million miles to get to some point that we can't justify turning to." Other times, he would turn the whole ship around. He'd be like, "I agreed to this, but you know what? Think about this. Because two or three episodes from now or next year, what you will have effectively said is X when you needed to say Y." We'd all sit there going like, "Shit. We just wasted a day yesterday. We're back to square one." That's Ed. By the way, that's the core DNA of what made *The Wire* what it was, was Ed arguing.

ED BURNS (CO-CREATOR): David would get very, very frustrated because I would come in—after the beat sheet was all done and the writer was off writing—I'd come in and say, "We got to change this. This works better." It would drive him crazy, but he'd change it. David handled everything. That left me free to handle just story, and that's all I was interested in. He would do post and he would deal with HBO and deal with the actors. I could just be free to do story.

DAVID SIMON (CREATOR): George is the barometer. When the morality of the show or the ethos of the show, when it's going wrong or when we're not honoring something or a character, that's where he'll assert [himself] in a way that can change the direction of the story-line or story arc. Once the universe is established, if we're getting too schmaltzy, he's on it. If we're being brutal just to be brutal, he's on it.

I've learned to listen to him. Ed and I could argue for hours, and George would be the third guy who would spin it one way or the other. George was the third vote. If you swayed George, then you were probably right. If you didn't sway George, it was time to rethink.

GEORGE PELECANOS (WRITER/PRODUCER): Not in the sense that I went one way or the other. The one argument was about the chips in the phones. That went on for a week with the SIM cards.

"Guys, can we move on? Like, this is ridiculous, you know? Let's get some cards up on the board." That was my role, was to be sort of the adult and say, "It's time to stop arguing. Let's just move on, because we've got to get some work done." There's that expression, David always uses it: "I'd agree with you, but then we'd both be wrong." He never will give up a fight, and Ed's like that, too. Even when they're wrong.

DAVID SIMON (CREATOR): I didn't get everything I wanted in the scripts. I lost arguments to Ed. Ed lost arguments to me. Ed doesn't like to lose arguments. He's pretty unrelenting. It becomes sort of a hive mentality if it works. If it doesn't work, then you don't have a writers' room. If it becomes just one person, you can't imagine the universe well enough. You can't imagine all these different characters well enough to have it have the breath that it needs to have. You gotta let air into the room.

You have to argue. The room has to be about argument. It has to be good academic arguing. It can get a little heated. You're basically arguing a story. You're not arguing self-validation. These are writers.

They're novelists by training. George is a novelist. George sits down, and it's him and the paper, maybe an editor behind him and that's it. That's the only thing between him and broadcast and publication. This is not that. What I'm saying is writers are about ego. What else has a greater vanity than coming to a sort of collective campfire and saying, "I have a story I want to tell. My story is good. Pay attention to me. This is my story. I've got a great story. My story is better"?

The whole act of telling a story is a grandiose thing in some ways. So, now you get a bunch of storytellers in the room, and they have to get along. They have to create one singular thing. It's at a point the showrunner has to be a little bit totalitarian and say, "I have to look out for the whole." But long before I do that, you need to be open enough and benign enough to let the arguments lead you where they're going to lead you. Those were the moments that made *The Wire* better than it might've been.

The casting of several new starring members stretched casting directors Alexa L. Fogel and Pat Moran. Chris Bauer had previously auditioned for McNulty. James Ransone was a young, talented Baltimore actor more than capable of pulling off a "Bal'more" drawl, and Pablo Schreiber left an original, indelible mark after his reading.

PABLO SCHREIBER (NICK SOBOTKA): The second season was a huge baby of Robert Colesberry. He was one of the main producers on the show. He was in the room with David when I had my callback. I guess part of the reason he liked me so much is when I came for my callback, there was an assistant of the casting director, Alexa Fogel. Alexa had this casting assistant at the time and her name is Jennifer Lafleur. She's actually an actress now, and it's funny. I flirted with her outside of the audition before I went in, and after I finished the audition. I left and I called the casting office after I had left and I asked for Jennifer and they put her on the phone and I asked her on a date. She said no because she had a boyfriend. And I guess she obviously told Alexa that this had happened, and when Robert Colesberry found out that I had done this, called the casting office to ask this girl on a date, he was very taken with my ballsiness or something.

CHRIS BAUER (FRANK SOBOTKA): I had [watched the first season] and was scared shitless by its authenticity and patience. If you bullshitted for one second in that aesthetic, you'd stand out like a dirty diaper. I didn't audition. They very generously trusted me enough to offer the part. I did, however, audition for McNulty while they were casting the pilot. Imagine a bloated, hungover, mumbling McNulty, who looked like he'd be single his whole life. Frank Sobotka was a much better fit.

JAMES "P.J." RANSONE (CHESTER "ZIGGY" SOBOTKA): My friend Leo Fitzpatrick was on the first season and he was Johnny, Bubbles's junkie pal. We sort of knew each other from New York. I would see posters [for *The Wire*] on the train, and I'd be like, "Oh, that's that show that Leo is going to do." You have to remember, no one cared about that show until the fourth season. No one watched it.

I was twenty-one or twenty-two, and it was probably my third legit job and definitely the biggest. It was the most corporate gig I've had up until then. I was just really young.

AMY RYAN (OFF. BEATRICE "BEADIE" RUSSELL): I was a huge fan of the show. I went to high school with Seth Gilliam. We were good friends, and so that was a cool moment, that first scene we filmed together in Daniels's office, and every time they block us next to each other, we just crack up.

When I am a fan of something, I turn to mush when I get there. I'd watched the whole first season, and I remember when I was on the show, we were working on this sound stage the second season of the show, I saw the orange couch stored up in the rafters, and it literally took my breath away, "Oh my God. The couch. The couch."

AL BROWN (MAJ. STAN VALCHEK): I was astounded when they got in touch with me, when it was time to start thinking about the second season. As an actor, I hadn't missed church for a whole bunch of weeks. As far as I knew, I was a day player, one shot and I was done. And suddenly, a year after that, pretty much that season was largely about me and another picayune argument, because I was only pissed at [Frank Sobotka] because the priest put his [stained-glass window] in the right part of the church and I ended up in the basement. I was trying to be teacher's pet, and Sobotka beat my ass to it. That's about what it boiled down to.

CHRIS BAUER (FRANK SOBOTKA): I loved Al and was obsessed with his accent, a very nice guy. I thought, *There's no way that guy could be an actor. He's gotta be the real thing.* It was as if they went and handed some commander at the nearest precinct a couple pages and told him, "Go." He's one of those Peter Lorre types who just stands there and talks, and the audience is transfixed. There were a lot of those bastards on *The Wire*. Naturals.

PABLO SCHREIBER (NICK SOBOTKA): What was interesting was feeling the vibe of the guys who had been there in the first season and a lot of that, like, "Who the fuck are these new guys and why is he writing stuff for them all of a sudden?" And then, when it came out, I think people who had watched it kind of religiously, a lot of people were kind of taken aback, because it was obviously the first time the show had shifted and changed like that, and a lot of people expected it to stay the same. So, a lot of people were sort of taken aback and frustrated by the shift. Then there was a whole other sort of people at the time who discovered the show for the first time with that season. And then they had to go back and watch the first season. For that whole group of people, who were watching at the time and discovering the show, it wasn't as disorienting or off-putting.

But yeah, it was interesting. Great actors like Andre Royo and Wood [Harris], some of the characters that weren't getting written for in the second season, they were like, "What's going on? Why are they writing for these guys? What's happening?" But obviously, everything, in retrospect, makes a lot of sense in looking at the canvas that he created.

ANDRE ROYO (REGINALD "BUBBLES" COUSINS): After Season One, we weren't a popular show, but it was a popular show in our hoods. When everybody would go back to their neighborhood, they were the street stars. We're telling a story about us and we're doing it in a way that's being looked at as really, really good. People are loving that they can relate to it. It's dope. We're feeling good, and not for nothing, this is the first time you're getting paid per episode. Most of us weren't at that contract where you get paid no matter what. At that point, you got to do an episode to get paid.

You get a call from David Simon or Nina, and they go, "For Season Two, HBO is not going to let us have series regulars on contract. We got to release your contract, and we're bringing in this new story. We're telling the storyline from a different perspective." The businessman in you is stuck and pissed off. *I got a contract and now you're telling me my contract is null and void? What's that about?* It is what it is. This is what the deal was. They told me, "This is what's going to happen. We're going to release your contract. We promise you in Season Three, you'll have all shows produced where you'll get paid, whether you do an episode or not. I need you not to fight Season Two. We're going to cut your contract and renew your contract."

My manager at that time was serious. She's like, "This is a business. This is how they do." She told me not to come back. She said, "What we're going to do, you're going to say no. You're going to do Two, but you're not coming back for Season Three. You're done with the show." I was like, "Word? Is that the move we want to make?" She was like, "Yeah. Guess what, Dre? You did Season One, and you weren't supposed to be one of the standouts, but people know you now from that season." She talked to me about the things I was scared of. She was like, "You don't want to be typecast. If you stay in the show too long, that might happen. Two, you see these people, they do whatever they want with the contract. They can say the contract is good. No, they're trying to fuck you. This is how the business is. I want to protect you. Don't go back." I was like, "Okay. Where am I going? What show am I going on next?" She was like, "We don't know, but the only way we're going to find out is you got to believe in me and you got to not go back." I was like, "Oh shit. All right."

Then, I'm looking at a daughter with her shoes that were too tight, who needs new shoes. I'm looking at my life like, *I can't. I got to go back.* I think the show is too important. If David Simon said they'll bring us back Season Three, then I got to believe him. She's like, "Okay. I doubt it." She started making phone calls. She started becoming a pest to the point where Nina Noble had to call me and go, "Listen. Did David Simon tell you about what's going on with Season Two and how we're going to bring you back in Season Three?" I was like, "Yeah." "Do you believe David Simon?" I'm like, "Yeah." "Well, then you got to tell your manager to stop calling us. We're not going to deal with the manager, and if we got to deal with the manager, then we can just release you right now. If he gave you his word, you got to trust him." It put me in a position where I had to fire my manager. I had to be like, "You can't call this guy. I know you're fighting for me, but I told you I'm going to do it. We believe these people." She was like, "I get it, Dre. I know I crossed the line. I just want to let you know that's how the business is. Just be careful." I loved my manager. She's the one that believed in me and got the ball rolling when I first started doing the theater to television. I was a little nervous.

I remember walking on set a little grumpy. I had a little attitude. I talked to [David Simon] and I asked the question, "What's this season about?" He had some interesting things to say. His point of view, which I believe to be correct, he was like, "Listen. I cannot tell a drug story. I cannot tell a story about the drug game and it be all about black people. That's wrong. I feed into the stupid lying stereotype that the industry has been doing for years, in that drugs is a black problem. It's not. It's not. I need to tell this angle, because white people are involved in this shit, too. This is not a race problem. It's a human problem. I don't want this show to look at it and just be a drug game and a violence game and it be all black people." I agreed with that, but it took me a minute.

MICHAEL K. WILLIAMS (OMAR LITTLE): Season Two, I was so ignorant to the game with David, his sophisticated style of writing and his take, which is why he even got into show business in the first place. It wasn't to be some Hollywood writer. He had a message to get out there. I was clueless to all of that. When he brought all the white actors in to tell the dock story, I was very ignorant. Long story short, I got very ignorant and bitter.

DAVID SIMON (CREATOR): Andre was furious. I tried to explain it. The guy who I explained it to and who started to get it, I had a conversation with Michael K. I said, "If we just stay focused on the Barksdales, we don't move the story around. We don't change the prism; we're a much smaller show. We will not be about what we're going to be about." I said, "This is the moment where we say, 'We'll do anything. This is where we claim the whole city for our own.'"

It's not that the characters are white. It's that the characters were at the point of importation of the drugs and the death of the working class. The union that you're going to see under pressure is going to be multiracial. There's going to be black stevedores. But it is important that it have a white presence, because the last thing I want to do is suggest that you can track the drug problem through America by following black people. That's a very reductive thing that I'm not going to say. I'm going to say you can track the drug problem into America by following class, and that, in a very fundamental way, the working class, white and black, is being devoured, and the underclass is growing because of the industrialization. I said, "If we don't suggest that the morality is permeable to all races at this point, we're saying some ugly shit that I don't believe in and we have no right to say."

I want to see Nicky Sobotka become a drug dealer like the guys

I knew down in Pig Town, [whose] dads were stevedores, and then they were on the fucking corner. I sort of said, "We're not forgetting you. We're not walking away from anything." But it was really hard. We never thought of it as a black show. We were doing Baltimore. So, I would say that to them, and they would be like, "But we did. We thought we had this. They had *The Sopranos.* We had this, and now you're fucking it up." I was like, "I'm not thinking about it like that."

LANCE REDDICK (LT. CEDRIC DANIELS): The race part of it was almost tangential. I feel like the more conscious attempts that *The Wire* made in making people look at that, was in terms of class.

GLYNN TURMAN (MAYOR CLARENCE V. ROYCE): I've got to admit that it crept up on me slowly while doing the show. I didn't watch the show a great deal before I got on the show. I had friends telling me about it. I'd tune in every once in a while. But once I got on the show is when I started reading the scripts that came through and found out that I was reading more than just my part, that I was reading the whole script. You get a script and you just want to read your role, but I would read it because it was like reading a book. And I realized somewhere during the course, I said, *God, over half the characters in this piece are black.* And it dawned on me, and the major thing was I never got a sense that it was a quote-unquote black show. But the question was: How did that happen? How is it that it doesn't feel like a black show and that over half of the characters are black and that it's a show that takes place in the hood, on the corners, and it still doesn't come across as a black show? What is that all about? And it's because all of the characters were so multidimensional and so nonstereotypical. And that the show never spoke down to its audience, no matter what level you were dealing with in the structure of society that the characters dwelled in. Everyone was bright and everyone had a point of view and everyone had a dimension that was a human quality no matter how steeped in chaos and mire that they were.

PABLO SCHREIBER (NICK SOBOTKA): People got really comfortable with the characters in that first season, and then, all of a sudden, they were forced to develop relationships with a whole new cast of characters. I think it really tested people's patience, and everybody has their own vision of what the show should be.

DAVID SIMON (CREATOR): I certainly think the show had a ceiling built in, because the majority of the cast was African American. Okay, race has got to be a part of any show. If you're writing about America, if you're trying to make a critique about urban America, you have to make sure that you acknowledge that. But I didn't even think we were really writing about race, if that makes sense. We scheduled a cast in Baltimore that we knew. We accepted the city on the terms that we knew.

I live in Baltimore. I still live in Baltimore. We made the police department the racial breakdown of the department that we have. In city hall, we structured it like it is. We just took it as a given. Nobody woke up in the morning and said, "Oh, we are going to make a black show." That's all just a form of ghettoization itself. "I'm going to make a black show." Fuck that. We are making a show about Baltimore, but we didn't pull the punch and go, "Oh man, we need to have sixty percent white people or we are going to lose a white audience." I think I always assumed that we would lose audience, and in a weird way, the HBO model allowed a new show like this to survive without degrading it. It was a luxury. If we were chasing advertising dollars and tried to maximize the audience, the show does not survive. But HBO brought people into the tent to watch it for what it was. It didn't bring everybody into the tent. More people came for *The Sopranos.* But as long as we added to the amount of people who subscribed or helped, we could be part of this little family and they'd leave us alone.

SETH GILLIAM (SGT. ELLIS CARVER): David Simon told us at one point, "You know that frustration you're feeling as actors is a frustration that Herc and Carver are feeling as cops, so you can use that."

DAVID SIMON (CREATOR): He was like, "Fuck you. I'm upset." "Use the frustration." "Fuck you."

But then, they get pushed into the Western District. And both characters have this arc. And that was the thing about certain seasons: Some people are going to come into the fore and be more active, and some of them are not. And if you tried to service everyone in the same way, then you would end up with five separate narratives that are the same. Not every tool for every job.

SETH GILLIAM (SGT. ELLIS CARVER): I'd asked him about it at one point, and he had mentioned that. And he was kind of smiling as he said it, like, "You'll understand when it all comes together."

DOMENICK LOMBARDOZZI (DET. THOMAS "HERC" HAUK): The second season, we probably were a little frustrated, because we were kind of reduced to second unit. We were just doing a lot of surveillance stuff. I was never really upset at that kind of stuff. I just wish Herc would turn into another type of guy or go down a different kind of path. Maybe not always be this rough guy. That kind of stuff, because after a while, that sits with you. You go to work, "Okay. What am I doing? Okay. I'm beating up Bodie again."

When you sit back and you think about it, it's genius, because it's part of David's genius. He never jumped [the] shark. Everything was true. Everything was solid. Everything was where it was supposed to be. People, they do not change. That's reality. What you want and what happens in reality are two different things. As an actor, I don't know any actor that doesn't get frustrated. You play a character long enough, sometimes you're going to see things differently, but second season was only because we were reduced to a second unit. In retrospect, I'm kind of glad we were, because we got to work with Bob Colesberry a lot. I learned a lot from Bob. I wouldn't trade the second season and what I had to do and all that time I spent with Bob for anything. He was the eyes of the show. David was the ears of the show. A lot of that vision, that's all Bob Colesberry.

ANDRE ROYO (REGINALD "BUBBLES" COUSINS): We didn't see David Simon after the first season. He was in the room, the think tank. Ed Burns you saw every once in a while. He'll come to set, but you didn't really talk to him, because he was scary. He just didn't talk. When he talked, you felt like an idiot. Bob Colesberry was our producer that was a go-to between the actors and everybody. Colesberry was a good mixture of both. He was like, "I'm smart like these motherfuckers, but I'm cool and personable. I can hang out with the actors. I can tell you the football scores without making you feel bad." He was this guy producing *Mississippi Burning*. He understood good storytelling. He was a cool dude.

PABLO SCHREIBER (NICK SOBOTKA): First day, I slept through my alarm. I guess what happened was, it was the early days of cell phones. I set my cell phone as an alarm, and then the battery ran out overnight. I woke up to being like an hour and a half past my call time, jumped out of bed, got in the car, sped down there as quick as I could and ended up getting stopped on the way and got a speeding ticket and ended up showing up to set two and a half hours after my call time for my first day of shooting. P.J. [Ransone] and I were kind of the new additions to the season, so we hadn't been there, and that was the first impression I was making, was showing up two and a half hours late. They were all obviously very upset and disappointed. I was petrified. I thought for sure I was going to shoot that day and be asked to leave the following, but they were very gracious in saying, "Just focus on your work and get the best work done you can and don't worry about this." And yeah, I don't remember the next time I was late the whole season.

CHRIS BAUER (FRANK SOBOTKA): I have a vivid and uncomfortable memory of my reaction to finding the dead girls in a can on the harbor front at the end of the first episode of Season Two. As the scene unfolded, Ed Bianchi, the great director, blocked the shot so that as the door opened to reveal the dead bodies, I was in position to express shock, dismay, and panic, a great "Oh, shit" moment. The first couple takes, I overacted so much he had to pull me aside and—if I remember his exact words, they were: "What the fuck are you doing?"

That was the last time I tried to show anyone how good I was.

ED BIANCHI (DIRECTOR): A big problem with the beginning of that season was establishing the yard where the cans were and the set we were shooting on. We weren't actually shooting on the set where the cans were. We were shooting on a parking lot right next to it, where we had our own cans, but a limited amount of them. We had to shoot half the scene in one place and then, for the reverse, we were allowed to go on the real yard, where the boxes were coming in, and shot that on another day. That was an interesting thing that we worked out between Bob and I. It really made you feel like you were in the real place, as opposed to being on a set.

AMY RYAN (OFF. BEATRICE "BEADIE" RUSSELL): We have these amazing women, these extras [playing the dead women]. They weren't dummy bodies. They were real people huddled up on top of each other, and it was scary. I only had gone through it once. The camera person knew where I was going, but I think that was such an extraordinary scene. It's so chilling because it happens. It's not just like Hollywood make-believe. I'm sure that happens more often than we really know about, and I just found it scary, like a horror movie.

PAUL BEN-VICTOR (SPIROS "VONDAS" VONDOPOULOS): I think it was the first episode when I had to slit that guy's throat. Bill [Raymond] and I had never worked together. We actually became friends, and ended up doing some other things together. I remember that first scene. We dragged the guy in. He's tied up in the chair, and when I do slit his throat, we had this whole blood rig that was geared up to his throat, so it would get nice and bloody. The first time we did it, when we rehearsed it in the moment, the actor who was playing the victim there, he really got into it. When I grabbed him, he really struggled from me and got out of my hand. We lost our rhythm, and the blood went everywhere and it didn't really work, so we had to do that twice, having to clean him all up, get everything all rigged up again.

DEBI YOUNG (MAKEUP DEPARTMENT HEAD): The engineer guy that was naked, he had his throat slit by one of the Greeks. Bob Colesberry, he came over to me. He said, "Debi, in this episode, I want, when his throat is slit, for him to bleed on camera." I'm like, "Okay." He said, "Well, he's going to be naked." I'm like, "Okay." Sandy [Linn Koepper] and I start thinking about it. We don't have anywhere to hide anything. We had to do all that.

We first worked out how we were going to get the blood to come out of the pump. Then we just had to figure out how we were going to do it. We were in an old warehouse. We took surgical tubing and we had blood that we'll pump through the tubing that we were hiding our contraption under, an old, dirty staircase in this warehouse. We had the tube run across the floor, and then we taped the tube up the back of the metal legs of the chair. Again, he's sitting there naked, a costume, of course, covering his private parts. We had beat him up in the trailer, got his face all bruised up and cut. When we got out there, we had to bring that tubing across the floor of the warehouse, to the chair, tape the tubing up the chair. We taped it up to behind the seat and taped it up his back. Then, we brought the tubing up under his left arm and had the tubing open up into his palm. We told him, "Once he has pulled that knife across your throat, bring your hands up to your throat," and that's when we started to pump. The blood just oozed out through his fingers.

AMY RYAN (OFF. BEATRICE "BEADIE" RUSSELL): When we were shooting, we were inside the warehouse, in the containers. It was January in Baltimore, and however cold it was outside in the water, it was even colder inside, because everything's just metal, like being in a big refrigerator. I was in layers and layers of silk, and long johns underneath. They put the whole gun belt gadget stuff on me, and even with all those extra layers of clothing, it pulled. I started to have plumber's crack. They pulled it out and gave me a plastic gun. It doesn't make you feel very tough for a standard [officer], but Beadie Russell was never really that tough.

CHRIS BAUER (FRANK SOBOTKA): By the end of the first episode I shot, I never thought for one second about performance, because my faith in the authorship was blind. Those words did all the work. Even a casual familiarity with text analysis yielded a strong sense of theme, and especially regarding Frank Sobotka, an Aristotelian batch of hubris that would ultimately take a character down.

JAMES "P.J." RANSONE (CHESTER "ZIGGY" SOBOTKA): The first scene that I auditioned for was the bar scene in Episode 201. A lot of the dialogue is so dense, and I was talking about all these characters that I had no idea about. The dialogue was really dense. I didn't really know what I was doing. I just was like, "Oh, I can do a Baltimore accent."

NORMAN KNOERLEIN (RESEARCHER): The whole Ziggy character came literally from stories from Walt Benewicz. There's a guy named Pinky. He was a complete oddball, but because he was related to the head of the union, he was able to get through. He would wear a suit to the bar in the afternoon. He, at one point, had a duck. This is completely true. He had a duck with a diamond collar, and he would bring it into the bars.

South Baltimore was checkers and union workers, and they worked in the Port of Baltimore. They lived in this really small neck of the woods, where everybody knew everybody. Everybody was connected. Everybody drank in the neighborhood bars. You'd have these little shops. Sometimes people would have bars in their front rooms, and it was like a converted town house. Pinky would come in there with this duck with the diamond necklace, and he'd give it vodka. One time they kept saying, "Get this duck out of here. Get this duck out of here." The duck drank too much vodka, fell off the bar, and died. The bartender's like, "You need to clean up this dead duck." He's like, "I don't know what you're talking about. That's not mine." Pinky left, and then he came back, because the duck had this diamond necklace, got the diamond necklace back, and then gave [someone] fifty bucks: "Go bury that duck in the backyard."

PABLO SCHREIBER (NICK SOBOTKA): I do remember having a great time with P.J. in that scene where he comes out of the bar really drunk. It was after he had been in the bar with the duck the whole time, and I come and basically slap him around a little bit. I guess that probably sounds like most of the scenes we had together.

JAMES "P.J." RANSONE (CHESTER "ZIGGY" SOBOTKA): They gave me this penis prosthetic and they brought it in my trailer. It was like the fucking size of my forearm. I was like, "This thing's insane. This could kill a person." It was really translucent, so it looked like it had just come out of some factory mold. It looked really fake. I had to wear it on this big harness. Then, we got to set, and I'd pull it out, and we had this German director of photography, a woman named Uta Briesewitz. I'd pull it out, and she'd go, "It's reading too light in the lens." Then these women, these really sweet middle-aged women who David Simon has worked with since *Homicide*, they would have to come over and shade in my fake penis as it was hanging out of my pants. Then they'd be like, "Oh, okay. I think that's a little darker." Then they'd pull it out again, and Uta would be like, "It's still too light in the lens." Then they'd have to come over and airbrush it. So, it became this beautiful work of art.

UTA BRIESEWITZ (CINEMATOGRAPHER): The color just didn't match the person that was wearing it.

JAMES "P.J." RANSONE (CHESTER "ZIGGY" SOBOTKA): Then, after we shot it, I was like, "Hey, can I keep that thing? Just as like, a souvenir, you know?" Because can you imagine, "I want the shark fin from *Jaws*." I was like, "I want this huge fake cock." Right? Maybe one day I'll show it to my kids, and then I'll be like, "This is what people thought your old man was made of." But then they were like, "No, you can't have it." They were like, "What if we need it for reshoots?" So, it's literally hanging in a warehouse somewhere, in case we were going to reshoot it.

PABLO SCHREIBER (NICK SOBOTKA): That was funny. Obviously, if your character is written with a massive schlong, then you either have it or you don't. Well, you know, maybe P.J. does and he didn't want to show his own. Maybe he wanted to keep his for himself. Either way, the stand-in penis did a great job. Everybody was very happy with his work. Everybody was very complimentary to the penis afterward.

JAMES "P.J." RANSONE (CHESTER "ZIGGY" SOBOTKA): Chris Bauer really sort of was the first person to come along and make me really respect, I don't want to say my own talent, but my own sort of process or abilities. He created sort of like a nurturing space, so anytime that we really got to dig into anything, the work just became really interesting for me.

I think we had a little bit more of like a father-and-son thing because he had his shit together a lot more than I did when I was in my twenties. He sort of helped me through some really dark times in my life, but beyond that, he's been the first sort of shepherd that I've had in terms of being able to respect myself—not myself, that's a lot, but to respect the artistry that I was trying to undertake. I don't know if I would have been able to do anything that I did on that show if it weren't for him specifically.

PABLO SCHREIBER (NICK SOBOTKA): I would immediately lock myself in my room and read the whole script from front page to back, because they were so involving and I was so into the story at that point. So, when Zig kills the guy, I remember reading the part where he went back and sat in the car, and I remember reading it for the first time. I'm not really an emotional reader. Scripts don't usually affect me emotionally that much, but I remember actually crying a little bit when he went back to the car, and I thought, *Oh fuck. That's it for him. We're not going to see him anymore.* And then, obviously, one of my first reactions was, *Well, shit. What's going to happen to Nick? How is this all going to play itself out? Am I not going to be involved in the show anymore?*

JAMES "P.J." RANSONE (CHESTER "ZIGGY" SOBOTKA): Ernest Dickerson shot that episode, and we had sort of already gotten into our rhythm. We knew it was coming to a close, both the show and our storylines. A lot of times in TV, when they call for you to cry, you can use fake tears. I use them a lot still. I'm not too proud to say that I do. When we were shooting the jail scene, I was like, "All right, I want to make this as authentic as possible." When Chris and I shot that jail scene, we had developed such a kinship. They shot my coverage of that first. They were like, "All right, we're going to shoot your side." And then they were like, "All right, once we sort of have what we want to view, we'll come around and we'll get Chris Bauer's side."

It's really tiring to cry that much. You gotta work yourself into a pretty dark state, and you have to stay there to make it conceivable. We're on Chris's side. I have the choice whether or not I just remove myself from that dark space and feel like I don't have to cry as much anymore. I was a pretty young dude, and I was like, *Fuck that, this dude has shown me gratitude and respect.* I think that there's a better performance of me that didn't get filmed because I was like, *I want to give you the best version that I possibly can every time so you have something to react off of.*

CHRIS BAUER (FRANK SOBOTKA): By the time we got to that jail scene, the weight of the story between us was so apparent, and the words so elegantly placed to avoid sentiment or indulging an emotional understanding beyond the characters' own understanding, that the scene played itself. It is an utterly loving embrace of people at their most human; witnessing the dissolution of their best intentions in excruciating pain because there's nothing they can do to stop the collapse of their lives. And why is it my favorite scene? Besides how permissive and supportive the crew and director Ernest Dickerson were, it's a beautiful love scene. I think of it now and I get moist in the eyes. They were fucked. Look at the writing in that scene. Sobotka says to Ziggy in a noble effort to rouse some fight and macho optimism, "You're a Sobotka." Ziggy answers "Fucked is what I am."

Gives me chills.

JAMES "P.J." RANSONE (CHESTER "ZIGGY" SOBOTKA): He said that a lot more poetically than I did, that motherfucker.

CHRIS BAUER (FRANK SOBOTKA): I have a vague but treasured memory of walking with David Simon down the waterfront while he told of a wonderful character's imminent demise. He said something like, "The audience doesn't get to decide who lives and dies. The story does." If only all writers in television felt the same.

Although The Wire's *canvas expanded, the show consciously tended to the storylines of continuing characters while still introducing new figures, such as Robert Wisdom's Maj. "Bunny" Colvin and Method Man's Cheese Wagstaff, who would play larger roles in future seasons.*

MELANIE NICHOLLS-KING (CHERYL): I got pregnant in between first-season and second-season shooting. I was concerned. I was like, *Uh-oh, I don't know where they're going with this. I don't know what their plans are for this character.* Not to say that lesbians don't have children. I didn't know where the writers were planning to go with it. I was worried that it would be a detriment to me being able to continue to play this character. Then I got the first script to Season Two, and it said our first scene together was Kima and Cheryl are investigating in vitro fertilizing. I was like, "Oh my God. That is total universe. Thank you." That's what would be going on. I was able to tell the writers.

It was funny because I was still kind of worried because they hadn't made a clear decision about who was going to actually carry the child. Because Kima is really a character, I assumed that they would probably have her go through that journey. I actually didn't tell them, the first episode that I went down to Baltimore to shoot, I didn't tell them that I was pregnant and it was only the wardrobe person who was like, "What's going on, because your boobs are huge?" I wasn't really showing in the belly yet. I was like, "I'm pregnant and I don't know what to do." Eventually it was like, "You need to share it with them." Also, I was like, "I don't want to deny this beautiful life that's inside my tummy." I told Nina. I felt comfortable going to Nina because she was female and an executive producer. I told her first, and she was amazing. She was like, "Oh, my God. That's amazing. Congratulations. That's perfect. Now we don't have to decide, because we've been going back and forth with it. Cheryl or Kima, Kima or Cheryl? Now we know. It's Cheryl. I'm so glad you made our lives easy. We don't have to put a belly on you. We can just use your belly." She actually said, "I wish you'd have told us earlier," because I don't think I told them until we were shooting the fifth episode or something. We could have shown the gradual increase of the belly. Then, the beautiful thing that happened is that Elijah, my son, ended up playing our son on the show.

ROBERT WISDOM (HOWARD "BUNNY" COLVIN): When Bunny gets introduced, at the end of the second season, I was down doing that movie *Ray* in New Orleans, and my manager got the call that David Simon and *The Wire* were offering a role. I had no idea what that role was, but I had gotten caught back up. I admit that after not getting the Stringer Bell role, I said, "Fuck that show." But I came into it maybe after the third or fourth episode, and I was a fan of it. They offered this role, and we took it and then I looked at it and there were very few words to the character, not too many tip-offs about who this guy was or what the scale of the role was. We had no idea about anything. I would go to these various locations. There was the murder of this kid in a drive-by shooting, and it was just going to these different sites of collateral damage that was happening in the hood, because of the violence and the drugs and everything that was out of control—I just stood looking at these scenes. David came in early in the day and just laid out kind of generally what would be happening. When I look back on it, the whole skeleton, it laid out beautifully: the skeleton of Bunny's arc and Bunny's story, in just that one episode.

MICHAEL POTTS (BROTHER MOUZONE): Brother Mouzone was somebody they had tried to cast for a while. I know my then-agents were trying to get me in for it, but Alexa didn't see me for that role. I didn't come in to read for it until very late in the game and I think I had a very persistent agent, who kept saying, "Alexa, see him, see him. He can do this. Let him read for this." I came in basically when they had pretty much given up on finding the actor for the role, and that first episode that I came in, I had just one line, just one word, just "Officer." And that was supposed to be it. He wasn't supposed to come back after that. That's as much as they thought. They didn't think they'd be able to cast the role or it wouldn't work as they had envisioned it.

ED BURNS (CO-CREATOR): I knew a guy, his father was a preacher and he was very articulate. He got involved with a spin-off of the Panthers and he started robbing federal guards to get their equipment, which is not the brightest thing in the world. He got caught, but when I was talking to him, he was very focused, revolutionary-type ideas, very firm, and I thought, *Maybe you can take that attitude, that strength, and take the discipline of one of [Louis] Farrakhan's people and mold them into this guy and then, find an actor who could play that part.* And we did.

MICHAEL POTTS (BROTHER MOUZONE): All I was thinking in my head, *If I can get three episodes, I can catch up. I can get all my bills paid and I can be even for the year again.* They gave me one word in the very first, and in the second episode, they gave me a monologue. Method Man said, "They bringing you in nice."

METHOD MAN (CALVIN "CHEESE" WAGSTAFF): When auditions went out for the first season of *The Wire*, I made a conscious choice whether to go audition for that show or do the job that I was doing at the time, which was *Brown Sugar*, that Sanaa Lathan movie. I stuck around to do that. It turns out that shit didn't even make the movie. It hit the cutting room floor. They put it in the extras on the DVD. That's the only way you'll know that I was even in the damn movie. But yeah, I blew my shot there, because me and Hassan, who played Wee-Bey, was there at the same time. He didn't like how they were utilizing him at *Brown Sugar*, so he kind of stormed off the set, left, and did *The Wire* audition and got it. So, I watched the first season, and I wanted to get on the show when the casting call went back out for it. I went in and read for Alexa Fogel, and it went pretty well because I had read for Alexa before, so I was comfortable. I had read for her for *Oz* before, and I got the part. So, when I went back to read for *The Wire*, I remember being comfortable. I remember the audition going well.

I thought it could have been better, but when I walked out, I remember seeing Mr. Cheeks, and I was like, *Aw, shit. This part must be for a rapper or some shit.* So, I kind of was turned off by it for a second. But then, when I heard I got the part, I was excited, and first day on the set, I guess they were expecting some big entourage or something like that, but once they saw I was regular and accessible, it ran pretty smooth after that.

ED BURNS (CO-CREATOR): You talk about a hero in the neighborhood. Holy smokes, and all my kids in school, all their notebooks, had that

Wu-Tang Clan symbol. It was remarkable. You would have thought he was the Second Coming when he showed up.

VINCENT PERANIO (PRODUCTION DESIGNER): Baltimore, despite what many people think, it's an extremely friendly place. The people are not jaded. They let you come into their house. Baltimore's interested that somebody's interested in them. Having the film about them and their neighborhood that nobody else cares about really picked up the attitude in the neighborhoods. They were excited about it. They didn't try to disrupt us or play loud music.

METHOD MAN (CALVIN "CHEESE" WAGSTAFF): Fans were a little rambunctious. Like, in between shots, I would have to either stay inside if we were shooting inside or go inside my trailer when people left, because I would basically be signing autographs every time we yelled, "Cut." So, yeah, it was a little crazy. They shot on location in Baltimore, so some of those streets they shot on were in real rough neighborhoods.

One day, this family, they were just playing this music loud when we were trying to get our shot, and I remember the crew constantly asking if they could [turn it down] and they was just beefing like, "We ain't doing shit. We live here. We ain't gotta do shit." So, I walk over there and I ask them politely, but I didn't ask them at first. First, I started kicking it with them. "Yo, what's up Method Man? Blah, blah, blah. What's good? What's good?" This, that, and the third. Then, I politely asked them if they could turn the music off while we get our shots off and shit. They were like, "Yeah, we'll do that for you." But don't get me wrong. They had goons on the set that would shut anybody down that would try and cause problems on the set. It just so happened that, that day, I kind of stepped up and did it in a diplomatic matter, where nobody was offended.

STEVE SHILL (DIRECTOR): The biggest dilemma for me as a white British man trying to interact with Method Man—I was like, what do I call him? Do I call him Mr. Man? Method? Or Method Man? This is a guy who's already a giant star. I'm like, "I'm going to show this guy the respect that he deserves, but as an Englishman I need to find the right way to meet him at the correct level." But he didn't need direction. The scenes that I did with him, the only thing you need to tell him is, "I think you come in here. You meet this guy here and you set your car on fire over there." That's all he needed to know. He did all the rest.

The Wire *carefully picked moments to unravel the myth of Omar and his beliefs. One opportune moment presents itself in the Season 2 episode "All Prologue." On the witness stand, Omar identifies Marquis "Bird" Hilton as the killer of a state witness, William Gant. The writing made clear that Bird had likely murdered Gant, and that Omar was not present at the time of the killing. Upon cross-examination, Bird's lawyer, Maurice Levy, describes Omar as "a parasite who leaches off the culture of drugs." "Just like you, man," Omar interrupts. "I got the shotgun. You got the briefcase. It's all in the game though, right?"*

The moment is one of the few times in the series that Levy, played by Michael Kostroff (the brother of Nina Noble), is flustered. Kostroff said he appreciated the scene and the ability to show another side of Levy, often remembered as conforming to Jewish stereotypes. "If we only told stories where people didn't fall into different stereotypes, it would be really false, so I had no problem playing what some may call a Jewish stereotype," Kostroff said. "I do believe that there are corrupt, successful Jewish lawyers. Rhonda Pearlman is also a Jewish character, and she's on the side of good. I think people noticed it more because Deirdre Lovejoy doesn't appear to be Jewish, so I think people don't notice the fact that there's two Jewish characters on both sides of the law. But I think we've gotten a little bit too careful about telling those stories. The Wire showed us black drug dealers and black elected officials and good guys and bad guys, and thank God for that range. But if we objected to the portrayal of black drug dealers, we wouldn't have that show."

MICHAEL KOSTROFF (MAURICE "MAURY" LEVY): A lot of these actors, I just found intimidating, but right before Michael K. Williams and I shot that courtroom scene, we had a good laugh, because I was scared of him and he was scared of me, because we'd only seen each other on the show, and he's the sweetest guy in the world, but I didn't know that. And he thought I was very mean and tough. So I took a deep breath and I walked over to him and I said, "Hi, I'm Michael Kostroff." He goes, "I was scared to meet you." I said, "I was scared to meet you, too."

MICHAEL K. WILLIAMS (OMAR LITTLE): I was intimidated. There was a lot of people I respected. He was one of them. He had done stuff on *Law & Order* and was out and about. I was like, "That guy. Holy shit. He was in my living room, my living room just two weeks ago."

MICHAEL KOSTROFF (MAURICE "MAURY" LEVY): The one thing about Levy is, he's a good strategist, and not only does he enjoy being a good strategist, but he enjoyed showing everybody the strategy that he's come up with and how he's going to win an impossible case. He never saw that coming, particularly from a street thug, and Omar presented a really, really valid debate at that point and took him down in front of people. It was just something that he wasn't accustomed to encountering.

I made a decision about Levy pretty early on, which is ugly to hear, but [it] really served the character. When I saw the phrase "You people" in the first episode, that tells me a lot, as somebody who's grown up around black people. I know what that means. "You people" is a racist term. I made the decision that he was very happy to work for these guys, but really didn't have a high opinion of black folks. What's delicious in particular to me about that scene is that he's taken down by somebody that he would have dismissed as not intellectual and not capable of forming that valid argument. That's what I loved about it. It hits him out of nowhere, because Omar is also a great strategist and also kind of brilliant. I think that's what I love, is that [Levy is] shut down by the person that he thinks is just a stupid animal.

STEVE SHILL (DIRECTOR): It was shot in a real courtroom that was actually active at the time. Normally, you would shoot overnight, but for some reason we couldn't. It was an active courthouse in Baltimore. The video village was around the back, and around the back was the corridor where defendants were being led back and forth from the cell holds to their respective courtroom. I'm sitting at video village with people being led past us in chains for real. It was frankly awful. It's one of the most awful things that I'd ever been involved in. I would say that this is a quintessential David Simon moment. He brought us there because this is one of the places where he had sat as a reporter for twenty years reporting on this stuff, and this is what he knew. He brought us to the real place, and by accident we ended up shooting there during working hours.

I can't tell you how guilty I felt for sitting there as some jerk-off television director making money fictionalizing what's happening to these people for real. David Simon's thrust was to expose the injustice. Even talking about it right now, I still feel bad about it. I had to move my director's chair out of their way so they could shuffle past in shackles. I feel like a piece of shit because of it.

Lawrence Gilliard Jr. passionately, yet unsuccessfully, argued with David Simon against D'Angelo's sudden and emotional demise. Many regarded D'Angelo, Avon's conflicted nephew, as the show's Season 1 conscience. Gilliard's fellow cast members described D'Angelo's death as even more shocking and devastating than Michael B. Jordan's Wallace's killing in the first season.

FRANKIE FAISON (ACTING COMMR. ERVIN H. BURRELL): Whenever anyone would die or get killed, that was always tough. It was tough to lose these characters, but you have to be true to the writing. People die or disappear. Those were always emotional scenes and emotional times, when someone would read the script and know that their number had been called.

STEVE EARLE (WAYLON): Yeah, D'Angelo. He argued with David about [getting killed off]. When he got the script, he fucking argued with him about it. He thought he could change David's mind.

LAWRENCE GILLIARD JR. (D'ANGELO BARKSDALE): The way I found out was we were in the second season, I think we were on like Episode Four or something. I was coming out of my trailer. I saw David, Nina, and Ed Burns; they were walking across this lot. Ed and Nina peeled off. David just kept coming straight for me, and he goes, "Hey, what's up?" I'm like, "Hey." "So, I've got some good news and some bad news. What do you want first?" I'm like, "Well, give me the bad news first." He goes, "You're not going to have to read beyond Episode Six." I'm like, "What?"

It was shocking. I was shocked and I was upset. I was disappointed. I said, "Well, what's the good news?" He said, "I wrote an amazing death scene for you." I'm like, "That doesn't quite trump the bad news." I've been around the game for a long time. I'm a professional, so I just thought, *I'll just move on beyond this.* Once I read the scene and I found out how it was going to happen, I just wanted it to be a good death scene. I wanted it to be memorable. I wanted to do a good job. That person exists in the world. I always want to be truthful to my characters.

DAVID SIMON (CREATOR): Nothing was funnier in its own dark way. I didn't laugh. He said, "My character is only—he's only twenty-six years old. He's got his whole life ahead of him." "Yeah." "There's so much more I could have done with his life." And therein lies the tragedy. It was really like he was pleading from real life, like any sane, life-loving human would. To hear it happen, that's exactly why it's such a tragedy.

WOOD HARRIS (AVON BARKSDALE): I thought this kid was going to be with us this whole ride. He got killed. It had unpredictability, and it added that element to the work that we were doing. It was just very unpredictable on *The Wire*. It felt almost like a horror movie. It's scary around the corner. It added a reality to it as the actors because we could not be presumptuous to think that we would be here the next week even.

LAWRENCE GILLIARD JR. (D'ANGELO BARKSDALE): You don't develop characters and have your fan base, your audience, fall in love with a character, and then kill them off. It's just not done, you know? It was shocking to me. It actually affected me more than I thought it would, because before *The Wire*, I was already working steadily in the business. When I found out about it, I was like, "All right. This is different. It was not expected, but I'll be working. I'll just keep doing my thing." I didn't realize how much it would affect me, because I really loved that character. Not only how much I loved the character, but also the writing was so good, you become spoiled. It had never happened to me before, because I was used to reading the regular Hollywood formula stuff. You know what to expect.

When you do a show like this, you're ready for good-quality writing and you're performing on such a level, with everyone who's at the top of their game. When you're done with something like that and you move back into that Hollywood system, everything you read is crap. It took me a long time. I passed on a whole lot of stuff. It took me a long time to realize, *Wait a minute. This crap is the norm. That's what I'm going to get. I have to find my way back to this.*

JAMES "P.J." RANSONE (CHESTER "ZIGGY" SOBOTKA): I shot that show when I was so young. That was my first big TV gig. It kind of fucked me up because I sort of expected that everything else would sort of be that way. Nobody cared when we were shooting it, so they weren't like, "You're shooting *The Wire*." You know what I mean? I didn't have anybody older than me being like, "You're doing this amazing, prestigious thing." It was like, "Oh, just go ahead and shoot this show that nobody cares about." I didn't realize that the bar had been accidentally set so high in terms of writing or storytelling.

ANDRE ROYO (REGINALD "BUBBLES" COUSINS): I love Season Two, but I know when Season Two aired, we got a lot of slack because people were like, "What happened to my story? What happened to our show?" People were like, "I had to sit through eight, nine, ten episodes of the slowest fucking show that I fell in love with. I fell in love with these characters, and they were all gone in Season Two. What the fuck is that about?" You had to sit in the bar and tell people, "It is what it is." They would get it. They would agree with it, but they were mad. They were mad. It also, to be honest, it brought in our audience a little bit. It brought the conversation to a bigger perspective because, let's be clear, white people were not watching this show the first season. Not the masses. I'm sure there were some, but when you see more than four black people on-screen, they're like, "That's not my story. That doesn't have nothing to do with me, so I'm going to change the channel." All of a sudden, in Season Two, white people are watching it and going, "This is dope. Who's that guy? Who's this Omar guy?" They start asking questions, and the black people go, "You don't know who they are? Let me tell you who they are."

You had these conversations, and that's what made Season Three big. You had two audiences who came together and started talking about this show and going, "This show is amazing. This show is not following TV standards. They can just go from any angle." It's all the same narrative. It's about the community. I don't think any other show at that time was doing it like that, just changing it all up. Because Season One or Season Two, there were no nominations. If you get a nomination or even if you win, it's harder to change up. If it's working for you, HBO might be like, "Don't change nothing. Leave it like that and keep doing it." [But] because we were still going under the radar, HBO was like, "Try and do something new. Try and figure it out. See if you can get nominated. If it ain't bad, then do that." It was David Simon's and Ed Burns's plan, but they didn't get that much resisting in the changing.

JAMES "P.J." RANSONE (CHESTER "ZIGGY" SOBOTKA): The first season, you follow these black drug dealers around the streets of Baltimore and you go, "Oh my God, they're trying to function as a business. Their capitalism is the same way everything else is." Then you shift focus to the white working class, right? What you really take away from that is those people are just as trapped in the machine of capitalism as the drug dealers are.

People go like, "The White Season." It's always weird to me because it's like, no. They're just like, incrementally a little bit more financially well off than the drug dealers. So, to me, the takeaway from that is people go, "Season Two is always the worst." The reason why I think people think that is because it's too much to reconcile the fact of whites in the same terms of social mobility as a poor black person. They hate to admit it to themselves. It's too much to reconcile the fact that white people are enslaved to their own social class as much as poor black people. They would have to give up the delusion that they can be wealthy one day, working honestly within the contexts of the system.

Think about where we are as a country today. People make these great hyperbolic comparisons to [Donald] Trump and Adolf Hitler, and it's really wrong. Trump has benefited completely from a system of debt, right? Borrowing against your perceived value. What he's really tapping into is exactly what I'm talking about: is the delusion that you think because you are a certain sort of skin color that you are afforded more social mobility than other races or cultures. And that's just simply not true. A politician will use that in terms of going, "See, the problem isn't me. It's these other people working right next to me." But if they were to compare their pay stubs, they'd see that they had more in common with that person than they would hope for.

AMY RYAN (OFF. BEATRICE "BEADIE" RUSSELL): At the end of the first year, because I had signed a contract for the duration of the whole series, David said to me, "You know, this isn't like network TV, where I can write an episode and some other character can say, 'Hey, congratulations, Beadie. You became a detective. You took the test.' In reality, that would be five years that you'd have to go from port police or something like that." He said, "I'm not going to do that. I have plans for you. Don't worry, but you're not going to be one of the detectives next year."

I was crushed, because I love the show. Wendell Pierce said to me, "You got to fight for your job." I was like, "Well, what am I supposed to do? I can't become detective overnight." I don't think it was every script, but David would put a few random scripts with a famous line from a movie, and just for fun, you'd see if people would figure it out, and Wendell had figured one out and he gave me the answer. He said, "Go tell David you know what the line is." I was really nervous, and I go up to David and I say, "David, there's a line in one of the scripts that says, 'Let's go.' And the other guy says, 'Why not?' Is that line from *The Wild Bunch*?" David does this double take, and he looked me up and down, he's like, "Ha, well, how did you know that?" I was like, "Oh, I was just guessing. Am I right?" For a second I was like, *Oh, my God. Okay, I'm going to make detective. He's going to change the roles.* He was so impressed. He said, "Somebody told you." I was like, "No, no. I'm right. Oh my God. I'm right." I never told him that story, that Wendell told me the answer. Maybe he'll find out from this.

Anyway, it didn't work, and I was finished on Season Two, but as you know, I came back and was peppered in through the years.

DAVID SIMON (CREATOR): In Season Two, the writers had a contest to see how many lines from *The Wild Bunch* we could get into the show. "Let's go" is one of the most famous lines in the film. We were deep in the season, and I think we got like ten, fifteen lines in. Some of the actors got wind that we were doing it. They recognized some of the lines. More lines like "Let's go." There were lines that really sort of stick out. She said, "I think I've got one of the *Wild Bunch* lines in the script." It was said to Nicky Sobotka by his uncle. I remember looking at her, going, "Are you a [Sam] Peckinpah fan?" And she went, "Oh, yeah." I said, "Really?" There was a little part of me that went, "Somebody give you that?" "No, no, no." "Very cool, Amy."

The large size of the ensemble cast made it impossible for the actors to know every single cast member intimately. Al Brown recalled sitting at a table with Dominic West between takes in the final season. West finished telling a story and departed. Brown turned to the person sitting next to him and asked, "What the fuck was Dominic trying to talk like some Englishman for? Is he auditioning for Shakespeare?" Brown had not realized West was British, even though the pair had been with the show since its beginning. But the deaths of major characters served as bonding sessions, with Sonja Sohn routinely gathering the cast and crew in mourning. The closeness of the actors largely broke into whom they portrayed on screen. Cops commiserated with cops. Crooks hung out with crooks. The cast would describe itself unilaterally as a family, but as with any family, occasional bickering occurred.

AMY RYAN (OFF. BEATRICE "BEADIE" RUSSELL): There was a real camaraderie with the whole group. A lot of laughs. I felt very close to Dominic in that way as well. It becomes almost sibling-like, and when our characters became romantic, it's kind of goofy, four o'clock in the morning, you're in bed together, and you just want to be home in your own pajamas. Like in bed with your own brother or something, not that I know what that's like.

LANCE REDDICK (LT. CEDRIC DANIELS): I definitely got annoyed with Dominic. I think it was really our personalities. I think it's ironic, but I don't think it's because of the nature of the roles we were playing. I'm an introvert, and Dominic's an extreme extrovert. He's the guy that's got to be the center of attention all the time, in my opinion, as talented as he is. I kind of just want to do my work and hang out. I just feel like there were times where Dominic got bored. It's funny, because this didn't happen when we were in a scene just the two of us. It only happened when we were in group scenes, where he was class clown. That just bugged the shit out of me. For me, everything matters.

DOMINIC WEST (DET. JIMMY MCNULTY): We had a lot of fun. It was long days in the hot sun, and we had to do something. I can't remember what I got Lance for. He was pretty serious. Lance, he's a very serious actor. He's a real professional and takes it seriously, so it was quite easy to get him.

LANCE REDDICK (LT. CEDRIC DANIELS): He's a great actor, but as personalities, we're oil and water.

DOMINIC WEST (DET. JIMMY MCNULTY): [Wendell and I] bonded pretty quickly. He took me around New Orleans a few times, and it was interesting. The difference between us and the nationality difference, I suppose, was what sort of drew us together in a way or what made it such an easy relationship.

RICK OTTO (OFF. KENNETH DOZERMAN): I don't think anybody plays drunk better than Dom West and Wendell Pierce.

DOMINIC WEST (DET. JIMMY MCNULTY): We were drunk. Well, we got a lot of practice in.

WENDELL PIERCE (DET. WILLIAM "BUNK" MORELAND): He's that sort of person that makes you feel like when he's dealing with you, that moment is the most important in the world at that time. That's what I really appreciated about Dominic. You can take him anywhere in the world. I took him to New Orleans for Mardi Gras once, and— Clarke Peters was the same way. The places that I took them was just like, "God, if the production company ever found out, they'd be like, 'Wendell, that was dangerous.'" We were in the back alleys and the little barrooms in New Orleans, just having a great time. I wanted to show them a different side of New Orleans, not something that was touristy. We had a ball of a time because Dominic is open to that sort of thing.

DOMINIC WEST (DET. JIMMY MCNULTY): This guy stopped me and Wendell in the street, going, "Hey, you're in *The Wire*, that's Wendell," and Wendell goes, "Yeah, yeah, yeah," and he said, "Look, man, my friend here. He plays McNulty," and the guy looked at me and went, "Oh, yeah man, you're the bitch ass. You're the crybaby. That's right, you're the crybaby."

WENDELL PIERCE (DET. WILLIAM "BUNK" MORELAND): The guy knew me, and I said, "Wait, meet my partner on the show. You remember him?" He kind of thought he remembered him, but he felt as though, "Well, you're actors, so you must have had an emotional scene." He's like, "Yeah, you were crying and everything. Yeah, I know him now." He just assumed that he had this big dramatic scene that he started crying. The guy was funny. Then, what Dominic didn't say was that I had him over on Orleans Avenue looking at [the] Zulu [parade during Mardi Gras] and a guy said, "Hey, Wendell. Wendell Pierce." I said, "Hey, listen, don't look at me. He's on the show, too." Dominic loved the fact that he'd be able to go somewhere, they'll jump on me and crowd around me and not recognize him. I said, "But, no, this is McNulty." This one guy said, "Oh yeah, the white boy." I had him over in the Lafitte housing projects, and everybody says, "Yeah, that's the white boy. The white boy from *The Wire*." For that block, for half an hour, he was, "Hey, baby, come over here. It's the white boy from *The Wire*."

AMY RYAN (OFF. BEATRICE "BEADIE" RUSSELL): One time, we went to New Orleans for publicity. The Essence Music Festival. I'm probably the only white person in New Orleans as well, and we were all at this club dancing, and Seth [Gilliam] said to me, "Can I ask you something?" "Yeah." "How do you feel right now?" "First time in my life I feel exotic. This is awesome." You know, I didn't feel shut out by the guys, and certainly if talk off set turned to a different topic that I wouldn't feel comfortable with, I would just walk away. There are lots of other women around on set working in the crew, our DP, Uta, she was at the helm the first two seasons, and Nina, there was a female force on that show even though it wasn't represented in large numbers on-screen, but the women who were there were strong and full of love and humor, and it was a nice group.

DEIRDRE "DEDE" LOVEJOY (ASST. STATE'S ATTY. RHONDA PEARLMAN): It was educational. I jokingly say I'm just a dumb white girl from Indiana. I have lived in New York for thirty years. It is not like I'm a kid. Showing up on a set that is eighty percent black men, I would be like, "Oh my gosh." That awareness was enough to make me just sort of be able to scratch the surface of what every black or Asian or whatever it is goes through every day. I have got to tell you, it is sobering.

JIM TRUE-FROST (DET. ROLAND "PREZ" PRYZBYLEWSKI): Both from the story and from my friends in the cast, I think I gained a much clearer window on the experience of the black characters in the story and the black actors in the show. If you're a member of the privileged majority, you can't, no matter how compassionate or insightful you are, you can't—let's just say, the closer you are to the world of people who are in the minority and the more you're exposed to it, the more you truly can relate, I guess. In my case, in art and in drama, I wasn't only exposed to the story, but I was a part of telling the story, and that was a real blessing as well.

MICHAEL HYATT (BRIANNA BARKSDALE): I remember Idris before he was Idris Elba. I remember having a conversation with him on set. It must have been the second season. I was comfortable with the guys that I was working with. He was saying he wasn't sure how much longer he was going to stay in this country. He knew French or some shit. I remember him saying there's an opportunity for him to do some work in France, and maybe he should take that. I was saying to him, "Brother, are you fucking out of your mind? People are going to love you as this character. You're not going anywhere, dude."

He was not at all conscious yet of the fanfare. He had not started receiving the fanfare from the show. He was just wondering where the fuck is his next job going to come, because nobody knew how long this was going to last. There was no promise of anything. He was trying to figure out what his next move was. I was saying, "I think you should stay here. I think people are really going to like you in this show." I'm sure I had nothing to do with his choices. I'm not suggesting that. I just remember that conversation and just remember thinking, *Dude, you're fucking clueless. You're not going anywhere. This is going to be really successful for you.*

IDRIS ELBA (STRINGER BELL): My understanding of the show when it got picked up was Stringer and Avon does one season. This is about Avon. I was like, "Okay." By the end of the season, they were obviously still writing it. There was more and more Stringer and Avon stuff coming. At that point, they were like, "We want you back for next year." I was like, "Really?" That became clear that my character was popular. Not just my character, but the whole Barksdale clan just became more and more popular with the rest of the show.

ANDRE ROYO (REGINALD "BUBBLES" COUSINS): What was funny about Idris was, from my point of view, we would have long talks at the hotel bar. When he first got on the scene, he was really, really nervous. We were all unknowns. Wendell was probably the biggest one we knew. It just was like, "I'm trying to hide this accent. I'm trying to be a believable Baltimore hood dude." He was just nervous. Nobody do hood better then Wood Harris. That was the dude. Idris was the number two guy, and he didn't think he was doing it justice. He felt like he was faking it. We were like, "Fake it until you make it. You're doing great." There were always moments where we would have to check each other and reassure each other that we're doing a good job.

5

A REAL ROM-COM

George Pelecanos described it as a pincer move when he and David
Simon cornered novelist Richard Price before a reading at a bookstore.
Pelecanos had mentioned to Simon that the pair should measure Price's
interest in writing for the show. To Simon, the addition of Pelecanos
had worked better than anticipated. Why not? he thought. Simon
and Price enjoyed a history. Simon's Homicide: Life on the Street
and Price's Clockers had debuted at around the same time. Clockers
snatched Simon's interest. This gripping novel, based in a fictitious
New Jersey city, captured the dual perspectives of police and an urban
community. Price and Simon shared an editor in John Sterling, who
once brought Simon to Price's downtown apartment, which featured
a view into Jersey City. Their first "play date," as Price later labeled
it, arrived the night of the Rodney King verdict. They watched the
unrest unfold from Price's apartment, and the eternally curious minds
then ventured to Jersey City to witness it firsthand. "Price had written
tons of movie scripts in the same vernacular," Simon said. "He was
supposed to write The Wire. Before The Wire, if they had given him
the charge to write a thirteen-episode cop show around a drug wiretap,
he could've gone in and holistically written it."

Price had already made a cameo in the show during Season 2, as a prison English teacher. He quickly mulled over the offer before accepting it and convened with the show's inner circle of Simon, Pelecanos, Ed Burns, and Robert Colesberry at a hotel in Tarrytown, New York, to outline Season 3's focus on the death of reform and the introduction of local politics. "I don't know where that money came from to send us up there, but that was nice," Burns said. "I don't think we were a big hit with HBO, I'll tell you that." Bill Zorzi eventually joined the group after Price departed. He originally planned to briefly stop by and say hello to Simon, a former Baltimore Sun colleague, and instead stayed involved through the show's run. Dennis Lehane, another renowned novelist, who authored Mystic River, also joined the writing staff. The experience in the room established an atmosphere of competitiveness. Many had already described The Wire as a visual novel. Now novelists worked on most of the episodes moving forward.

Yet, for all the additions, the show would soon be shaken by a devastating, sudden, loss.

DAVID SIMON (CREATOR): We went to get George, and George worked out great. After that, George was introducing Price at a bookstore in Washington. Price was touring on, I want to say, [his novel] *Freedomland*. He said, "Let's go get Price." He just said it like that. That was George. I was like, "Man, Richard Price is like a literary lion." He was like, "Let's try it." So, we both went to the bookstore and we pulled him up, and he said, "Yeah, I'm interested." And then it was like, "Let's go get Dennis Lehane." At a certain point, I was just joking, like, "Who do you want now?"

GEORGE PELECANOS (WRITER/PRODUCER): It's very obvious why you want Richard Price. He'd already written *Clockers*, and all his other books fit right into what we were doing, but if you read Dennis's books, the best part is the dialogue, and it's very natural and it's witty. We thought he'd be good for this, and it didn't matter that they were respectively from New York and Boston. I told them, "Don't worry about it. You don't need to know the street names. Just put

"STREET, BALTIMORE" in the slugline. We'll plug in the street name later on. That's not why we want you. We're not coming after you because you know Baltimore through and through. You know people. That's why we want you."

I think David went after Walter Mosley, [too], and I don't know what happened there, but he didn't write for us.

RICHARD PRICE (WRITER): When [David] and George asked me to do it, I didn't want to do it, because my fear was that they thought, because of *Clockers*, I knew so much about the world of *The Wire*, and my feeling is I gave everything. I emptied my brain out on that book. It felt like if I wrote an episode, it's gonna be "The Emperor's New Clothes": "Well gee, I guess he doesn't know as much as we thought he did." I said yes because how could you not? I killed myself on that first episode. Did ride-alongs in Baltimore. Like cops in Baltimore are any different from cops in New York or LA.

DENNIS LEHANE (WRITER): A few years earlier, I was hanging with David, Laura [Lippman], and George at a writers' conference, and David was talking about a show he'd pitched to HBO under the guise that it was a cop show. It was, at that time, in late development stages, I believe. Dave had this idea that he wanted to hire novelists for his writers' room because he thought most TV writers had probably picked up bad habits working on bad shows for network TV. Fast-forward to a few years later, and George had written the penultimate episode of Season One and raved to me about the experience. He mentioned that David was interested in having me in the room for Season Two. Problem was that I was buried in *The Given Day*, and it was at a fragile point, where any distraction could conceivably have killed the book, so I declined, but said, "Please come back to me." And they did. And I hooked on for Season Three.

RICHARD PRICE (WRITER): I had never been in a writers' room before. My whole experience with TV, I wrote a pilot in 1981 for NBC, and

I didn't even know what I was doing. I had never done TV before, but I had known the characters just from watching. I could do the characters. Somebody said to me, "It's like watching [Donald] Trump long enough on TV. You could do him. You could do a credible imitation of him. Anybody could." I just had integrated so much of each individual character that I could do it very fluidly. I'd never been in a writers' room before, and before Season Three they had a meeting. It was Ed Burns, Pelecanos, and Simon in Tarrytown.

It was an interesting process. They have six characters. "What's the theme this year? What institution are we going to focus on?" In Season Three it was Hamsterdam. "Okay, so, what's the overall arc for Omar? What's the overall arc for the Barksdales? What's the overall arc for the mayor's office? McNulty, etcetera, etcetera." For an overarching meeting in Tarrytown, you can't get too intimate. You can't ever get to a point in an overarching meeting to say, "Well, in Episode Six this is what happens exactly." Because even right before you write Episode Six, you're still gonna be off, because you've still gotta [consider] what happened in Five. Every time you write, there's a good chance some of your stuff is gonna go an episode later under another guy's name and stuff from the episode previous is gonna be shoved into yours. It's sort of an assembly line. The story trumps the author.

WILLIAM F. ZORZI (STAFF WRITER): It was sort of a fluke that I ended up being in Tarrytown, which was the twenty-third and twenty-fourth of July of 2003. It was at the Dolce Tarrytown House. I had been in Long Island and Queens for a funeral for the morning of the twenty-third—a father of a friend of mine had died. I knew David was up in Tarrytown somehow, so I thought I'd just drive up and kind of drop in.

I just dropped in, like to say hi. That's how I kind of stumbled into it, and David was good enough to put me on the table as a staff writer eventually. The rest is history or something. I did all the political stuff. Ed and George had no desire to have anything to do with politics.

GEORGE PELECANOS (WRITER/PRODUCER): Nina controls all the stuff, like where you stay. She tried to book us into a hotel up there that didn't have liquor, didn't have a bar, and we promptly booked ourselves into a different hotel. That's one thing I remember. She might dispute it, but I have brought it up with her recently. I've never forgotten that.

We did find a place where we could drink at night, even though it was kind of in, to me, the boonies. For all I know, it's a nice place, but it looked like just a hotel sitting on a bunch of land. We also played handball, and Richard Price was very competitive.

RICHARD PRICE (WRITER): Mainly what I remember from Tarrytown is it was like the most anti-*Wire* setting in the world. It was a corporate events hotel. Everyone's having motivational meetings and bonding sessions for their sales corps, and stuff like that. We're sitting there going, "Well, who's Omar gonna fuck this year? Yeah, I think a Barksdale is gonna die." Everybody else is studying the acronyms for success and getting on the links. We're sitting there killing people in Baltimore.

I remember, at one point—I used to play a lot of racquetball—I wound up on a court with Burns and Pelecanos, but I didn't bring any shorts, so somebody lent me their shorts, and they kept falling down to my knees on the racquetball court. It was maybe the most memorable thing that happened to me there.

ED BURNS (CO-CREATOR): I have a very good sense of story. I don't know where it comes from. Maybe being Irish. I don't know where the fuck it comes from. I know this world. I know this world intimately. I know that I can sit in a room and make a story, and it's fun to do that. There's a competitiveness there. There's bouncing off of each other. When you have a room with the talent that we had, we can always make the story. Richard Price is probably the sharpest, quickest, funniest guy you'll ever meet. When he gets on a roll, there's no story. He'll have you on the floor laughing. He's just amazing.

GEORGE PELECANOS (WRITER/PRODUCER): All these people are writers, so they're pretty vain, and they all think that their ideas are the best ideas. And they all think that they're the best writer in the room, which is as it should be. There's dealing with the personalities and kind of pushing your ego aside, because, after a while, since everybody gets to know each other, it's not so polite. It's like, "That's a stupid idea. We're not going to do that." All those types of things that you thought you put behind you back in high school.

RICHARD PRICE (WRITER): In a script, there's no writing. It's just dialogue and directions. There's not one sentence of prose. There's no writer of a script. It's a one-hundred-twenty-page memo to the director: "Do this. Say this." What *The Wire* had that *Clockers* didn't have is, I kept *Clockers* on the worm's-eye view. It rarely left the trenches. It rarely got higher than the Homicide Squad, if it did at all. He went top to bottom. It was like he went from the general's tent to the grunts. I always admired that about the ambition of the show. I couldn't have written it. I didn't know anything about how the DA's office works, the interoffice politics in a police department, how City Hall works—any of that. That's a lot of Ed Burns because he had been a homicide cop. Before that, he was a military man. Zorzi had the city desk at *The Baltimore Sun*. Simon was a police reporter for the most part. They each had different areas of experience. I did best with the guys on the street, in my opinion.

DENNIS LEHANE (WRITER): Richard is the reason I'm a writer. He's foundational. No matter how many times we've hung out, worked together, chatted each other up, I can never feel comfortable around the guy. It's fucking embarrassing because I'm a pretty social dude, good at putting people at ease, but Richard must think I need Adderall because I simply can't chill around him. I was fourteen when I read *The Wanderers* in the basement of my house in Dorchester, and the world was fundamentally altered between when I picked that book up and when I put it back down. And to follow his writing for my very first teleplay twenty-odd years later—that was just too daunting to contemplate. So, I blocked it out. I read the notes on his episode, saw where he was going with it, and then just put my head down and banged out my ep'.

RICHARD PRICE (WRITER): It's a real rom-com, you know? I was intimidated by both of them because of what they'd done on the show. I guess George had been reading me, but I'd also been reading George. I read *Homicide* and read *The Corner*.

DENNIS LEHANE (WRITER): I'm an urban writer. I'm fascinated by the ways a city does, or doesn't, work. I love the street slang and the hum of city life, the sense that within that density, a million stories are waiting to be told. The particulars of Baltimore—the names of specific streets or neighborhoods, its local patois—all of that was filled in by David or Ed.

RICHARD PRICE (WRITER): *The Wire* was kind of painless, other than my own stage fright of giving me an episode that didn't make me look like a horse's ass. It was a writers' show, and Simon was very respectful of people he wanted to work with. Because he was the big poo-bah of the show, he took all the crap from HBO. He's Patton; I'm just a solider. Tell me where to go, and I'll execute. That was very painless, because I like Simon. I like Pelecanos. I like the subject. I really dug the characters. It's easy. It probably took me two weeks to write an episode.

DAVID SIMON (CREATOR): As soon as the second season happened, Ed was thinking about education. "We've got to do education. We've got to do education." We were always thinking seasons ahead, because guys had ideas of stuff, of slices of the city they wanted to get to. I knew we had to get to politics. You can't do education without establishing what oversees it. By then, you want City Hall as fast as you can get it after Season Two. But Ed was hungry to do education, and I always wanted to end on the media, because I wanted the whole show to be a critique of what we're not attending to and why.

ED BURNS (CO-CREATOR): I didn't like politics.

RICHARD PRICE (WRITER): How could you not like writing Omar? No, I really liked writing about some fucking corrupt councilman. It's Omar. Everybody loves Omar.

ED BURNS (CO-CREATOR): Every moment we saw of politics was one less moment we conceived a character that I liked.

WILLIAM F. ZORZI (STAFF WRITER): Once David drove the point home that he wanted a political storyline, I spent a lot of time with Ed, and I'm sure Pelecanos had many a laugh at our expense, really. He would just walk out. First of all, Ed has amazing stamina. He could sit there for hours upon hours upon hours and just spin up scenarios about plotlines or thoughts that he had about politics or "try this one on for size"—that kind of thing.

We spent a lot of time sitting in that room on Clinton Street, just the two of us, after George just sort of left shaking his head, going over possible political storylines. I don't know that any of them really made it. It helped shape who the Carcetti character was, but there wasn't a lot of room—nor was there the inclination to make room, except by David's doing—for the political storyline.

Ed and George were absolutely more concerned with the actual investigation by the unit and the characters who had already been

David Simon, a journalist at heart, only reluctantly recognized television as an effective medium to present discussion. "I'm more interested in the arguments," he said about the show's surviving popularity. "I wish that were the legacy of the show." KRESTINE HAVEMANN

D'Angelo (Lawrence Gilliard Jr.) teaches Wallace (Michael B. Jordan) and Bodie (J. D. Williams) chess by drawing an analogy to the Barksdale crew in one of *The Wire*'s most memorable scenes. DAVID LEE/HBO.

Andre Royo as Bubbles, the heroin addict and informant who never stops battling to right his life. "I want Bubbles to be a human first, addict second," Royo said. "I wasn't trying to play the addiction. I was going to play the person." DAVID LEE/HBO

Members of Season 1's police detail: Cedric Daniels (Lance Reddick), Leander Sydnor (Corey Parker Robinson), Kima Greggs (Sonja Sohn), Ellis Carver (Seth Gilliam), and Michael Santangelo (Michael Salconi). Reddick recognized the show's potential to be special early on and remains upset over *The Wire*'s lack of awards. "I'll be pissed off about it until the day I die," he said. DAVID LEE/HBO

Set decorators found the original iconic orange couch in a Dumpster and established it in *The Wire*'s pilot before discarding it. An expensive scramble ensued to replicate the couch with this replacement once HBO picked up the show.
DAVID LEE/HBO

Jimmy McNulty (Dominic West) and Bunk Moreland (Wendell Pierce) investigate a crime scene. Pierce, from New Orleans, and West, a native of England, developed a quick rapport on and off the screen. "Our chemistry, it's been a great friendship from the bat," Pierce said. "He has a great curiosity about things. He's very well read, loves to go out and have a good time. I think we share that approach to life." DAVID LEE/HBO

The city of Baltimore served as the show's biggest star. Pictured are some of the city's vast number of row houses, many of which became vacant during Baltimore's population drop-off. "Some of the lighting to me was almost like a painting from the past, like from the seventeenth century, a Rembrandt look about it, the darkness of the house and the sunlight searing through the boarded-up windows," said Vincent Peranio, the show's production designer. "I think the show was bleak and beautiful in the way that looking at ruins in a ruined civilization are." DAVID LEE/HBO

Wallace (Michael B. Jordan) speaks to D'Angelo (Lawrence Gilliard Jr.) in The Pit. Jordan's Wallace lasted only one season, but David Simon rightly predicted the character's impact would be enduring. Jordan later blossomed into a movie star. DAVID LEE/HBO

Michael K. Williams beautifully played the many sides to stickup artist Omar Little. Several real-life figures known to the show's creators formed the character's background. Williams believed that Omar would be killed off early in the show's run; however, he lasted long enough to evolve into President Barack Obama's favorite television character. NICOLE RIVELLI/HBO

Idris Elba did not recognize the budding star power in his portrayal of Stringer Bell, the suave gangster who strived for legitimacy, during the show's early run. "People are going to love you as this character," Michael Hyatt, who played Brianna Barksdale, recalled telling him. "You're not going anywhere, dude." PAUL SCHIRALDI/HBO

The discovery of a container holding a dozen dead women drove Season 2's plot by linking the police detail and the docks. "They weren't dummy bodies," said Amy Ryan (Beadie Russell). "They were real people huddled up on top of each other, and it was scary."
LARRY RILEY/HBO

Chris Bauer originally auditioned for Jimmy McNulty before being cast as Season 2's Frank Sobotka. "Imagine a bloated, hungover, mumbling McNulty who looked like he'd be single his whole life," Bauer joked. "Frank Sobotka was a much better fit." LARRY RILEY/HBO

Robert Colesberry in his small, recurring role as Ray Cole. Colesberry played a much larger, significant role behind the camera. His sudden death in 2004 following complications from heart surgery caused deep heartbreak among the show's creators, cast, and crew.
LARRY RILEY/HBO

Members of Season 2's police detail: Lester Freamon (Clarke Peters), Ellis Carver (Seth Gilliam), Beadie Russell (Amy Ryan), Rhonda Pearlman (Dede Lovejoy), Herc Hauk (Domenick Lombardozzi), Roland Pryzbylewski (Jim True-Frost), and Kima Greggs (Sonja Sohn). "I went to high school with Seth Gilliam," Ryan said. "We were good friends and so that was a cool moment, that first scene we filmed together in [Cedric] Daniels's office and every time they block us next to each other, we just crack up." LARRY RILEY/HBO

David Simon on location with Andre Royo (Bubbles) and Leo Fitzpatrick (Johnny Weeks). "Every time we went to Baltimore I thought, *Man, this has to be the worst block of Baltimore*," Fitzpatrick said. "And then we'd find one that was worse. It's fine for a TV show. But when you think that people actually live there and that this is people's reality, that's a mind blower." PAUL SCHIRALDI/HBO

Michael Potts as Brother Mouzone, the calm enforcer eternally dressed in a bow tie who became a threat to Omar. "They gave me one word in the very first, and in the second episode they gave me a monologue," Potts said. "Method Man said, 'They bringing you in nice.'"
PAUL SCHIRALDI/HBO

Frankie Faison as Ervin Burrell and John Doman as William Rawls. The characters portrayed bureaucratic careerists in the police department. Faison, behind the scenes, added levity while shooting some of the show's more serious scenes.
PAUL SCHIRALDI/HBO

The Wire often blended fact with fiction. Here is the "real" Jay Landsman as Lt. Dennis Mello. David Simon awarded another character Landsman's name. Landsman, a longtime Baltimore homicide detective, instead depicted Mello, which in real life was the name of the first black officer in Baltimore to reach the rank of captain.
PAUL SCHIRALDI/HBO

Some assumed that the show's great reformist had arrived with the introduction of a white mayor (Aidan Gillen as the originally idealistic Tommy Carcetti). "Um, just wait," Simon would say. "*Hero's* a big word." PAUL SCHIRALDI/HBO

Michael K. Williams met Felicia "Snoop" Pearson in a bar and encouraged her to come to *The Wire*'s set. The show's creative forces urged her to leave behind a past of illegalities for acting. In an *Entertainment Weekly* column, Stephen King labeled Pearson, "perhaps the most terrifying female villain to ever appear in a television series." PAUL SCHIRALDI/HBO

Delaney Williams pictured as the fictional Jay Landsman. Landsman served as a middle man caught between his bureaucratic commanders and his squad of subordinates. David Simon regarded the character as one of his favorites to write dialogue for. PAUL SCHIRALDI/HBO

Season 4's the Corner Boys: Dukie Weems (Jermaine Crawford), Randy Wagstaff (Maestro Harrell), Michael Lee (Tristan Wilds), and Namond Brice (Julito McCullum). The season featured each boy confronting life-derailing issues and hurdles.
PAUL SCHIRALDI/HBO

Marlo (Jamie Hector) holds court with Chris Partlow (Gbenga Akinnagbe), Monk (Kwame Patterson), Snoop (Felicia Pearson), O-Dog (Darrell Britt-Gibson), and Cheese Wagstaff (Method Man). Hector quickly recognized Marlo as a character who was economic and efficient in everything. "What Marlo really wanted is power, just pure, uncut, unstoppable power," Hector said. PAUL SCHIRALDI/HBO

Andre Royo's Bubbles, sober and working near the end of the show's run. "You don't know if he turned it around," Ed Burns said. "That's the thing. Most guys do detox fifteen, twenty, thirty times before it might work. It's not like walk in, walk back out." PAUL SCHIRALDI/HBO

The cast of *The Wire* consisted of a deep and talented range of African-American actors. Andre Royo and Robert Wisdom decided one day to preserve that breadth with a photograph. "Everybody felt, especially with 20/20 rear view, that it was really worth doing and they were proud that we were able to pose," Wisdom said. COURTESY OF ANDRE ROYO

established, what they were going to be doing and what their arcs were going to be. I don't think they really much gave a shit about Carcetti. Ed is sort of a funny cat. It's a push me–pull me thing. He's completely resistant, yet he's willing to sit there for hours and days and discuss the possibilities of, "Well, here's an idea." These guys were not obstructionists. I'm not trying to paint them in that way. It just wasn't important to them. Politics seemed like, "That's not what our show is." I can't remember the specifics of them saying that, but I would be willing to bet body parts vital only to me that both of them said to me, "That's not our show."

GEORGE PELECANOS (WRITER/PRODUCER): I was really against it. I fought David tooth and nail on that one. I just think growing up in Washington, DC, as I have, politics are really boring, and when I say it's boring, I think it's pretty basic.

DENNIS LEHANE (WRITER): We were trying to break a transition in an episode once, where McNulty and Greggs needed to gather the information necessary to figure out Bubbles's whereabouts. We'd been at it for a couple hours, just banging on the box, and it was turning into a time suck, all over this minor transition. So, I said, "I know it's not pretty, but what if we just have McNulty and Greggs happen across a CI [confidential informant] and ask where Bubbles is? And the CI says, "The soup kitchen on such and such?"

So, Ed Burns, who hates anything that smells even a little bit like it was something he ever saw on a shitty network cop show, leans back and folds his arms and stares across the table with a kind of bemused contempt. And he says, "In twenty years as Bal'more police, I never, not once, just happened to come across a CI who was conveniently in possession of the location of another CI on the other side of the city. I mean, who is this guy, fucking Huggy Bear?" And there was much snickering and pained looks of pity and commiseration for me and my dumbass idea. And for the rest of the week, Ed called me Huggy Bear or Starsky or Hutch. The takeaway there was: Don't cut corners, even if it's a lot harder not to. Taught me more about how to write good TV than just about any lesson I can think of.

CHRIS COLLINS (STAFF WRITER): A traditional writers' room is where writers get together every single day from—let's say, for regular office hours, nine to five. A bunch of writers sit around a table. They talk about ideas, pitch stories, that kind of thing. For instance, you might take two weeks to break an episode on *Sons of Anarchy*, which I was executive producer on. On *The Wire*, it took about two to three days to break an episode. We would get together for two or three days. The show basically always started out from some point of view of David or Ed that was based on some sort of historical reference or personal experience. Then it would jump off into the fiction. We would start with that kernel of fact. Then they would somehow twist it into the fiction of the show, the mythology of the show. Those episodes were very fast. David and Ed were lightning fast in the room. I've never seen anyone, in the twelve years I've been doing this professionally as a writer, turn stories as fast as they do.

DAVID SIMON (CREATOR): In the beginning, there would be days before we even wrote a beat. We would just talk about who the characters should be. First thing was: What were we trying to say? What are we trying to say about the death of work, the blue-collar story in Season Two? What are we trying to say about reform in Season Three? What were we trying to say about the drug war? Then, that would induce a discussion, argument. Nobody would put a card up on the board for days. After three or four days, we put a card up.

Then we'd argue about that. By the time you get to Episode Five, now you've opened some doors and you slammed some of those shut that you can't open again. You've made choices. By the end, I think it was moving pretty quickly, because we committed to certain stories that we were going to tell and we had abandoned other ones that we weren't going to tell. I didn't feel that way about it. If Chris says that about the beginning, boy, it didn't feel that way to me.

DENNIS LEHANE (WRITER): Working with David was great. Smooth as glass. I've been told that's maybe not everyone's experience, but Dave and I worked real no-muss-no-fuss together. As far as I was concerned, I was in that room to service David's and Ed's vision, not my own. And it happened to be a vision I believed in, which made it all the easier. The biggest difference between the writers' room on *The Wire* and some others I've worked in subsequently is how little time we wasted. We came there to work, man, and to cut to the chase and figure this shit out as fast as we could, so we get film in the can. We investigated a lot of possible paths in terms of story, but we rarely got lost down those paths. I've been in rooms where they'd been up and running four months and still had no idea what the major beats of their "A" storyline were.

GEORGE PELECANOS (WRITER/PRODUCER): The very first scene we did in *The Wire*, the political scene, was in that deli with Burrell and Carcetti sitting at a table negotiating with each other. After we shot it, I was being a smart-ass, but I said, "That's it, right? We've said everything we need to say about politics. They negotiated. Each guy wanted something, and they came to an agreement. That's all it is." I sort of fought him for a long time, and I shouldn't have, but I didn't know. Once I saw it coming out, I saw what he was trying to do, which was broaden the world. You can't really tell the whole story unless you bring the politics into it, because now you've got the panorama of this city, and that's what we were missing before. He was right and I was wrong, and I told him I was wrong.

DENNIS LEHANE (WRITER): George is funny that way. I remember he was initially against the middle school thrust of Season Four, too. But that was something I know David counted on in George, that he would push back against Dave's wonkier instincts. You can't value your own voice until people you respect question it. And you should always have at least one person around you, creatively speaking, who feels comfy speaking truth to power. *The Wire*, if mishandled, could have very easily started to feel like homework for the viewer. George and, to a lesser degree, I pushed for the show to retain its roots as a cop show. David never saw it as a cop show. George and me did. Not just a cop show, by any means, but a cop show in its DNA. The yin and yang of those competing ideas helped make it richer, in my opinion. As for the political stuff, I grew up in the shadow of a Democratic machine in Boston, so I know how that works, but I didn't know it the way Bill Zorzi did. I could play the music, but I couldn't compose it. So, I just waited to hear the tempo and ran with what I was given. I enjoyed that aspect of the show: Clay Davis and Carcetti and all that. Good stuff.

The second season had closed with Nick Sobotka leaning on a fence, anguished over the death of his uncle, Frank Sobotka. Steve Earle's "I Feel Alright" next played over a montage punctuated with several brief, vivid shots of the decaying, neglected docks. Robert Colesberry, at the persistent urging of David Simon and Nina Noble, directed the episode and pieced together the montage. "I loved the montage they concluded with," said Karen Thorson, Colesberry's wife and a producer on the show. "It's a pity. That's, for me, the saddest thing when I think back on my life with Bob. I would've liked to have seen him go forward with that, and he would have done well. He would've done better and better, and I can only imagine what other things he would have directed and whether he would have remained a producer. I think he would've remained a producer-director. I think he would've remained in television, but at least he got there. It hurts my heart to think of that lost opportunity for him."

Colesberry, the man Simon eternally credits as the eyes of the show, died suddenly in February 2004 following complications from heart surgery. Thorson, Simon, and Noble were among those at his bedside in his final hours. The loss sent the cast and crew, just weeks from starting to shoot Season 3, into deep mourning. Colesberry had established the show's visual template. Beyond that, he had been a teacher and mentor, someone who possessed a quiet, steadying influence. Colesberry had

calmed down an antsy Dominic West. He had gone horseback riding with
Clarke Peters. He had offered the right advice when he sensed someone
was hesitant to ask. He had an impressive past, having worked with a
number of well-known directors, and seemed primed for an even brighter
future. As a producer, he had been soft-spoken, subtle, and discreet, Simon
wrote in an appreciation of Colesberry for The Baltimore Sun: *"He*
made his points after everyone else in the room had already had their
say. Bob could back you into a better idea and convince you that it was
probably your own. And he was forever pathfinding through the forest of
overgrown ego that flourishes on any movie set." Thorson, Simon, and
Noble privately spread some of Colesberry's ashes on the set during the
first day of filming Season 3. The writers wrote in a wake for Det. Ray
Cole, the minor character Colesberry played on the show, in the third
episode of the season. In it, Jay Landsman (Delaney Williams) delivers a
eulogy peppered with tributes to Colesberry and his work on films such as
Mississippi Burning *and* After Hours.

AIDAN GILLEN (MAYOR THOMAS CARCETTI): We met at Bubby's, in
Tribeca, for breakfast. We had a good long chat, about an hour. He
was outlining this character he said they were thinking of introducing and that he was a politician. I'm thinking, *Wow, I've never played
a character like that before.* And I hadn't—hardly any establishment figures, but lots of the opposite. I hadn't seen *The Wire,* and as Bob
described it, I remarked that it sounded like the John Sayles film *City
of Hope,* and Bob said that he was involved in the production of that
film. Having that touchstone prompted further movie chat and general chat, and at the end, we bid our farewells. He said they'd keep in
touch, and I walked away thinking, *Fuck, that sounds good.*

About six weeks later or so, I asked my agent what the story was, so
she put in a call, and the word came back that Bob had died just the
day before, which was astonishing news, obviously, as he'd seemed
so vital. A few weeks later, I got that call to come in and try out the
scenes. I got cast, and the first day on set was actually a memorial service for Bob. There was a red sports car parked on the set, which was

inside a big warehouse space, and I asked, "Whose car was that?" It was Bob's. Then, on the show, they gave his character, Ray Cole, an Irish-style wake, including the song "Body of an American," by the Pogues. For someone I only met for an hour, it feels like I knew him a bit more than that would afford, and the upshot of that hour was that he and Alexa Fogel changed the trajectory of my career, and I'll be eternally grateful for that. It was nice getting to know his widow, Karen [Thorson], a bit over the subsequent few years.

SEITH MANN (DIRECTOR): I do not know who handed Bob Colesberry my short film. He got ahold of it and reached out to me and invited me to a coffee. We went and talked. He was very complimentary about the film, very cool, and said, "Come shadow on the show." I said, "Great."

I'll never forget, on the way in, Ed Bianchi came in, and that was his next meeting. He introduced me. He said, "Hey, Ed, this is a young director." I remember it was cool because he called me a director. I had a twenty-two-minute short. This guy had obviously directed I don't know how many episodes of television. That was the one and only time I talked to Bob Colesberry. I never saw him again because, unfortunately, he passed away.

A couple months later, I get a call from Nina Noble saying, "Bob was a big fan of yours, and out of respect of his memory, we'd like to invite you to come shadow on a show. We have a place for you to stay in Baltimore, and Ed Bianchi has already agreed to let you shadow him."

JEFFREY PRATT GORDON (JOHNNY "FIFTY" SPAMANTO): The night that Robert Colesberry passed away, there was an HBO function in New York, and I was with Chris Bauer, Andre Royo. Omar was there, his assistant. It was a very social, very light atmosphere. We were either at a bar going to the party or leaving the party and going to a bar, and I remember walking down the street and Andre Royo got a call, and as we were walking and talking, he was on the phone. He hangs up and says, "Guys, I've got some bad news." We all stop on the corner in New York, and he said, "Colesberry just passed away."

I got chills on my arms now. We all just stood on this New York street corner with jaws on the ground, like, "Holy shit." It was like the carpet ripped out from under you.

NINA K. NOBLE (EXECUTIVE PRODUCER): He created the visual style of the show. He was involved in the first meetings and the first research, and he hired the first cinematographer that we had, Uta Briesewitz, who I think is really the one who created the style most people recognize in *The Wire*, in terms of camera work and lighting, and Bob also came from movies and, I think, really found his element. He was really happy working on *The Wire*, and it fulfilled a lot of his creative urges in terms of directing, in terms of helping guide other directors and other filmmakers in collaborating with David. It was very sudden, surprising, and devastating to lose him, both as a friend and a coworker. We were not prepared for that at all.

THOM ZIMNY (EDITOR): He loved his working day. One of the details I remember with Bob is he'd wake up very early and read *The New York Times* and get to set early. He loved his work and was passionate about the process. That was intoxicating, because it just made you feel part of this bigger process. When he passed, his presence still was there in spirit with the season.

DOMINIC WEST (DET. JIMMY MCNULTY): He was a mentor to me, and I remember going in the first year and saying, "Look, I don't think this is the job for me. I think someone else could do much better and I really want to go home. I miss my daughter." And he took me in hand and said, "Look, I've been in this game a long time, and this is a really unusual and really exceptional show, and I think you'd be making a mistake." He really reassured me, looked after me, and then he took me up to his house and we had this amazing weekend. My daughter came over. I felt particularly close to him and indebted to him.

When he died, you realize that everybody felt the same way. He treated everybody that way. He was really unusual. Producers tend to be either total assholes or they are at least quite superior and, I don't know what the word is, but set apart, but you'd never know he was the boss. He was always sort of behind the camera or just quietly encouraging people. When he died, I suppose we all thought that was the end of it, that was going to be the end of the show, and fortunately it wasn't. David took that decision, I suppose, and was pretty brave to do so. Bob, we all thought he was too big a personality and too big an influence on us all to be missed, but Karen, his wife, came on board as the editor, and I think that helped.

CLARKE PETERS (DET. LESTER FREAMON): Quiet, and he had this little Philadelphia kind of lilt, soft-spoken. He was just one of the lads. Just as bowlegged as I was. That was something we all shared in common, people who are bowlegged. We're like a private group that nobody understands. Women think that you look attractive, but you know what, it's painful to have that allure. I really liked that man. I really liked him.

DELANEY WILLIAMS (SGT. JAY LANDSMAN): I didn't know him that well. We weren't friends or anything. We're just colleagues, but every time I dealt with him, he made me feel like a better human being. It was the end of a very long night, and I was working episode to episode, and he and I happened to be walking back to base camp, where the trailers were. He turns to me and says, "Do you have an agent?" And I said, "No, I don't. Most of my work's here in DC and Baltimore. I work mostly onstage, some television when it comes to town, and when I go out of town. I pick up the work." He said, "You need to get an agent." At the moment, it was just something he said. Moments later, we're apart, I'm getting dressed, and I'm thinking, *Wait* *a minute, that's the executive producer of the show telling me I should make his job harder. What kind of human being does that?* It was in the string of almost every conversation I had with him, where he was thinking about me as opposed to himself.

ALEXA L. FOGEL (CASTING DIRECTOR): It was just such a shock. There was a big transition time for everyone. It's just hard to kind of align again.

DOMINIC WEST (DET. JIMMY MCNULTY): He very much set the tone for the sort of collegiate, democratic nature of the show, that everyone was equal, everyone was contributing, and there was no room for starry behavior.

ANDRE ROYO (REGINALD "BUBBLES" COUSINS): When he passed away, that threw us all for a loop. It also brought David Simon and Nina Noble out to [the] set. It brought them out from the cave and forced them to come out and try to make sure the actors were cool and [to] talk to the actors and make sure we still feel that team spirit, that family spirit.

DAVID SIMON (CREATOR): [Noble] took over picking the directors. She became the arbiter of how we would get the camera to move and how we would light. She became more involved in the creative function of the show, as Bob was. Not only because the writers think of things that are impractical or impolitic or disruptive to production, but because production can often offer insights the other way. And she became more and more essential, because she had to. So did Karen. Karen became involved in a lot of the aesthetic discussions and took over the credit sequencing and began giving notes about the visual episodes.

Everybody tried to fill in, but Nina was effectively my partner in terms of trying to achieve story from even before I met Bob. She'd never been completely without creative input. I always relied on her for her assessments of story and of acting and what we had, what were our assets, where we were weak, where we can improve. I always had her in my ear from the beginning of *The Corner*, with Bob. Bob, Nina, and I, we started as a little trinity there in terms of director, producer and writer, producer, line producer. Then, when the director-producer wasn't there anymore, I had to take some functions, and Nina had to take some key functions. The influence of Bob in the writers' room, when we'd sailed off course or when something started to sound like it was derivative of something else we'd done, that was when Bob, in his own quiet way, would set us right. He was remarkably ineloquent about everything but film. You had to listen as Bob talked like this, but if you didn't interrupt him, he landed it exactly. You ever been with somebody, "Eh, you know? That's sort of . . ." Don't interrupt him. He's going somewhere. With film, he understood right away.

He was eyes. I was ears. I had to become a little more eyes and learn a little bit more of what I was asking my directors to do, and Nina had to become more specific about what we were looking for in our personnel and what to tell them. It used to be the tone meetings were just to discuss the script and the ideas of the characters. It was the writers talking to the director. Then Bob would get with them about the template of the show visually. The tone meetings, we began incorporating rules about what the camera can do, what it can't do in our tone meeting. I was shocked to hear myself vocalizing that fairly quickly into Season Three. He taught me an awful lot, I've got to say.

UTA BRIESEWITZ (CINEMATOGRAPHER): I pretty much owe everything to Bob Colesberry, because I was doing indie movies. When you do indie movies, maybe you do one or two a year. That was more than ten years ago. It was not as vivid a landscape as it is today, with all the outlets that you have today, and also it was before the digital revolution. It was harder to get an indie film off the ground. My paychecks didn't come so regular, and sometimes I was almost struggling a little bit to pay my rent. I was starting to get concerned, like, *Wow, will there ever be a career for me that I can actually support myself with?*

Bob Colesberry gave me that. Once I started working on *The Wire*, I got a real paycheck, and I got it for a long time. It put me on the map, and after that, I had no problems getting other jobs.

KAREN THORSON (PRODUCER): I know that David Simon was deeply wounded, had lost a friend, but he felt alone out there making the show. His mother told me that several years later. In fact, it was not too long ago, maybe three or four years ago. I was sitting with Mrs. Simon and she said that David really mourned the loss of Bob and was worried that the show wouldn't go on without him, but as you can see, it took a different turn and it worked out all right.

ED BURNS (CO-CREATOR): I think Colesberry really affected David. They were very close and they were professionally very close. I stayed away from David and Bob. I did. Bob and I had our own little thing.

DAVID SIMON (CREATOR): Nina and I turned to face HBO and say, even if we didn't feel it, "We're fine." We needed to do that politically, to keep them confident. But we definitely missed him. I remember the first episode of Season Three, Uta and Ed Bianchi—Ed Bianchi was directing, and Uta was shooting, and I'm looking through the monitor now and I don't have Bob next to me. There was something wrong, and I knew it was wrong and I didn't have the vocabulary, and on the [spur of the] moment, I had to invent my own vocabulary for expressing why the camera movement is problematic.

DENNIS LEHANE (WRITER): Bob Colesberry died while I was in the earliest stage of the script, so we had to regroup, and David sent me the new beats that incorporated the death of Ray Cole, the character Bob played on the show. He also sent me a list of all the projects Bob had been involved in as a producer—it was an impressive list—and

I incorporated some of them into Landsman's speech. I was pretty anxious about that storyline. I told David I thought I wasn't the guy to write it, but he asked me to do a first pass, and Bob was such a great guy—you never come across anyone who didn't love the guy—that I did the best I could. Then David took those scenes over and made them his own personal tribute to his friend. He also added the Pogues's "Body of an American" to the bar scene at the end, because it was Bob's favorite song.

DELANEY WILLIAMS (SGT. JAY LANDSMAN): That was a pretty long and hard day, I'd have to say. Kind of a well-remembered scene, I guess, for my character, and certainly it is for me. The scene takes two or three minutes, and of course we shot it for probably eight hours. We basically monologue for eight hours straight. I guess the hardest part for me was that I was the only one who had to stay sober. We're shooting in a bar, and I had all the words. Dom and Wendell, they had their own lunch. Lunch for me, I just had to stay in the business of the scene, I guess is the only way to put it. It was emotional and it was kind of a touching moment. At the end, we raised a glass to him, to say goodbye.

It wasn't integral in the story, obviously, but it was central to the experience for the people working on the show. In that regard, it was really important. It's a pretty long monologue for a television show, so it was a lot of work, and you had to get it right every time, so I had that sort of pressure. The hard part was actually getting to do it, for me. Because, at the time, I was hired episode to episode. I could expect to be hired, but I didn't know, so I wasn't on a contract. During the downtime between seasons, I obviously had to work. The mind is conflicted, as I was doing a play at the time at Arena Stage, in DC. Unfortunately, I think it was the third or fourth episode of the season, of that next season after Bob passed, that we did this, and I had been written into the previous episodes, but I couldn't do either of them because the play wouldn't let me out to do it. I had to go through hell or high water to get the play to let me out of the one night to shoot that. We did it Friday night, like all through the night, which is the time I should've probably been onstage. My understudy had to do the role in DC while I was working on the show, and it was one of those things that fortuitously came together. Both of them are businesses. I just needed that day off because that scene was that important. Whether I worked again on the series or not, I wanted to make sure I was there that night.

KAREN THORSON (PRODUCER): Joe Chappelle came on board as a director-producer type and was helpful. He definitely had his own aesthetic. It was different than Bob's, but he brought some good ideas to the show.

I do think that the visual style definitely changed, and I don't think we were quite as adventurous because we were wounded. We had talked about going to widescreen and that we were going to do that Season Three, and we just didn't do it. We didn't do a lot of bigger changes because we were wounded, and if we didn't have to fix something, we had to do so much healing, why add to the burden?

I was, of course, doing as much healing as anyone, and I was just grateful for the job because, for me, the work is what pulled me through. If I didn't have the structure of the work, I don't know what would've happened to me. It saved me. I put all my energy into the show, because when you're in that kind of pain, when somebody dies that's close to you, if your day is twenty-four hours and maybe for three hours you don't think about it, that's a good day. Having the distraction and the focus of the work was really important to me.

6

NO ONE WAS EVER SAFE

David Simon recalled some assuming that the arrival of a white mayor to The Wire marked the introduction of the hero who would reform an inept system. "Um, just wait," Simon would say. "Hero's a big word." Instead, in Season 3, Tommy Carcetti (Aidan Gillen), along with Maj. Bunny Colvin (Robert Wisdom) and Stringer Bell (Idris Elba), portrayed how little individual reformists are often able to influence archaic institutions. Carcetti started as a boyish, idealistic city councilman, but by the end of his arc, he allows his political ambitions to consume any original altruistic intentions. The Wire's third season delved into Baltimore politics, depicting the overseers of a political system that allowed the police department to lurch aimlessly onward. The show arrived at the topic with most of its creative minds staunchly opposed. "They never convinced me," Ed Burns insisted as late as 2016, and he may as well have spat when he said it. But Simon remained steadfast in expanding The Wire's horizon and mirroring the actual happenings in his Baltimore. The addition of Bill Zorzi to the writing staff aided that effort. No one knew the ins and outs of the local political scene quite like Zorzi. He was the son of a political journalist who had never accepted as much as a free doughnut at a presser during nearly two decades chronicling politics for The Baltimore Sun. Simon and Zorzi poured months into hammering authentic dialogue that politicians would use, though the most iconic line was created by an actor, when Isiah Whitlock Jr. (who played corrupt state senator Clay Davis) liberally stretched the word shit, *which became one of the show's most memorable catchphrases.*

For many locals, the examination of politics severely blurred fact and fiction. In one scene, the incumbent mayor, Clarence Royce, briefly ponders the morality of the de facto legalized drug markets created by Colvin and colloquially known as "Hamsterdam." A health commissioner cautions him, "Better watch out, Clarence, or they'll be calling you the most dangerous man in America." Kurt Schmoke, a former Baltimore mayor, depicts the health commissioner. In reality, Schmoke's mulling of decriminalizing drugs nearly ended his political career, with Rep. Charles Rangel labeling him America's most dangerous man. In another scene, Robert L. Ehrlich Jr., Maryland's governor at the time, plays a security guard who tells a waiting Carcetti that the governor cannot see him that evening. The scene mimics the circumstances in which Martin O'Malley, the former Baltimore mayor, sought an audience with Ehrlich.

O'Malley would become forever linked to Carcetti's character. He ran for Baltimore's mayor in 1999, triumphing in a predominantly black city over two black council members once Schmoke decided against reelection. O'Malley's friendship with Councilman Lawrence Bell III mirrored The Wire's *pairing of Carcetti and Councilman Anthony Gray. Once mayor, O'Malley, like Carcetti, pivoted ambitions toward becoming governor. (Unlike Carcetti, O'Malley also made a failed bid for the presidency, in 2016.) Simon and Zorzi have asserted through the years that Carcetti is sourced from several real-life Baltimore politicians, O'Malley included. O'Malley, for his part, denounced the comparison, labeling himself in 2009 on MSNBC as, "The antidote to* The Wire." *Simon once offered O'Malley a cameo on the show, in the same vein as Ehrlich Jr. The offer was declined.*

WILLIAM F. ZORZI (STAFF WRITER): Carcetti is based on [Martin] O'Malley, yeah. He's based in part on O'Malley. He's sort of based on a number of different politicians.

AIDAN GILLEN (MAYOR THOMAS CARCETTI): I think on my first day, [David Simon] said something like, "Okay, this is the deal. You were Bob Colesberry's last casting call, so whether we really wanted you or not, we had to give you the job."

SEITH MANN (DIRECTOR): I shadowed a couple of times, and David introduced himself to me. He said, "Bob was a big fan of yours, and his secret plan was for you to direct an episode [in Season Three]. That's not going to happen. We're just finding our way without him, but we wanted you to come have an opportunity to learn all you can." That was great, too.

I was very green. Fresh out of film school, had never worked in television, had never been on a television set, and didn't really know how it all worked, but I was really interested in television. I shadowed Ed Bianchi first, and then Ernest Dickerson. Jamie Hector was in my short. *The Wire* was a big break for both of us. The first day, he's on set, and I'm shadowing Ed. My belief is you behave as a shadow. Shadow goes where the director goes and doesn't say shit. That's a shadow, right? I was sticking pretty close to Ed, and so Jamie, he was eating lunch and we're talking. He's like, "Damn, you and my man so tight, I swear you going to turn him black." We just laughed about it. A couple episodes later, I'm shadowing Ernest Dickerson. Jamie comes up to me and says, "Damned if you ain't do it."

Eventually, George Pelecanos pulled me to the side one day and gave me some advice. He said, "Look, I think you can do this and I think you can be great at this, but it's not going to happen if you don't talk to David about letting him know you want to direct." Self-promotion has not necessarily been one of my strong suits historically.

That was way outside of my comfort level, but at the same time, for him to take the interest and give me some advice, I kind of got to at least act on it. I proceeded to have a fairly awkward conversation with David and Nina, expressing my desire to direct. Neither one of them committed to anything. Truth be told, I don't know if that conversation had anything to do with it at all, but [I got a chance to direct] when they finally got their pickup for Season Four.

AIDAN GILLEN (MAYOR THOMAS CARCETTI): I remember Bill Zorzi's eyes kind of out on stalks when I walked into the room, the writers' room, off the plane from London to start as Carcetti. I looked more like Ziggy than Carcetti—big mop of hair and scruffy clothes, etcetera. Someone said, "Get this man's hair cut and get him down to Brooks Brothers immediately." I was Bill's responsibility, and I knew he was going to be writing on the political strand. He took me on a crash course tour of local politics over the next few days. I had lots of questions, as I wasn't familiar with the American local government scene. He led me through it with great knowledge and wry wit. He filled me in on lots of local political characters and lore, where you'd eat, what sandwich you might have. He'd been a political writer at *The Baltimore Sun*, just as David Simon had been a crime writer, and I knew I was in good hands.

If I had any query on what might be going on in a particular scene, he would answer an email at any hour, day or night, and he would do it comprehensively. I really mean that. One night, I'd asked if he could write something for me to say at a street rally that was down for shooting the next day but didn't have written dialogue, as it stood. Bill said sure, and I went out to the bar with my brother. Come in at two a.m., and there's five pages of dialogue slid under the door.

WILLIAM F. ZORZI (STAFF WRITER): My wife says that I don't hide my feelings very well. It's always obvious what I think. When he had stepped into the room and sort of looked like he had just come off some punk-rock bender, I was like, *Holy shit. This guy can't be our councilman.*

AIDAN GILLEN (MAYOR THOMAS CARCETTI): My first scene, it was with Frankie Faison, and he was gentle with me. We'd gone out the night before to eat, which he'd suggested, God bless him, 'cause I guess he knew it'd make me feel more at ease, which it did. We were at a crab joint, and he taught me how to smash them proper with the hammer, and we had bibs on. I ate one of the bits I wasn't supposed to, in my enthusiasm. Have you ever eaten a crab lung? Anyway, luckily it didn't kill me. The scene was a good one to kick off with, as it was Burrell giving Carcetti the lowdown on what might lie ahead.

ERNEST DICKERSON (DIRECTOR): It was just great doing scenes with Glynn Turman [Mayor Clarence Royce], who's an actor that I grew up watching all the way back at *Cooley High,* and Frankie Faison, who I first met on the set of *Do the Right Thing* and just always loved his work. To see a black mayor and a black police commissioner doing Shakespearean power moves around each other, as an African-American filmmaker, that's the kind of stuff you just dream about directing. Plus, when you have two actors who are obviously having such a great time working with each other and playing with each other and doing these scenes with each other, it was cinematic heaven. I don't want to get corny with it, but I'm sitting there and I'm thinking, *Damn, man, this is the best show in the world.* It was the best job in the world to see these guys, these two pros, really play these scenes. These are the kinds of scenes you hardly ever see in any dramatic medium: cinematic or television. For me it was a privilege to be able to do stuff like that.

FRANKIE FAISON (ACTING COMMR. ERVIN H. BURRELL): Glynn Turman is an actor that I've been wanting to work with my whole life. He's an actor that I have admired, his work and the arc of his career. I love Glynn. When I found out he was coming onto the show and he got the role, it was almost like it was magical. I had never met Glynn before, and I've been in the business a long time, and he's been in the business a long time, even a little longer than me.

When we met, it was such an amazing chemistry. Glynn and I were just very good friends, and we were also very respectful of the body of work that each of us were bringing to this experience. Some actors you work with, it's like working with family over and over and over again. He and I have that kind of relationship, and every time I see him, it's more than just acting, bonding to do a show. It becomes something much more than that. Then, whenever we were on set together, he was always funny, entertaining, exciting, but it was also very professional. We both bring a lot to the table on the work process, but we also both know how to just relax and enjoy ourselves on the set. That whole thing was magical for us, and hopefully it was magical for people around us who were shooting and filming in scenes with us.

GLYNN TURMAN (MAYOR CLARENCE V. ROYCE): They break in on me and I'm getting head. How much more memorable can a motherfucker [scene] be? Shit, I guess you don't get exposed to that degree often in the biz, and that was indeed a memorable moment, as attested by my wife. "You did *what?*" It was a great moment, well done, and it did take me by surprise in the writing. You're reading it—I said, "Wait a minute. Wait a minute. Wait a minute. What? Let me read this again. How are they gonna do this?"

WILLIAM F. ZORZI (STAFF WRITER): I have to credit that to David. That was based on a rumor.

GLYNN TURMAN (MAYOR CLARENCE V. ROYCE): Simon is probably one of the smartest people that I've had the pleasure to meet and certainly one of the most creative producers-writers that I've had the pleasure of working with. And I knew it early on, when it was first call to the first day on set. I had been doing a movie called *Sahara* that we were shooting in Morocco with Matthew McConaughey and Penélope Cruz. I wasn't finished with that when I had to come to Baltimore to do the first scenes and then go back to Morocco to finish the *Sahara* movie. So, *Sahara* had the first dibs on me as a result, so to speak.

I had a goatee and a mustache, and David had come up to me and said, "Glynn, can we lose the goatee for Mayor Royce?" And I said, "David, I'd love to, but I've gotta go back and finish shooting *Sahara*, so I can't take it off." Right there on the spot, he kind of scratched his chin a little bit and he went, "Okay. I'll tell you what. Next season, you're gonna be in a mayoral race against a younger man. We'll have you lose the mustache and the goatee then, when you try to get reelected." So, he looked that far down the line. He knew his storyline so well that he could see a year ahead where his characters were going. That's when I said, "Who the hell is this guy?"

DAVID SIMON (CREATOR): I can't say we had Royce in our head. But we had like a Clarence "Du" Burns in our head. That's the real guy. And then we had a white insurgent who was really the last sort of white liberal insurgency on the Democratic side in a time of high crime. That was Marty O'Malley. Things were happening in Baltimore that we were tending to.

KURT SCHMOKE (HEALTH COMMR./FORMER MAYOR OF BALTIMORE): It was somewhat ironic to sit there, the former mayor, and playing the health commissioner, while [Turman is] playing the mayor. I was impressed with his ability. He moved from being very jovial on set to, once the cameras were running, to being in character, very serious and committed to conveying a strong message as mayor.

GLYNN TURMAN (MAYOR CLARENCE V. ROYCE): I was able to personalize who this guy was, and he was loosely based on Schmoke. Schmoke was not as strident as Mayor Royce was. Mayor Royce was a little more arrogant and sort of entitled in his approach to his power. He felt that he was entitled to the power that he had, and I never got that from Schmoke.

I had the opportunity to work with Mayor Schmoke and talk with him about some of the things that happened and how close they were to what he had going. One of the things that has stuck with me in talking with him was talking about Hamsterdam. He said that he wished that he had phrased it all differently. Because it was indeed a brilliant idea, and I think the country is actually employing, under a different name, some of those policies. But he thinks that had he couched it under a health situation, a health resolve, that it would have flown.

REG E. CATHEY (NORMAN WILSON): Norman is still one of my favorite characters. Before, I had done Querns in *Oz*, which I loved doing, Querns. But first of all, what was great about *The Wire* is that you had all these different black characters on the same show. When I was living out in LA, I would audition for the black guy on the show, and that would be the only black guy. He wouldn't have any black friends. Maybe he'd have a black wife or black girlfriend. He was the black guy, and usually he was upstanding and honorable, because everyone wants to have a good role model. But in *The Wire*, there were all different types of characters and different types of human variables, and it was fabulous to play. In terms of Norman, to play a smart man, a man with brains, a man who drank and smoked and made mistakes and told truth to power because he just didn't give a fuck anymore—it was so much fun. And then David would joke with me that he would give me these one-liners and then he'd come up to me before, these perfect little one-liners, and say, "Okay, we're not going to spend a lot of time on this. I want you to get it right in one time. Don't be fucking around. But no pressure."

ISIAH WHITLOCK JR. (STATE SEN. R. CLAYTON "CLAY" DAVIS): First season, I did maybe, like, one episode. I think the second season, I made a couple of small appearances. I was doing *Othello*, doing a Shakespeare play, and just said I was going to let it go. But everybody kind of corralled me and said, "It's a great opportunity, and you should do it." Because they were going to run my storyline. Once I got my head wrapped around that, then I agreed to go ahead and keep working on it. But there was one moment when I said, "I'm going to go off and do my own thing." Fortunately, I went ahead and did the show.

GEORGE PELECANOS (WRITER/PRODUCER): A lot of black guys say "shit" like [Whitlock's Davis]. David wrote it originally. He just gave it to him, and Isiah ran with it.

ISIAH WHITLOCK JR. (STATE SEN. R. CLAYTON "CLAY" DAVIS): Nine *e*'s. Yeah. I don't know where I came up with nine *e*'s, but I said, "Okay, if I'm going to live with it, I'm gonna have to spell it." I always tell people, "If you write it to me, use nine *e*'s. If you do any more than that, you're not saying it right."

MARLYNE BARRETT (COUNCIL PRESIDENT NERESE CAMPBELL): In rehearsal, it did take a couple of minutes. Like, "How long are you going to do it for? How long is it going to last? I just need to know rhythmically. Is it going to be a sheeeeeeeeee-it? Is it going to stop?"

ISIAH WHITLOCK JR. (STATE SEN. R. CLAYTON "CLAY" DAVIS): My uncle used to say it all the time. But he wasn't the only one. A lot of people used to always say that. It was a very, very funny way that he would always say it. He would always say it—at least every time I spoke to him. It was just part of his language. So, I remember when I did the film for Spike [Lee], I got the opportunity to use it, and the rest is history. But that's not something I really came up with. A lot of people used that.

It kind of started for me in Spike Lee's film *25th Hour*. And then I did another movie for Spike. To be quite honest, I've done it in every Spike movie that I've done. I've done about four. But I think it really took off when I used it in *The Wire*. That's where a lot of people know it from. But it makes people smile. At first, I didn't quite get what the big deal was. I said, "I always thought everyone says that." A friend of mine says, "Everybody does say it, but it's the way you say it that makes it special." I'm glad people are happy with it.

FRANKIE FAISON (ACTING COMMR. ERVIN H. BURRELL): I liked [Burrell]. I thought he was a good guy. I always saw him as a nice guy. He was just caught between a rock and a hard place. Circumstances, they always reveal to him how he should act. As time went by, I began to see a little bit more rough edges about him. Not that I still didn't think that he was a nice guy, but he was a guy who was driven to succeed and to reach the highest levels he could reach in law enforcement. I kind of got it when I used to walk down the street and people would say, "Man, what is this guy doing?" I used to say, "What do you mean? He's a teddy bear. He's a sweetheart." I see him going home from work, going home to his wife and kids and just playing in the backyard and eating meals.

The trick is, you may be thinking you're portraying something, but the way it's viewed by the audiences at large—they go by fact, by what they see, what they hear, what the character is doing. They go by that. You didn't see very much backstory with Burrell, outside of the law enforcement arena. That thing was for me. It was only for me alone. I had it somewhere in my memory bank as something that I could use, but it never showed or revealed itself. In very rare instances did it reveal itself throughout the life of Burrell in this series called *The Wire*. There was not a lot of opportunity or chance to reveal that. I wish that there had been, but there wasn't. That's just the story that you have.

I found a lot of things, a lot of information, kind of about myself and kind of about society at large, through the character Commissioner Burrell. Anytime a character can inform me in that way, then I think it's been a very successful role for me to play.

ISIAH WHITLOCK JR. (STATE SEN. R. CLAYTON "CLAY" DAVIS): To be quite honest, I never thought [Davis] was going to be convicted. There was a moment where I really honestly believed in everything I was doing. I believed the character, everything that he believed, that I was actually doing some good for the people. I know there were a lot of people who are going to dispute that. But in the playing of it, I really believed that what he was doing was right and that I wasn't going to be convicted. To me, that's the only way you can approach a character like that. You've got to have some belief that what you're doing is right, and I think that's what kind of made the character believable, is that I believed so much in what he was doing. Otherwise, if you go the other way, people can kind of dismiss the character, so I had to make sure that I made him likeable, so people wouldn't dismiss him, that everybody, no matter where he was, everybody had to be aware that he was in the room. I think that kind of translated to the people watching it. When Clay Davis shows up, you know he's there for some reason or some purpose. You have to take notice.

JOE CHAPPELLE (DIRECTOR/CO-EXECUTIVE PRODUCER): It was a really galvanizing mix of really experienced, really great actors, professional actors, people who knew their craft and then, in the same scene, working with someone who had never been in front of the camera before, but was so authentic and so real in that moment. Seeing those styles sometimes in the same frame working, to this day, it just kind of blows my mind how cool that was and how dangerous it was in the sense that it was like, *Oh man, this could just fall apart because we were dealing with many nonprofessionals in front of the camera.*

MICHAEL K. WILLIAMS (OMAR LITTLE): It was Season Three that I had to get humbled. I had to go through some things. When I got there, I realized that, "Mike, this ain't even about you. This is bigger than you and your career and all this shit." I started looking at the story of the people that *The Wire* was telling and the people it was affecting and how it was affecting. This little dude from Chicago, Mr. Senator, or Barack Obama, mentioned that it's his favorite show, and then he's president of the United States. All of that kind of just came about. I was like, "Okay, whoa. Like, whoa. That just happened." It put me on my quest. That was the beginning of my enlightenment, when I started realizing that I can be of service through the gift that I've been given to express myself through art and the story that I tell through art. It became something other for me than just about my career.

ROBERT WISDOM (HOWARD "BUNNY" COLVIN): Not one word in *The Wire*, not one single word, was ever improvised. Every "fuck," every "shit," every whatever term—everything was written. And it was performed.

DOMINIC WEST (DET. JIMMY MCNULTY): I was always just trying not to fuck up. I think everybody was. What's amazing about David as a writer is that every single character, from a cop to a gangbanger to mayor, we had to learn meticulously every word that he wrote. Otherwise, I'd no idea what this character was like. You watch it and you think—particularly, I think—in the street scenes, that a lot of it must be improvised, but I think I'm right in saying that none of it was ever improvised, and no one ever went off the script. It just shows you what great writing it is. He has an incredible ear for the way people speak and the way different people speak differently.

DOUG OLEAR (FBI SPEC. AGENT TERRANCE "FITZ" FITZHUGH): One of the things Dominic West said to me was, after a couple of takes, "Fucking Dougie, they never fucking say anything to you. You always ad-lib. You always swear. You always bring in all these fucking things. If I do one thing, they're like, 'Excuse me, Dominic, that's not in the script.'" I'd laugh at it because I'd work hard on my small scenes and I would always improvise. There's outtakes that [Ernest] Dickerson shot—and we must have done fifty takes, and they just kept shooting because they would keep laughing at the swear words that I would bring up and the names that I would call them, like "circus clowns" and "dick holes." Whatever it was, it was never in the script, but they always kept it.

WENDELL PIERCE (DET. WILLIAM "BUNK" MORELAND): There are only two lines that I know of that were ad-libbed that made it into *The Wire*. There's only two that I've been involved with. One season, Clarke is walking away with his bowlegs, and I said, "Yeah, I made him walk like that." We were always making little jokes. I said, "Look at him. *I* made him walk like that." David said, "I can't believe all these hours we've worked on this and some fucking actor in the spur of the moment just comes up with this great line and I just had to leave it in." They were on us about the words, man. Every piece is important. All the pieces fit. "All the pieces matter." That was the mantra. He was very exact about the dialogue.

The other is when I was laughing after catching Snoop and [Chris] Partlow, and I had the handcuffs on them and I'm laughing. "What you laughing at, man?" I said, "I'm thinking about some pussy." Snoop says, "Me, too." I was already laughing. You ever see something like some major slam dunk by LeBron James or something, the whole place erupts? That's what it was like. She says, "Me, too," and everyone's like, "Ohhh."

Richard Price sat in on a writers' meeting for his first episode, and at one point, he noticed a quiet man in a running suit jotting down notes. Price took the man as an HBO representative dispatched to monitor the meetings. "Turned out that that was the real Omar," Price recalled. "His name was Donnie. I'm thinking he's an executive." The show often collaborated with its inspirations, which meant that people previously arrested by Ed Burns occasionally served the show as advisers. Donnie Andrews, one of the primary avatars for Omar, had once terrorized Baltimore drug dealers, but he had maintained a code that dictated he never involve women or children in his exploits. He once contracted a double killing to fuel a burgeoning heroin habit. When the murders weighed heavily on his conscience, he turned himself in to Burns and received a life sentence. In prison, he worked to pivot his life by providing insider information to police and counseling inmates on addiction. Andrews met Fran Boyd, the mother featured heavily in The Corner, *through Ed Burns and Simon. The pair wed in a union documented with a feature in* The New York Times. *Andrews was freed from prison in 2005 after Burns, Simon, and others advocated for his release. He joined* The Wire, *where he worked as a consultant and occasionally*

*appeared on-screen as an associate of Omar's. Melvin Williams also
sought redemption, and a role with the show, after leaving prison in 2003.
On The Wire, Williams portrays the Deacon, a calming presence and
community mentor.*

*Andrews died from complications following heart surgery at the age of
fifty-eight in 2012. Williams passed in 2015, at the age of seventy-three.*

CHAD L. COLEMAN (DENNIS "CUTTY" WISE): Donnie said hi and he
chuckled, and I got a chill, because I knew he had killed people. He
wasn't trying to be intimidating. He was very quiet, like, "Hi, man.
Hey, how you doing?" I said, "Oh shoot. Okay." *Tread lightly until you
get to know this man because you don't want to say the wrong thing around
this dude.* Then he began to tell me what he was all about. These are
some incredible human beings. God rest his soul. I was with him last
up in Harvard. This man was putting it together where he was going
to be the one responsible for us going around to all these universities.

MICHAEL POTTS (BROTHER MOUZONE): One of the actors who was
working with Omar was actually someone that Ed had arrested back
in the day. He knew a lot of the people that some of the characters
had been based on. He would tell me that some of the guys who used
to be in the life would call him and go, "How did they know that?
You must have been telling them." He would say they would be getting on his case about "They shouldn't know that."

One day, between takes, because we were mic'd up, he covers
his mic and he goes, "I know the guy you're based on. You're doing
real well. I'm sure he likes what you're doing." I said, "Does he really
exist?" He goes, "Oh yeah. I know the whole family." He kept covering up the mic and looking around as if he was an informant or
something. "You do realize this is make-believe? This is TV. Why are
you nervous?" He said, "I know the whole family. I can take you to
meet him. Nice family. I know them. I know the brothers. You look
like them. Nice family, but don't cross them." He literally did this: He
said, "Don't cross them, the whole family." He said, "Next time you

come, I'll take you to meet them." I said, "Maybe." Because, clearly, I don't want to piss them off. He said, "No, no, no, I guarantee you, he's smiling at what you're doing."

ED BURNS (CO-CREATOR): Melvin, he got in touch with us, with David and I, when he came home, did sixteen years. He wanted to kill Barry Levinson, the guy who did *Rain Man*, because he did a movie about Baltimore and he had this guy play Little Melvin in the movie, wearing this green suit. Melvin was extraordinarily offended by that because Melvin had hooked up with the Gambino family and they had taken him to places where you got suits—this is back in the sixties, and you're paying six hundred and seven hundred dollars for a suit back then. He wanted to kill him, Barry Levinson. We said, "I don't think that's a good idea, but if you want, we will create a role for you." He was the most robotic in the precision. If he did this on a word and we shot it again, he did it exactly right every time. It was perfect.

WOOD HARRIS (AVON BARKSDALE): That was weird, because I'm kind of like him in stature in real life. It was just odd. I know it was probably more surreal for him, looking at somebody that's taking on that role. He wasn't one for a whole lot of words. I didn't talk to him a lot. He was quiet and he was to himself.

BENJAMIN BUSCH (OFF. ANTHONY COLICCHIO): I never felt that the show depicted this animosity between the law and the street. There was this strange sense that the criminals knew they were committing crimes, [that] they were supposed to avoid the police, but if they got caught, that's just the way it went. The police, frustrated though they were with the crime, knew that it was just part of the job. Their job was to hunt those guys down. I guess the way to symbolize that, for me, was that Melvin, having been put in prison, partially by Ed Burns, comes out and plays a character on the show who is redeemed. He plays a formative pillar of the underground, the street side. That's his character. He was about as dark and dangerous a character as you could have run into in the streets of Baltimore back then.

Ed was a young police officer and he was a younger man. Despite prison, despite all the wreckage caused by the two forces going against each other, there was no hate between them. I thought that was kind of fascinating, that relationship between the law and its opposition. They didn't oppose the police. They were just trying to get around them.

JAY LANDSMAN SR. (LT. DENNIS MELLO): I'm not as forgiving as David and Ed were. Both of them are dead now, Melvin and [Nathan "Bodie"] Barksdale. But I didn't particularly care for them. I never liked Melvin, and I hated Barksdale. Barksdale's a scumbag. The time that he spent in jail didn't break the ice for what he should have spent in jail. Donnie's a great guy. There's a guy that truly made amends for his ways. But Barksdale has always been a scumbag. So was Melvin. I didn't like that they used Dennis Wise. They made Dennis a kids' coach. Dennis was the most vicious man I ever knew in my life. Cutty was Dennis Wise. He was known as "Two to the head and you're dead." He was a hit man in West Baltimore. He used to just walk up behind somebody, blow their head off.

DAVID SIMON (CREATOR): These were sort of nods to the universe. Usually, we mangled up the names. Avon Barksdale doesn't exist. It's very funny. Nathan Barksdale later on tried to put out a video and said, "I'm the real Avon." The real Avon was Melvin, more Melvin. It was Melvin and six other guys. We used the name "Barksdale" because there were like twelve Barksdales. It was just a West Baltimore name. We gave Bodie a different name. I think he had the last name of Broadus. It was a nod to [hip-hop artist] Snoop [Dogg, whose birth name is Calvin Broadus]. We gave him the nickname Bodie, which was Nathan Barksdale's street name. But I was just listening to a lot of that West Coast stuff at the time. I think when we were naming the characters, [Snoop Dogg's] "Gin and Juice" was playing on the stereo, and I went, "Eh, your name is Broadus." That's how little interest we had in the precision of the last names. We mangled stuff up.

Then we see people trying to do a one-to-one ratio, like Jay is doing there, and it doesn't make any sense to us. Let me say this: Nathan Barksdale was not a good guy. When he showed up on parole, [he] walked up to our site one day and said, "I want to do something in the show, because he used my name," we gave him a small role. We were like, "Okay, we're all about redemption." And he terrified the Wardrobe. I mean he terrified the Hair and Makeup. He was unrelentingly discomforting to the people on the show. Jay's right about the real Barksdale, but Avon Barksdale was a character that had that surname but had nothing to do with Nathan. The only way that Melvin got on the show—I mean there was no Melvin Williams on the show. Melvin, he actually played the role of the deacon, because I wouldn't let him play a gangster. In our heads, that's what I'm saying, it's all mangled up. We were taking surnames because they sounded real to us. We weren't really thinking about how they matched up to the actual people.

Filming The Wire *produced daily unpredictable experiences. Some of the show's actors had family members in law enforcement. For them, their experience with the show brought to the forefront the many dangers and paradoxes their loved ones continually faced.*

Others spent so much time with police in preparing for their roles that they felt like cops. Robert Wisdom (Maj. "Bunny" Colvin) hung close to the real Jay Landsman. "He's the real deal," Wisdom said. "He took me under his wing and led me and became my best buddy. We were joined at the hip. I bounced questions off of him for veracity. Between him and Ed Burns, I was being held." Wisdom visited enough barbecues that after a while the real officers started referring to him as "Major."

Bunny Colvin offers his approach to reform in one of the major

Season 3 storylines through the creation of Hamsterdam. The character creates three small zones where drugs can be sold with immunity if dealers stay confined to the area and operate peacefully. The compromise is made to allow officers the freedom to keep peace in other neighborhoods and to pursue legitimate criminals. "He came up with that idea and lost his job because of it," Wisdom said. "If you rode around Baltimore and you looked at people who were prisoners in their own homes because of what was happening, you tried some radical shit to try to help those people out, and it made a certain type of sense. We were locking up guys for bullshit. I mean, literally, for bullshit. And they were right back out on the streets. It was really such an impotent system that a radical measure had to be taken if you wanted to say you were going to leave something behind."

DOUG OLEAR (FBI SPEC. AGENT TERRANCE "FITZ" FITZHUGH): My dad was a cop. He was paranoid. My dad would put locks on the house, and you wonder why. You work in the county courthouse and you saw some stuff. Shit happens. I remember when he started out early; he worked at a state prison. He was a prison guard and moved his way up. At one point, he was guarding a prisoner at a hospital, and they were on twelve-hour shifts. His shift had just ended and he left, and the other guy took over, and the prisoner had to go to the bathroom, and the guy was a young kid. He took the handcuffs off the guy. The guy grabbed his gun and shot him in the head and jumped out the window. My dad left five minutes prior to that. Stuff like that, they see all this stuff. I have a real profound respect for these guys. They're thrown into this world, and it's a tough thing. It's a really tough thing to navigate through that and keep your sanity.

RICK OTTO (OFF. KENNETH DOZERMAN): My father spent thirty-six years on the job in the Baltimore Police Department and ended up retiring as the major in charge of the Homicide Department. That was a good memory for me. To have had the experience growing up the son of a police officer, you can really get a sense of what his life was like. My dad did a good job of not bringing his work home. He could be moody, so in that sense, the job affected him. He's mellowed now. He's been retired a few years, but he was really, really just tough. From what I understand, he was a very fair police officer. He was very hardworking. You either really liked him or you thought he was the biggest asshole in the world. There was no in-between.

I took my role on the show very seriously, and I wanted to sort of honor the best I could, what it's like to be a police officer. I did, probably, a thousand hours over my time on the show, on ride-alongs with the guys in the police department that I'd set up through my dad and two buddies that I knew. It was enlightening to me to understand what he did every day for twelve, fourteen, fifteen hours, sometimes twenty-four, forty-eight hours at a time, depending on what the severity of the case was, and how police officers really do sacrifice. I mean, I think there's some bad apples. There's no question about that. We can look at the news on a daily basis and see that. I also think there's a large number of white officers that work in areas that they don't live, their children don't go to school in, they don't shop there, etcetera. For the sole reason that their skin is white and the people that they're primarily policing are minorities, they're looked at as if they don't care about the community. But they do care.

In present-day Baltimore, my experience is there are some assholes out there, no question about it, that treat people disrespectfully no matter what the color of your skin is. But, all in all, they mostly just want to make a difference to the people in these communities and get home to their families.

Sadly, this so-called war on drugs, mandatory sentencing, and the privatization of prisons and militarization of police forces hasn't ingratiated law enforcement to most inner-city communities. I remember just listening to my dad when he would tell stories on how he would walk a foot beat and you would know everybody in the neighborhood and know the seven people that were constantly in and out of trouble. You could impact them. So, maybe in two years, there were only four people in trouble. You could actually change lives, and I think it's less about that now, because of lawsuits and because of cameras everywhere.

All I would say, the greatest gift it gave to me was an understanding of what it really is like to be a police officer and what it was really like to try to make a difference when sometimes no matter what you do it isn't going to make a difference. Not only that, it's not appreciated by either the size of your paycheck or the amount of grief you get from the public at large. The other interesting thing for me that's sitting here right now is the fact that people complain about the police, their tactics, or abusing civil rights. But they're also the first ones that people call when there is really a problem, and they show up. That is a really interesting paradox to me. The real issue, I think, has to do with poverty and a sense of hopelessness that is far too prevalent in our inner cities. I hope, in my lifetime, that will change.

ROBERT WISDOM (HOWARD "BUNNY" COLVIN): When you have the sheer volume of these kind of incidents happening, it becomes overwhelming for a city, because nobody knows what to do. So, that's when you have the Bunny, who's just way down in some little corner of some division, who just says, "I'm going to try and do something here." I don't think he even got how futile that effort could have been, but he saw it as his reason for being. If one person could be helped, it was worth it. If one kid could be saved and [if] all of these people who made the decisions to live with drugs in their lives could all just go over there and do it out of our sight and we shift our forces to keep it contained, it's worth it. It's twisted, but it's worth it.

RICHARD PRICE (WRITER): They found a street [for Hamsterdam] that they didn't have to set-dress at all. It just looked like Dante's hell. The problem was, right before they started shooting, they realized that you could see, on a rise, the back of a museum. The museum called the city, complaining, and refused to be in a shot, and the city came back and says, "You can't shoot there." They looked at each other. *What are we going to do?* They moved literally fifty yards that way and found the next street, where you couldn't see the museum. It was the exact same thing. I think they lost an hour.

ED BURNS (CO-CREATOR): That was Hamsterdam. It was David's idea, and I remember where it came from. We were sitting on Vine Street, which is off of Fayette Street. You look up the hill, and there was this setting sun, this big orange glow, and a local drug dealer had just serviced about thirty, or forty, or fifty addicts. It was like the walking dead how they were all moving around. We were sitting on the steps of this old vacant house and David said, "Maybe they should move them all into one place." And I said, "David, they already did. Look around. They're all fucked up." That's what we did in Season Three.

GEORGE PELECANOS (WRITER/PRODUCER): It's just funny about Hamsterdam because when I wrote that scene where the kid says that, that wasn't discussed or anything in the writers' room. It's just I always try to figure out a way to get out of the scene and I thought, *Well, some of these kids, they don't know what Amsterdam is. They don't know what it is and so they would mispronounce it.* I just wrote it. "I ain't going to no Hamsterdam," and one of the kids that delivered it was a Baltimore kid. He wasn't an actor, so he did it perfectly.

David called me up and he said, "How'd you think of that?" I guess I got a laugh out of him. I just said, "Look, I was just trying to get out of the scene. It's no big deal." Our thing was: don't ever write a boring scene, even if the material is boring. I hated the political stuff. I hated writing those scenes, because it's just people talking in a room, but we would always say in the writers' room that every scene counts. Don't ever throw away a scene, because then it's going to be the scene where somebody gets up to take a piss or goes to the refrigerator to get a beer and we don't want them to leave their seat.

BENJAMIN BUSCH (OFF. ANTHONY COLICCHIO): What was amazing was how closely *The Wire* paralleled what was happening in Baltimore. There was a lot of surgery going on in the streets up there, and what they were depicting, with the flushing out of some of those poor neighborhoods, to gentrify them, was happening in real time. They actually put the Hamsterdam set in a place that was about to be leveled. And during the show, it was. All of those row houses which we shot in were knocked down months later.

CHAD L. COLEMAN (DENNIS "CUTTY" WISE): We would be in neighborhoods, and I swear, I'm literally standing there going, "God dang. I know there's nobody living there." And the people would stick their head out the window.

CHRIS COLLINS (STAFF WRITER): We were on a block that was just full of abandoned row houses. Then I looked over and I see this guy come out of this row house with a broom. Then I see two pots he put out there, with plants in them, next to the door. He just started sweeping the doorstep.

That guy is just hope right there. There's a guy that's living in the middle of nowhere. He's taking time out of his day to come out and sweep his front stoop when every single house around him is abandoned. It was a powerful image for me, that this guy did not give up.

LEO FITZPATRICK (JOHNNY WEEKS): Shit, man, because I was there shooting a television show, it didn't seem that bad. But there are people that live in the building next door and the one next to that. Every time we went to Baltimore, I thought, *Man, this has to be the worst block of Baltimore.* And then we'd find one that was worse. It's fine for a TV show. But when you think that people actually live there and that this is people's reality, that's a mind-blower. That's crazy. Of course, there was set dressing and that sort of thing, but there was nothing built on a stage. Those were all real buildings. Whatever was on the floor was on the floor. I definitely worried about putting my face on it at times. Hamsterdam, it was surreal to shoot there because when you were shooting, it felt very much like a set. But when you left, when you were going home for the night and you saw all the actual residents and the people coming out of the woodwork, you were like, "Holy shit, this is fucking real."

ANDRE ROYO (REGINALD "BUBBLES" COUSINS): It was one of those times I'd been away from home for a while. I was living in Brooklyn. I invited my wife and daughter. My wife had never been to a set before. She came and—I think I was upstairs. I was shooting a scene with me and Johnny. He was getting really high. After the end of the scene, they say, "Your wife and daughter is downstairs." I was like, "All right. Cool." I'm coming down the stairs and I'm looking for her. We're on location. Everything is on location, except for the headquarters, the police headquarters. We're on a block, a regular block. It's not dressed. It looks the way it looks because that's the way it looks. I'm looking at my wife and she's talking to some random addicts, or regular people. She thought they were extras. She's talking to them.

I'm like, "Come here. What are you doing?" She came over, and when she walked toward me, I forgot I had all this stuff on. She saw me, and it just hit her. It hit her, and she started tearing up like, "You look so bad. Does it hurt?" She's looking at my face. I'm like, "No, it doesn't hurt. Why you talking to those cats?" She's like, "I was asking where you were." I was like, "They wouldn't know where I'm at. Those are not actors." She just looked around. She's like, "This is not a set?" I said, "No. This is a block." She just saw that, and it really hit her. She's like, "It's crazy that people live like this. This is somebody's house. This is somebody's house you're in. This is what people see when they wake up in the morning every day. I thought you built this. I thought this was a Hollywood backdrop." I was like, "No, this is life." It brought her to tears. Same with my daughter. My daughter saw me, forgot I had [makeup], she came and gave me a hug and looked at my face, and she thought Daddy was hurt.

ERNEST DICKERSON (DIRECTOR): The dealers hated us, because a lot of times we were shooting right down the street or a couple of doors down from a working crack house. That always interrupted their business.

LEO FITZPATRICK (JOHNNY WEEKS): The people in Baltimore didn't really give a fuck we were shooting the show in Baltimore. They were more frustrated that we were shutting down their streets and the corners that they worked on. Me and Andre shot in probably the worst places in Baltimore. It's where actual drug dealers worked at night. You roll in with your twenty trailers and police escorts. These drug dealers would be getting pissed.

There are really nice areas in Baltimore, too, and there's really bad areas. The two just kind of ignore each other. It's sort of like, "You stay on your side of the street, and I'll stay on my side of the street. We won't talk about each other."

CLAIRE COWPERTHWAITE (SCRIPT SUPERVISOR): Because the shoots were long, I remember there was always a challenge for me to get home at night because we would do several company moves. I was staying in the Inner Harbor, and I didn't know the area at all. I would drive to the location, do a couple of company moves, and then, at the end of the night, there were no directions for me to get back to my apartment that they put me up in. I had no idea where I was. I would be stopping, "Excuse me, Mr. Crack Dealer?" They would come up to my window, and they were like, "You buying?" "No, honey. No, no, no, I just need directions." They were like, "Girl, you in the hood." I said, "Honey, I've been in the hood all day. I know. My feet are killing me. Do you know where the harbor is?" They're like, "No, no, man, I don't know." So, I take all these kinds of points that I thought they might be able to get me in the right direction. "Do you know where the harbor is? Do you know where Johns Hopkins is?" I knew if I knew where two areas were, I could get back home.

Every night, I'd be asking some crack dealer, some prostitute, some whatever that's on the corner, how I could get home at night. That's what I did every night. I'd wind down my window, "Hey, can you come here for a second? Hey, hey, can you come here for a minute?" They'd look at me, stay on the corner because I'm this white woman and they're thinking, *Hmm, this is odd.*

VINCENT PERANIO (PRODUCTION DESIGNER): We scouted many funeral parlors in the neighborhoods. Certain ones were just gorgeous, beautiful, Victorian houses and others modern, where they had multi-funerals in different rooms and a main area where people would mourn. When we found this one in the heart of our neighborhood, it was just a corner row house, and the people lived upstairs, and it's just two rooms downstairs that were the viewing rooms. When we went to scout it, there was already someone set up in the funeral, and it was a kid that had just gotten shot, a young man. These people said that they get a lot of those. They get a lot of young black men. And it was so unlike any other funeral parlor I've been to. It was just a room set up.

CLAIRE COWPERTHWAITE (SCRIPT SUPERVISOR): We're in the Baltimore City Morgue and we have to stop shooting because they have to bring a real dead body of a seventeen-year-old who hanged himself. Because we were shooting in this location, you never knew what was going to happen or who was going to be there. There was always a level of realism wherever we shot, because there was somebody who was real there. The real homeless guy is in our shot.

UTA BRIESEWITZ (CINEMATOGRAPHER): We were working in a morgue downstairs, where they process the bodies and everything. Anyway, out of nowhere, they are wheeling body parts right past me that they have found somewhere underground. I don't know where it was. I just said, "Please, guys, give me a warning next time. I want to prepare myself for what I look at," because images really stick with me. What images really, really stuck with me was when we were shooting upstairs, in one of the offices. Our script supervisor, Christine Moore, was sitting at one of the desks and she was looking at photographs and she said to me, "Uta, you should come over here and take a look at these photographs." I said to her, "I don't think I should look at any photographs that are connected to the morgue," And she goes, "No, no, no, you should take a look at these photographs."

I walked over and I took a look at the photographs that she was referring to. They take these photographs when they have dead bodies. They take these photographs from straight above the person, so it's like a portrait, but it shows the upper torso. There was this big stack of photographs of African-American men in their prime, really young, maybe age seventeen, no older than twenty-five. Beautiful young men, and all dead. One had a bullet to the head. Another had two bullet holes to the chest. They were already cleaned up, so you just saw these black holes there. It was not messy. It was not bloody. All these men looked like they were sleeping. It was this big pile, and I went through this pile, and it was just one young black man after another. This was when it really hit home for me, what a tragedy this all is. How many lives lost with the war on drugs. It hit me really hard. I will never forget these portraits of these young black men falling victim to what's happening in Baltimore.

CLAIRE COWPERTHWAITE (SCRIPT SUPERVISOR): You didn't know if that day was going to be a really sad day or you were going to laugh a lot or you were going to be heartbroken or you're going to be afraid or you're going to be appalled. You just never knew from day to day.

CHAD L. COLEMAN (DENNIS "CUTTY" WISE): Times where you would hear *pop, pop, pop, pop,* and you didn't know how close it was. It felt close, and it gave me that kind of "oh, shit" moment. It was real like that. It was times we had to shut down because of that.

JANICE KINIGOPOULOS (HAIR DEPARTMENT HEAD): We were in a community where the houses were so close together that if we were there at two in the morning, a lot of the kids would come out because they were hungry. It's naturally upsetting, but I have to say, Nina was always so cognizant and aware of the neighborhoods and trying to help any kids that they could.

CLAIRE COWPERTHWAITE (SCRIPT SUPERVISOR): This little boy from the show who was sick had come up to me. A lot of the kids would hang out together. He was the cutest thing. He said, "I was wondering, Ms. Claire. I was wondering, maybe, if you could be my mom." And I was like, "Oh my God." It took my breath away. I was wanting to cry right there and then. I said, "You know what honey, you have a mom, but how about if I be your friend? Friend is much more fun. Let's be friends." That was hard.

As the show advanced, the writers noticed an evolving mentality on the Baltimore streets. A new crop of dealers came of age. They appeared detached from the previous generation, the elders who had played the game with a sense of decorum and unbreakable rules. The writers charted a crew to rival the Barksdale organization and reflect this transformation. Robert Colesberry had noticed Jamie Hector in a short film and advocated for his casting as Marlo Stanfield. Stanfield was consumed with accumulating power. Hector played him beautifully, terrifyingly, and with restraint. Gbenga Akinnagbe became Marlo's number two as Chris Partlow, a quiet, efficient murderer. Most improbably, Michael K. Williams came across Felicia Pearson one night and accompanied her to the set. Pearson was Baltimore inside and out. She was tiny in stature, spoke with a raspy voice, and dressed like a man. She had been convicted of second-degree murder at the age of fourteen and served nearly seven years at the Maryland Correctional Institution for Women, in Jessup. The show offered her a small role depicting an enforcer in the Stanfield organization, for which she kept her real name. For a while, Pearson continued dealing drugs even after being cast. "I wake up in the morning, get dressed, leave my work on the block to walk into a world about make-believe work on the block," Pearson later wrote in her book, Grace After Midnight. *"But because I ain't that sure the make-believe work is real, I keep my real-life work. My shop stays open." Her role on the show eventually increased, as did her attempts to leave the drug game behind.*

GEORGE PELECANOS (WRITER/PRODUCER): If you look at the first couple seasons, even though a lot of those guys, like Poot and Bodie, are young, they're still almost Old World gangsters, because they're following guys who have been around for a while. They have a code. They have their own sense of morality. We were always reflecting what was going on in Baltimore at the time. As the show progressed and as time went on, we were seeing a lot of guys coming up in Baltimore who had no morality, who were just doing executions and didn't care who got caught in the crossfire, and that's where the whole thing came from in that sequence where there's a shootout on a Sunday morning. That's a no-no. You don't do that. So, we were just trying to show the change.

ED BURNS (CO-CREATOR): Melvin [Williams] has some style about him because Melvin's people worked, and he lived in a working neighborhood. The next generation, a little bit less. The next generation, even less, and then you come to the Marlos—nothing.

JAMIE HECTOR (MARLO STANFIELD): We sat down and we worked on the material. When you don't have much to work with, you got to figure it out. As an actor, you can try to do something a thousand different ways, especially if it's your first series regular and your first project. It was not my first project, but we'll unpeel layer after layer after layer after layer to try to figure this person out. *Why did he say that? What's the setting? What's really going on? Where's he going right now? Where's he coming from? What's his life about? Who is this dude with two lines?* Now let's flash back through the rest of the season and figure this cat out. We don't even know who he is. We've got to narrow this down. For him to walk out and a guy's about to get murdered, and he only says a couple of words, that's when we realized that he probably wastes nothing at all, not even words, not food, not time, not money, nothing.

FELICIA "SNOOP" PEARSON: I met Michael K. Williams. It was a nightclub called Club One. Mike was sitting over there. He was just ice grilling me. You know? I didn't know who he was. I heard about the show. I seen them shoot the show, but I never was into it, because I was just outside. I wasn't into the TV thing like that.

MICHAEL K. WILLIAMS (OMAR LITTLE): I was so immersed in Baltimore culture, I could spot it a mile away. It had become more than just a TV show. I had moved down there. I had friends, people I could stay with in the off season, on hiatus. Baltimore really became a second home for me. The first time I'd ever really experienced that outside of my neighborhood, that love for a community and people.

When I looked at her, I instantly knew that she was the quintessential Baltimore. Then her beauty. You know, when you just look at somebody and you just know that, damn, they're supposed to be in your fucking life? They're supposed to be in your life. She was one of those people. I took one look at her and I knew that she was supposed to be in my life. I was right. I was right. I love her.

ED BURNS (CO-CREATOR): Felicia has a very positive energy. I mean, she exudes energy. When Michael brought her to me—she's got that hoarse voice: "You ain't going to believe this, but I just got out of jail." I said, "I believe you, because I see the tats well enough." She goes "Ha-ha." Her laugh is a killer laugh, right? We put her in. She didn't make it the first round. She got locked up in New York for a stolen car. The next script came up, [we] put her back in. She was right as rain all the way through.

I tried to get her to start to envision a broader range, but that was tough. I definitely wanted her to get out of Baltimore. It took her getting arrested again before she made that move. Michael's been a real good influence in her life. The girl's got something. She's got a magic to her. That was an easy call.

FELICIA "SNOOP" PEARSON: First time I had met David Simon and Ed Burns and Nina, when Mike told me come on set, everything was looking crazy, and I was like around all these white people and all that. I ain't never been around all these white people. You know what I mean? I was kind of nervous.

ANTHONY HEMINGWAY (DIRECTOR): Sitting here thinking about Snoop puts a smile on my face. I love to call her by her government name, Felicia. And she hates it. Snoop's first day on set was one for the books. It was her first day ever on set. She was so nervous, vulnerability at its best. It was actually really cute, because she was so determined and did not want to let herself or anyone else down. Once I saw that, I had to support and help her succeed. That's when our relationship started. Trying to handle my own AD [Assistant Director] responsibilities at the time, I couldn't get more than a few feet away before hearing my name in her distinct Baltimore accent. I have so many great memories with Snoop, but day one is definitely a highlight. Watching her work through her on-set nerves, I kept encouraging her to be herself and that truth is what comes out in the performance. It felt so real [that] I then had to start saying, "It doesn't have to be that real." I told her she was gonna scare everyone on the set.

ED BURNS (CO-CREATOR): We had a script coordinator change. The old script coordinator was used to Felicia making her own lines up and doing her own thing. This one was a little bit more like, "No, you can't do that." They became the closest of friends, but it was like, the script coordinator would come in: "What do you do with this person?" Felicia would come to me, "She's driving me fucking crazy."

CLAIRE COWPERTHWAITE (SCRIPT SUPERVISOR): My first day on set was the same day as Snoop's, Felicia. My whole impression was she was an actress. On the very first day, she says her dialogue, and soon they're like, "Holy shit." I don't understand a word this person's saying. First of all, I thought she was a guy. That was the other thing, too. She dressed that way. I turned to them, I said, "So, yeah, is this show subtitled, because I have no idea what she's saying?" I then go up to Snoop. I said, "Hey, how are you? My name is Claire. I'm Script." She gave me this look, this once-over. And then with the deadpan eyes, not saying a word, as if I had just been somewhat dismissed, she didn't say anything.

I said to her, "You know, you should say this." She looked at that, looked at me, and I'm like, "Okay." I walk away. I then sit back on the chair, and she gets the gist, but doesn't say it, and I'm like, "Okay." That's my job, it's to make sure the actors stay on script. I say, "So, you have got the gist, but the line is actually . . ." "Dang, girl. I got to say this word for word?" I think she's an actress, and I'm like, "Well, normally writers like it when you say their words, but you know what? This shot could be different." I go up to David and Ed, because some shows let you play a little bit with the words. "On this show, you're cool with them getting the gist of it?" "No, no, no. It's word for word." I said, "Uh-huh. So, Snoop?" "Oh yeah, we forgot to tell you, she's real." I'm like, "Real? What the hell does that mean? Real?" And they're like, "Yeah, real."

I looked around where we're shooting, which was the first scene with her, where she finds a power-actuated nail gun. She starts to board up the abandoneds. I'm thinking, *Hmm. How real?* They said, "Oh, yeah. She just got released from prison." And I said, "Ahh." Remember, I'm this middle-class white woman. I'm like, "Did she do something really bad?" And they're like, "Yeah, she killed someone when she was sixteen." I'm like, "Oh my God." I'm like, "Okay, alrighty. Well, okay. I'll be back." The next scene that we had right after that, she was in a car and she was mic'd, and I had headsets on, and she didn't quite grasp the whole headset-mic thing, where if you're speaking in a car or somewhere private and the microphone is on, the people that are wearing headsets can hear you. She has to say her line again. I'm like, "Oh God. I have to go and tell her she's not doing this right." I'm walking up toward the car, and I hear her on my headset, "Dang, here that girl come again, man. She frustrate me." I'm like, "Oh my God." I knock on the window. I'm like, "Hey, not to frustrate you, but it's really good if you could say this one line." By now, she knows how to say it. The next scene was the next episode. She's supposed to kill somebody. Let me tell you, there wasn't anybody better than she was. She was awesome. I mean awesome. I was complimenting her. I'm like, "You really know how to do this. God, you're amazing." Then it clicked for us. We became extremely good friends during the shoot. She had the most amazing look of hers. She had this angelic face, but with these eyes that had seen too much in her lifetime. It was this overall kind of sadness on one side, but hope on the other.

FELICIA "SNOOP" PEARSON: They just wrote me in. I was like, "Wow." I give my hats off to Nina, Ed Burns, most definitely. David Simon, all three of them. Everybody. Everybody. That changed my life. That moment that I met them, it changed my life forever, and I thank them for giving me the opportunity. They seen something in me, and I didn't even see it in myself.

MICHAEL K. WILLIAMS (OMAR LITTLE): My most proudest moment of having anything to do with *The Wire* is knowing that I met her five days out of prison for fucking manslaughter, for murder, and was able to have something to do with changing the trajectory of her life. She could have made some other decisions coming out of prison, you know what I mean? I had something to do with her not doing the same thing that got her in the first place. That will be the greatest reward I will ever have from *The Wire*.

JAMIE HECTOR (MARLO STANFIELD): She had the whole entire set in stitches, and she was in her hometown and it's like the microphone is on. Once she got comfortable, shooting with her was just fun.

METHOD MAN (CALVIN "CHEESE" WAGSTAFF): When I met Snoop, Snoop wasn't even working that day. I hear a knock on my trailer and shit. I open the door, and Snoop: "Sup, Meth? What's good?" I think she had some weed or some shit like that. But we were just kicking it, you know what I mean? She was basically like telling me how she got the job and all that shit. It was just like speaking to one of my nephews. No lie. And she harder than some of these niggas on these streets. I'm telling you, boy.

GBENGA AKINNAGBE (CHRIS PARTLOW): It was our chemistry off-screen. Now that I think about it, she and I would play. We'd play all the time. She'd say some wild things to me, and I'd say some wild things to her, and she'd say some wild things, and my mouth would be open, like, "What?" We would just play. I remember she took me to a strip club in Baltimore once, sat me down at the stage, gave me a stack of ones, and was just like, "Have fun," and left. It was wild.

You spend a lot of time with somebody, you learn about them. One thing I learned about her is she is a survivor. She's hard to kill. It's hard to kill her spirit. This one time, we were slap-boxing, because that's what she and I do. We play in between takes. It's like, "All right, cool. We're gonna slap-box." She's smaller than I am. I was a Division I wrestler, but she's tough. Don't street-fight her. We were about to start going, and she was like, "All right, cool." First thing she does when we start slap-boxing, she stepped on my foot, stomped on it to hold it there, hit me like three times within two seconds, and then went running. I was like, "Oh okay. That's how you survive. I can't trust you. That's what it is. You don't play by the rules." She's no joke. I couldn't move anywhere, because she had stomped on my foot. I was like trying to move my foot. Meanwhile, she's bopping me in the face like one, two, three. Then she runs off.

ED BURNS (CO-CREATOR): Gbenga turned down a role [to play Slim Charles] because he was taking a test. Shit, man, we got to find something for this kid to do. That's when we created Chris Partlow.

GBENGA AKINNAGBE (CHRIS PARTLOW): I didn't realize they didn't do it that much. I was very honored to be on that show, even before I found out that they went out of the way to make sure I was on the show. Then, in retrospect, having been an extra, I was really ignorant at the time. I didn't know that that kind of trajectory didn't happen very often.

It's funny because people talk to me and they meet me and they think I grew up going to a private school in New Jersey, an only child or something like that, but it's the opposite. I grew up in Maryland, in and out of institutions and schools. I was in a large family that never had enough. A lot of what you saw in the show, I had lived. It was like reliving it, but as a completely different person now. I was fortunate enough to get a wrestling scholarship, which took me to college and helped change my life. Now I'm looking back at my childhood through this TV show in Maryland. It was very strange and, in many ways, jarring for me. Then, also, because I'm different now, people are treating me different, treating me better than they would treat me if they thought this is where I came from. It was disturbing. I was fortunate. No one in my family that I know of was addicted to drugs or [impacted by] gun violence, but we lived in that poverty and saw those things all around us. The story told, in many ways, elements of my childhood, but going back and experiencing it as a different person now, it was jarring. It was strange.

ED BURNS (CO-CREATOR): It was Gbenga and Jamie Hector. I mean, I used to watch their faces to try to get the nuances that made these— I'm talking about sweet, do-anything-for-you people into, holy shit, and I could never figure out how it just happened, but it would.

JAMIE HECTOR (MARLO STANFIELD): Getting to know [who Marlo] was and getting to know the way he thinks and gets to operate was fun.

When I would walk outside the house where I lived at in Baltimore, when I would step outside of there, then I would approach people like that. They didn't know me. The show wasn't on yet. They didn't know of the show. People weren't seeing Marlo Stanfield yet. It's a young lady walking down the street, and I wanted to go approach her just to see how she'd respond, or I wanted to go and buy something in the Gallery, I would approach them the way he would.

That was fun. Going into the Gallery, if I wanted to purchase something or buy something in the mall, it was just basically, being that he was so economic and being that he wastes nothing, everybody would respond accordingly, right away with respect. Walking in a store, knowing exactly what you want, knowing exactly what you're going to get. "No, I don't got time for small talk." Just get this, get this. "Thank you. I'm out. Bye." That right there would be also appreciated. It'd be like, "He's an a-hole," but of course behind his back. Just exercising all of that was just fun.

GBENGA AKINNAGBE (CHRIS PARTLOW): Chris, in his mind, it was just business, but he's obviously a sociopath. The way I described it, it was like Snoop was a psychopath. Snoop, the character, got a thrill from the hunt, from the kill, and so on. That's what drove her. Chris, he didn't care. He could have sat down and had dinner with your whole family or killed your whole family, and it would have affected him the same way, which is disturbing, very disturbing. Psychopaths are easier to track, because if there's something that they like to do, there's usually a ritual behind it, and you can track the ritual. A sociopath may never kill. They blend in to society. They learn to fake emotions.

That's, to me, a disturbing phenomenon. I'm not saying I'm a sociopath, but I wouldn't tell you if I was. These are all elements that go into making these characters, and so, that being said, Chris, it's not like he was like, "Oh, I'm just going to go out and be a badass drug dealer" or whatever. To him, it was just like an everyday thing. Business, eat some food, talk to Marlo or whatever—it's just an everyday thing, and his business happens to be this dark, dark world.

Blink, and you would have missed it. In Season 3's tenth episode, "Reformation," Brother Mouzone dispatches his associate Lamar to various gay bars as unwilling bait to catch Omar. Omar is nowhere to be found, but the camera pans to find Dep. Commr. for Operations William Rawls in the background at one of the bars. In most cop shows, the homosexuality of a deputy commissioner would have been a dominant storyline. The Wire, of course, was not most shows. It left the strand dangling. The audience barely had time to recognize what it had seen before the show quickly shuffled along, never mentioning it again, beyond Sgt. Jay Landsman laughing after reading RAWLS SUCKS COCK *graffitied in the bathroom the following season.*

With such a deep ensemble cast, many characters were left without an overt backstory. This allowed the actors to ponder their origin stories themselves. Director Ernest Dickerson once asked Michael Potts (Brother Mouzone) how the disappointing Lamar came to be associated with Mouzone. "It became clear that he wasn't the brightest bulb," Potts said. "Why would I have him as my second? That's what I came up with: Clearly, he's family. He's a nephew. He has to be family, because he gets the wrong magazine every time." As Frankie Faison (Acting Commr. Ervin H. Burrell) said, "They touched upon that with Rawls and other minor things, but then it's just dropped, so you didn't know what to think. You just don't have time to delve into the most intricate aspects of everyone's personal life. You would have five or ten more seasons of The Wire."

JOHN DOMAN (DEP. COMMR. FOR OPERATIONS WILLIAM A. RAWLS): I was surprised when he showed up in the gay bar. That surprised me. That came out of left field. I hadn't seen the script, and I showed up on the set, and the AD [Assistant Director] came running over with this big, shit-eating grin on his face and said, "Have you seen the new script?" I said, "No," and Ed Burns was sitting there, and all of a sudden, I saw his head pop up and he looked at me and came rushing over and said, "John, we have to talk." He took me into a little room on the side, there on the set, and told me what they were planning to do. He said, "How do you feel about this? We're not really sure we're going to do it. We're going to shoot it, but we may not use it."

I thought to myself, *It's not going to make a damned bit of difference what I say here. If they want to use it, they're going to use it.* So, I said, "Oh, I love it! Let's do it. Why not?" Then, after we did it, I was thinking, *Boy, this could go in some very strange directions. What am I going to be required to do with this?* Then, the next script came, and there was nothing. And the next script came, and there was nothing. Finally, a third script came, and there was nothing. But I had to go through in my mind all of the possible scenarios. Now, it was like, "Well, why aren't we doing something with this?" I went to David and I said, "David, you know, this whole gay thing . . . I'm up for anything, whatever you want to do." He just kind of looked at me, with this faraway look, and walked away. Of course, in his brilliance, he never touched it again. It was perfect, what he did, he just dropped that little seed in there and never touched it again, but it planted the seed in the audience's minds.

DAVID SIMON (CREATOR): We discussed it. First of all, we said, "Okay, we're going into this gay bar. Who should be in there? Who would be possible?" So, we actually had the discussion. We went through the entire cast. When we thought Rawls, we said, "Man, that's perfect." We went back through all those moments with all of his sexual metaphors of him berating guys, and we would read them with this new sense, and the more we got into it, the more we were like, "That's it. That's the opportunity." Then we had a second discussion about should we use it.

ED BURNS (CO-CREATOR): I just liked the idea of you just panning that camera across that barroom scene and just catching him like that and keep right on going. Hit Rewind. And if we were given more seasons, it's something that you could work with. Daniels would find out about it; he could use it. I mean, you plant little things that way, so that the characters have someplace to go that you can use.

JOHN DOMAN (DEP. COMMR. FOR OPERATIONS WILLIAM A. RAWLS): I don't know what his reasoning was, but it showed another whole dimension to the Rawls character. Maybe it explained a lot about why he was like he was.

Seasonally, The Wire proved unabashed about offing characters who carried major story threads, as with the deaths of Wallace, D'Angelo Barksdale, and Frank Sobotka. The death of Stringer Bell in Season 3's penultimate episode proved that no one was safe. Long before the soaring popularity of Idris Elba, David Simon had decided that all attempts at reform in Season 3 would die, from Hamsterdam to Elba's Bell. He meets his death in the end-to-end magnificent "Middle Ground," an episode that earned Simon and George Pelecanos an Emmy nomination. The cold open features a Western-like protracted standoff between Omar (Michael K. Williams) and Brother Mouzone (Michael Potts) that is beautifully framed by director Joe Chappelle. Stringer, fumbling in his attempts to leave drugs behind for legitimate business, calculates that Avon Barksdale's escalating beef with Marlo Stanfield (Jamie Hector) threatens his operations and he offers Avon to Maj. Bunny Colvin (Robert Wisdom). Meanwhile, Brother Mouzone forces Avon to serve Stringer to him in order to protect his drug connection to New York. The two betray each other, yet they convene for one last conversation, during which they reminisce on a balcony about their youth as Baltimore's lights dance and flicker in the background.

Bell's end comes once Omar and Brother Mouzone corner him at an appointment. The character's death received what amounted to an obituary in The New York Times, long before newspapers routinely reviewed episodic television. Charley Scalies, who played Season 2's Horseface, recalled walking into a deli shortly after Stringer's death aired on television. A woman rushed him, jabbing a finger in his face, and demanded to know why Bell had been killed. "It scared the shit out of me," Scalies said. "She looked at me as I was The Wire, and she was going to tell somebody from The Wire that she didn't like it. She just charged after me. Turned out to be a lovely lady, but she got excited." The death came as a surprise to Elba, too, as did the original way that writers planned for Omar to commemorate the victory.

ED BURNS (CO-CREATOR): When Idris and Wood, when those two were fighting in that room, they thought that the furniture was break-apart furniture, because they smashed into the table and just shattered it.

They thought it could just be put back together. That's how good, how intense they were in this particular scene. They were like, "No, that was actually a table."

WOOD HARRIS (AVON BARKSDALE): We might have broke some furniture, but we weren't going at it for real. I will say about the chemistry that me and Idris have, is that you won't see that again unless you see us again. It'd almost be like Robert Redford and Paul Newman in a sense, where they did a lot of movies together and you just don't see that energy from any one of those actors apart necessarily. When we had that fight that he's talking about, I don't recall it being anything but good acting. We were just acting. I don't recall even breaking something. That's what I mean by being in the moment. We were in the moment. A lot of TV shows are behind a clock, and they rush through. Nothing really felt rushed on *The Wire*. It felt like you were making a movie every week.

If things got broken, that's good, though. If things got messy, that's good. We were definitely trying to keep things messy. Me and Idris, sometimes we'd look at a scene and figure it out as individuals and then come together, and the chemistry works. Particularly someone like Idris, [he's] a sharing actor. Some actors are not necessarily sharing actors. They wait for their opportunity to say their lines. Not Idris. Idris is available. I think we share that in common, where we're both available actors in terms of we're listening first and then the moments come from listening and not just the scripts.

IDRIS ELBA (STRINGER BELL): We approached that scene like a play, and the cameras stood back and didn't really get involved. It was like a theater piece. We had the whole space. The tension was really real, but it was delicate. We ended up with arguably one of the most explosive scenes I've ever shot, to be honest.

JOE CHAPPELLE (DIRECTOR/CO-EXECUTIVE PRODUCER): For the scene on the rooftop—there, that's the heart of the season for those two characters anyway. When I got to the scene in the episode, which was the penultimate episode of that season, you're getting to the climax of the book, getting to the climax of the movie. So I approached it with that in mind.

GEORGE PELECANOS (WRITER/PRODUCER): I think that's not only the best thing I wrote for *The Wire*, but it's probably one of the best things I've ever written, including in my novels. That comes from being on the show for three years at that point and sort of knowing everything intimately, including the actors, and as good as it is on the page, it's dead. It's just words on the page until they bring it to life. Idris and Wood Harris—I knew they'd knock it out of the park.

JOE CHAPPELLE (DIRECTOR/CO-EXECUTIVE PRODUCER): There was one thing I just wanted to get: a look at a certain point where they both know they are betraying one another. They don't know the other one's betraying them, but they each know what they are doing to the other guy. I just wanted one more take. And I think it's the take that's in the movie, especially in Wood's coverage. It's just the way he looks at Idris. It wasn't like I asked them to do this one. In television, even on an HBO show back then, time is always an issue. It's not like a feature, where you can go and get to come back tomorrow to pick up the scene. You have to get it done. I just remember going for an extra take or two on that particular scene, just so those guys got to really dig into it, which they did, obviously, and it's spectacular.

WOOD HARRIS (AVON BARKSDALE): I just remember how I felt that day, like *wow*. I was thinking, *What's going to happen between me and Stringer? Is somebody going to die?* You really don't know. I know the look that he wanted: a look of concern of what the matter is. I just remember turning around at the end of the scene, as Idris walked off, and having to give this gaze, this gaze of discontent in a sense. I had a lot of fun that day.

IDRIS ELBA (STRINGER BELL): Growing up with Wood, you might just be having a great conversation and be so relaxed, and although that scene has lots of tension and lots of stuff going on underneath it, it was a very casual scene to shoot. I think we realized it was one of our last scenes, obviously, by the words. It wasn't our last scene to shoot in reality, but it just felt—it was a process. It was a night shoot on a day when we both wanted to go out and have fun or whatever.

GEORGE PELECANOS (WRITER/PRODUCER): If you look at the way he shot that scene, you have the master shot and then he goes tighter and tighter, and the lenses are very long lenses. You see the lights of Baltimore behind them, blurred out, completely blurred out. And you're one hundred percent focused on these guys. It's like when they're speaking, you're in their heads. It was brilliant.

WOOD HARRIS (AVON BARKSDALE): When Idris got killed on the show, we both were contemplating over who would die. In fact, we wanted one of our characters to die. I just remember us talking about it and me thinking, *No, I think they might kill my character.* When you know a series is going to be over and done, for a character to get killed, it's a good thing. Moving forward, all the fans know that you won't be seeing that character anymore. It's a good period to put on the end of a character's life.

ED BURNS (CO-CREATOR): It was a logical thing to [kill Stringer] because we had used the character. We had brought him to the point where anything else would be downhill. To me, it would make sense to kill him. We crafted the relationships in such a way that just as he was trying to get out, the wall will close down upon him and he would have this death, which I think was a big shock to Idris. I don't think it's fair for a character to go beyond a high mark of his journey, just stretch the arc out for the sake of keeping the character there.

DAVID SIMON (CREATOR): They told me the script was still down in the production office. I had to finish some pages. Then I was going to go out to the trailer. He was getting things done in the makeup truck. He was working on the current episode. They told me his script hadn't been delivered to him yet. I said, "All right, I'll go out in an hour." It turned out he read somebody else's script. Normally, you want to go and at least have the bedside manner to talk to him personally.

IDRIS ELBA (STRINGER BELL): I was at the studio. I was making music, and David called me and he didn't know I hadn't read it. He was like, "I just wanted to call you and talk to you about Episode Eleven or whatnot." I was like, "Oh, yeah. Okay. Cool. Cool." At that point, I hadn't read it. I had got the script, but I hadn't read it. He must have presumed I read it. He started talking to me, and he must have realized I didn't know. I hadn't brought it up on the call at that point. He said, "I'm sorry, Stringer doesn't make it to Season Four." That's when I realized what he was talking about.

It wasn't the most ideal way to understand that. He was very careful and caring about letting me know. I was a little emotional about it because I was like, "Why are you killing Stringer? I don't get it. What's the point? What's the storyline?" He had a master plan, which he hadn't really shared with me at that point. It wasn't a big deal, but it certainly was a surprise. You know what? Death is a surprise. You don't know when you're going to die. I think that was a key moment for me as an actor, because this is my livelihood. This is a very, very popular character at the time. It's being taken away. It was being taken away at a time when the character itself was changing his ways. He was becoming not only a gangster, but a very smart businessman. I suspect *The Wire* must have saw this in me and killed his character or it becomes the show.

I didn't know that at the time. I didn't really get that. There was no bad beef with me and David. David had some ideas about the way we shoot the death, which I didn't really agree with, and so we got into talking about that. From his point of view, he didn't do anything wrong. I think he, as a writer, had to make a really difficult choice to behead a character that he loved. He really loved Stringer Bell. He was one of his favorite characters to write—well, so he told me—and it was a tough decision for him as well.

GEORGE PELECANOS (WRITER/PRODUCER): Ed Burns would always come up with these things. He would come up in the writers' room and say, "I was talking to so-and-so today and this new thing, the last couple of weeks, is after these guys executed someone, they'd piss on him." So, I wrote that into the script, where Omar pisses on Stringer Bell after he kills him. It's a sign of disrespect. Idris didn't like that, either. I don't blame him. He said, "Ain't nobody pissing on me." We were like, "Well, it's not pissing on you. We're gonna make a dummy of you and urinate on that." He's like, "Nobody pisses on my double, either." So, I cut that out of the script. And it's fine.

IDRIS ELBA (STRINGER BELL): That felt a little unnecessary. It just started to turn into a TV show for me, you know. Had I thought about it outside of the reaction, maybe I wouldn't have been so opposed to it, but the truth is we never shot it and it didn't need it. The death was impactful enough. The urination part felt like overkill.

DAVID SIMON (CREATOR): We didn't see that as being a statement about Stringer and death. You're dead, you're dead. We saw it as being a moral lapse in code by Omar, which we thought would have been an interesting addition and would have countered some of the mythos of Omar Little. And that's what George argued for, and that's what I argued for. But Idris said, "I don't want to do that. I really don't want to do that." And he was utterly unconvinced by everything George and I said.

ED BURNS (CO-CREATOR): That was my idea. It was between Mouzone and Omar. Each had a reason for doing what he was doing. Omar was going to take it personal, so, therefore, how do you express that visually? When the script came out, David should have went to Idris and said, "This is it. This is the way it's going to be," and he didn't. Idris had a lot of people saying, "They're mistreating you," and, "They're fucking you up," and stuff like that, and that's not true. His character's dead. What happens to a dead man, the dead man doesn't care.

MICHAEL POTTS (BROTHER MOUZONE): He didn't like the idea of him being killed, but he was really upset about [the character's body being urinated on]. He came to me and told me, and I think he said it to Michael also, "Just to let you know, if they keep that in, I'm going to walk, because I'm not going to get pissed on. So, if they insist upon that, I'm walking. I'm not going to continue doing it." Okay, so lots of discussion back and forth and what have you, and they decided no pissing on him. Just shoot him.

GEORGE PELECANOS (WRITER/PRODUCER): That was pretty bad. In the run of the show, he was definitely the most upset about his death. He was really pissed off, and David and I had to go into the trailer and sort of talk him down. He was mad. His career was really taking off because of the show. We would go on set in the middle of the night, and we shot in the neighborhoods. Women would be hanging out of the window in these neighborhoods and they'd be screaming at him like he was the fifth Beatle.

DOMINIC WEST (DET. JIMMY MCNULTY): Killing off Idris, I always thought, *The lucky bastard, he gets all the best lines and gets all the great* *scenes and he only has to do three years. I have to do five fucking years of it.* I was pretty jealous of him. Then I had to say all sorts of lines like, "Who was this guy?" When I was going through his apartment, and he'd be reading [The] *Wealth of Nations,* and I'd go, "Who was this guy?" *Why are we glorifying this fucking gangster?* I thought it was a bit glorifying. I was rather reluctant or a bit riled to have to make Idris look so good, but he made himself look good, so he deserved it.

DAVID SIMON (CREATOR): I had a long talk with Idris in that graveyard where we filmed the scene where he meets Colvin. We actually walked around the graveyard in the evening, and I tried to explain to him we were not punishing him and that he was genuinely a leading man. We had been incredibly fortunate to get him in servicing the show, servicing the story. It was the right thing for the narrative as a whole, but that he was going to have a career and that's when he gave me the line about "From your mouth to God's ear." He didn't believe it. He took it bad, but I've seen him since then, and a little perspective on where that was goes a long way. If you were into the show when Stringer got killed, that was something.

In order to make a story matter, you can't just kill the people, you can't disappear the people, the characters that people want to disappear. The audience is a child. If you ask the audience what they want, they'll want dessert. They'll say they want ice cream. They'll want cake. You ask them what they want the next minute, they'll say more ice cream, more cake. You show them that they like something else. "You like fried chicken? Here, taste my fried chicken." Then the next ten things they order will be the fried chicken. "You like Omar?" "Yeah, I love Omar. Give me more of Omar." No, I want to tell you a story, and the characters are going to do what they're supposed to do in the story, and that's the job of the writer. That's the writer's job. That's the storyteller's job. You don't write for anybody but the story, for yourself and for your idea of what the story is. The moment you start thinking about the audience and the audience's expectation, you're lost. You're just lost. So, you've got to just put it out of your mind and tell the story that you think you're there to tell.

BENJAMIN BUSCH (OFF. ANTHONY COLICCHIO): The thing with *The Wire* was that it didn't care who you loved. It never worried. It allowed art to define its decisions, not commerce. No one was ever safe.

GEORGE PELECANOS (WRITER/PRODUCER): It was like four in the morning on Howard Street, which is kind of desolate. Every place we shot was a little bit dangerous if you weren't around security on set. So, I get off and I'm walking to my car down a dark alley and I hear somebody running behind me. I turn around, and it's Idris. I say, "I just want you to know all this stuff is business. It's just to make the show better, and that's all I'm ever concerned about." And we shook hands. He's a really cool dude. When I got nominated for an Emmy for that episode, he sent me a bottle of nice Scotch.

RICHARD PRICE (WRITER): One of my favorite things that David did—one of the sentimental tropes—is that if you take a kid on the street corner, and this kid is dealing and he's holding together the business, he's got inventory, he's got sales, he's got police pressure, he's got higher-ups pressure. If this kid can keep numbers in his head and make money, they say, "Well, if this was a white kid and you put him in Wharton and he came out, he'd be running the world." What David did, and it's very sentimental to say that, but what David did, he took Stringer Bell—and of course you'd see Stringer Bell in a corporate setting—he took him to the cleaners, everything but his underwear robbed.

I loved that, because everybody wants to feel good and say, "If you took this young kid," but no. It might be true if the kid was born in another body, in another world, but he wasn't. There's a ceiling. There's a very low ceiling. I liked that so much better than if Stringer Bell became a business power in Baltimore, went legit successfully.

That's what I love about the show. It always foiled expectations. Just when you thought you were gonna get an uplifting story, you got smacked in the face.

MICHAEL KOSTROFF (MAURICE "MAURY" LEVY): There seemed to be a pattern that people who started to pursue goodness were often the people who got offed. Stringer was starting to see a way to not kill people and to run a business, and he gets killed. D'Angelo wanted out; he got killed. So, the really horrible people tend to survive.

GEORGE PELECANOS (WRITER/PRODUCER): Season Two, the ratings went up. I'm going to say something that no one else will say, but because we had a white cast in that season, America was more ready for that. But then, Season Three, the ratings went down again.

Most people had still not tuned in to The Wire. *It was a show that could still be canceled at any time. But the cast members noticed and appreciated its uniqueness, knowing they had never worked on a show like it before and likely never would again. Robert Wisdom and Andre Royo talked one day about the show's depth of black actors. They decided to document the range, and turned the event into a celebration.*

MICHAEL POTTS (BROTHER MOUZONE): Robert Wisdom, in that third season, he was trying to organize a whole picture. He wanted a portrait of all the actors. He goes, "This will never happen again, brothers." He was going around saying, "We've got to take a picture of this, because this will never happen again. Look at this."

ROBERT WISDOM (HOWARD "BUNNY" COLVIN): That was Andre Royo and I. We were just shooting the breeze one day and just marveling at the full array of talent that was coming together. This was the third year, and we came up with the idea to document this moment. At that point in television history, it hadn't happened, and we figured it would probably be a long time before it happened again. A show that didn't pitch itself as a quote-unquote black show. So, we went about trying to organize it.

I was inspired by the Harlem musicians photo back in the day. There was a photo where all the jazz musicians of the day came together in Harlem. And when you look at who showed up, it was just incredible. So, that's what we set up to do. Everybody from Idris to Wood Harris showed up. There's some people who didn't understand what we were doing. But I think everybody felt, especially with twenty/twenty rearview, that it was really worth doing and they were proud that we were able to pose.

ANDRE ROYO (REGINALD "BUBBLES" COUSINS): Me and Bob would sit around talking. He's someone I would learn from. He would talk about music. Bob was one of those characters you see in a lot of movies. Me and him, we liked each other. We would talk about, "Let's not be afraid to celebrate us." It wasn't just the black actors we had. It was the range. One day, we had a black actor, it's his first acting job. On the other side of the spectrum, we got Glynn Turman. We're like, "Oh, shit. That's a lot of people. That's a lot of range. That's a lot of history." We were talking like, "Let's get all the black actors together and take this shot. Let's make sure we have moments we can remember about this show and the times we had. Let's get all the actors together."

We made it an event. I wanted a deejay. We rented a space, got Dona [Adrian Gibson], our costume [supervisor], who was a great cook, to cook some food. We made it a party. We sent out an email. People came in on their days off.

A few people were nervous about it. They felt like they didn't want to exclude the white cast, because we have a big cast. We're all part of the family. It wasn't that we're excluding the white cast members, it's just a rarity that we see this many black actors in one show that have a storyline. It's a rarity. It's not a rarity for a white cast to be together. Back then, you turned on the TV or look at billboards, and the majority of people you saw was all white. But I had called David. I talked to Dom West. I was like, "Would this bother you?" They were like, "No. Go for it." David Simon showed up and was proud he had that many black actors. It was a great time and a great day. We can't be afraid to celebrate ourselves.

The headspace required to portray characters with defined faults weighed heavily on several of the cast members. Director Peter Medak came across Dominic West in England early in The Wire's *run. "You know, I'm not going to keep doing this," West said of continuing on the show. "I'm going to quit." Medak asked West how many years he had signed on to play McNulty. "Don't worry about that," he responded. "Nobody can force me to do anything."*

ANDRE ROYO (REGINALD "BUBBLES" COUSINS): There was moments I was depressed and didn't know why. The balancing of my life and Bubbles's life was daunting. There was days when I just felt dark and I wanted to run away. I would sit and talk to Idris or talk to Seth [Gilliam]. He was a real cool dude who's been around the business a long time. When we weren't getting the accolades we felt like we should have got, people started to feel a little depressed. *What the fuck are we doing wrong?*

DOMINIC WEST (DET. JIMMY MCNULTY): I was constantly whining and grousing about it and telling [Simon] I didn't want to do it, and he was the most generous-hearted man and a very exceptionally humane, warm guy, as well as a brilliant guy. He put up with all my whining and complaining and was great. Then, one day, he said to me, "You know, Dominic, in about ten years' time, twenty years' time, you're going to be sitting in some bar, in one of our horrible, wet, rainy London bars, and you're going to be sitting at the bar stool, and it's going to be late in the day, and you're going to say to the barman, or anyone who will listen, you'll say, 'I was once in a show called *The*

Wire. I dunno if you ever heard of it, but I was the lead actor.' And that barman is going to look at you and go, 'I think it's time you went home now, sir.' "

DAVID SIMON (CREATOR): Yeah, that's a bit that I stole from Terry McLarney, homicide detective, whom I consider a very good friend. He's used that on me a couple of times. I've used it on Dom. I've used it on a lot of people. I used it on Chris Albrecht when I was trying to get him to renew the show. I said, "One day, you're going to be in a bar and you are going to tell people you were the guy who renewed *The Wire* when nobody was watching it, season after season, and the guy's going to say, 'That's really great, sir, but it's two a.m. You've got to finish your drink, get out, and go home.'" I know it made him laugh, because he told me later. And, really, they had no good reason to renew it.

7

THE BASTARD CHILD OF HBO

David Simon authored Stringer Bell's death and the collapse of the Barksdale organization as The Wire's de facto series finale. He, of course, yearned for more seasons to tell his story under HBO's economic model, which did not rely on advertisers. The network could support the show's budget, as long as it attracted some additional paying viewers. But the show's ratings had never impressed, often bleeding viewers from its lead-in. Viewership peaked with 4.3 million viewers at the start of the second season. The Baltimore Sun reported that an average of 1.9 million watched Season 3's episodes. Simon voiced uncertainty that HBO would continue the series and deliberated writing books to finish a story he intended to complete. "I know [HBO] isn't particularly pleased with our numbers," Simon told the New York Daily News. "Why would they be? But, at the same time, I'm not sure what on HBO, besides maybe The Sopranos, could have gone up against the buzz saw that is Desperate Housewives and Sunday Night Football . . . What could have gone up against Desperate Housewives? Desperate Housewives is pretty. I'm not about pretty." Indeed, in initially greenlighting a show that no one else would have touched, HBO chairman and CEO Chris Albrecht displayed impressive foresight. But he left the show dangling for months on a fourth-season renewal. Soon, a website, www.savethewire.com

popped up, inviting viewers to plea for the show's continuation, and even provided the mailing address for Albrecht's office. "I have received a telegram from every viewer of The Wire—*all two hundred fifty of them," he joked at the Television Critics Association winter press tour in 2005.*

Simon did not relent. He requested a spin-off. He wrote intensive memorandums on the show's intentions and purpose. He pitched Albrecht and Carolyn Strauss on completing the show in its totality—a fourth season with a focus on education and a fifth on media. Finally, the network signed off on continuing the series. "It's been frustrating," Simon said to The Baltimore Sun. *"HBO has in the past been a unique little cocoon for writer-producers—providing a certain comfort level for shows that were critically and creatively viable. Well, that cocoon kind of got popped open and a little bit of cold air came in, and it got uncomfortable for a while. . . . But now it's sealed up again and warm and cozy." The delay exacerbated concerns among the show's actors over its hierarchy at HBO and a lack of appreciation for their efforts.*

NEAL HUFF (CHIEF OF STAFF MICHAEL STEINTORF): There was some kind of rumor going around at the end of Season Three, that there might be a spin-off show called *The Hall*. Aidan's the one who told me about it. I could have very easily hunkered down and stayed in Baltimore and done that for the foreseeable future.

WILLIAM F. ZORZI (STAFF WRITER): After Season Three, there was some question in HBO's mind as to whether they wanted to go forward. A bunch of time passed, and during that time, I wrote two episodes—this notion of writing a political show based on this Carcetti character.

DAVID SIMON (CREATOR): *The Hall* would have been seventy-five percent politics and twenty-five percent into *The Wire* world. I thought there was enough material to do two shows side by side and go from one to the other, to just sort of ration it. Nobody wanted to do the politics. Nobody. The only person that wanted to do politics was me, and Zorzi. George hated politics. Ed hated politics. I don't know what Ed thinks now. I know that George came to realize that doing the politics made *The Wire* about more than cops and robbers. Again, sometimes a story's got to eat its vegetables.

AIDAN GILLEN (MAYOR THOMAS CARCETTI): There was a pilot script written for that after Season Three. It was very good, and of course I would've been very happy if it had happened then. It didn't, but a lot of what was in it ended up on Season Four, which was a great season. Yes, if it came up again, I'd jump to do it.

DAVID SIMON (CREATOR): I remember going to Chris [Albrecht] and saying, "I want to split the shows, and one part of it bounces into *The Wire*. It alternates, and I'll give you a city municipal show about politics." It was just the most amazing thing. "So, I would have two shows nobody would be watching?" [Albrecht said.] I'm thinking of expanding the universe and they're really going, *How do we get out of this?*

ANDRE ROYO (REGINALD "BUBBLES" COUSINS): We did get canceled Season Three. We were done. After Season Three, we were over. We always felt like they didn't know how to gauge what audience we had, because at that time, it was about the water cooler talk. That's how you described good television. It's water cooler television. The next morning or Monday morning, you're at work talking about "Did you see that? Did you see what Tony [Soprano] did?" For us, our audience was BET, young black kids talking about our show. That's our story. All that wasn't countable.

DOMENICK LOMBARDOZZI (DET. THOMAS "HERC" HAUK): Every season, we had a wrap party. It was kind of like, "Well, shit. We don't know if we're coming back for another season." Some of the best wrap parties I ever went to were *The Wire*.

NINA K. NOBLE (EXECUTIVE PRODUCER): Every season was a struggle. Every season, we weren't renewed. At the end of the season, we would just say goodbye to everybody and "hope to see you again," and then it would be anywhere between two and four months they would keep us waiting, and usually David would have to go out to LA and pitch the theme of a new season and try to get an order. It was never automatic.

BRANDY BURRE (THERESA D'AGOSTINO): We knew that we were the bastard child of HBO in the best sense. It wasn't *The Sopranos*. It wasn't *Sex and the City*. We were doing something special, and it wasn't necessarily being recognized at the time.

BENJAMIN BUSCH (OFF. ANTHONY COLICCHIO): It was always that worry at the end of each season. When is there going to be Season Four? Is there going to be Season Five? It was one of their cheapest shows, when you look across the board. They were shooting *Rome* at the time. They had *The Sopranos*. These were high-end, high-cost shows. *The Wire* was very inexpensive by anyone's estimation. It lived in dangerous days. We always were amazed by that, that the industry, which now also considers it to be the gold standard, just refused to acknowledge it. I think we're still trying to figure that out. What was it? Was it the content? Was it the message? Was it the fact that it wasn't a happy show? *The Sopranos* was dark, but it was a gangster show. It had a genre. *The Wire* created its own genre.

CHRIS ALBRECHT (CHAIRMAN AND CEO, HBO): After Season Three, you went, "This story is over, man. What are you going to do?" Then, when [David Simon] came in—it's always really impressive and important when a very talented writer-producer comes in, and has a very clear, strong point of view about something that's pretty interesting. So, David had that. He said it's two more seasons. That was the other thing. It's not one more season. It's two more seasons. "Oh, Jesus Christ. Let's get rid of this guy."

DAVID SIMON (CREATOR): Carolyn called me, and I said, "Oh my God. We have such a great storyline. You can't do this." She said, "Well, look, [Chris Albrecht is] pretty convinced. He doesn't see a reason to go on. He feels like you're never going to get better reviews than you just got. Stringer's dead. The Barksdale storyline is over." I said, "Can I come in and argue?" She said, "Yeah, you're entitled to that. I'll make sure he hears it." So, I went into a meeting with them, and at first I prepared a storyline of characters for Season Four and Season Five and why we should finish this. "Education and media. If I can just get two more seasons of the show, we'll have a cumulative effect and we'll make an argument." And I concluded with the same joke about sitting in a bar.

I went into the room and just kept talking, and he didn't tell me right away. He says, "How much do you need?" He says, "Can you do it in less?" I'm like, "No, we can't. We need this. We need that." He said, "All right, let us think about it." He liked the media story, and Carolyn liked the education story, and they were both engaged in that story. That's kind of a miracle. Normally the dollars and the issues—you don't have an audience, fuck. They both talked to me about the story for about thirty-five minutes. I got up and shook his hand and said, "You won't regret it." He made a joke about, "I'm already regretting it," which made me feel good, and then I walked out of the room and heard a couple days later that they were going to renew it. Another thing is they asked about the actors. I said, "I'll get them all back. They'll come back to finish the show." I didn't know if that was true, but I promised him that. I went and got the actors back. Give them credit. No agent came to us and said, "Okay, he's coming back. He wants double." Didn't happen.

CHRIS ALBRECHT (CHAIRMAN AND CEO, HBO): Again, no one was writing about the show; very few critics had any appreciation or any time for it. The audience was, even for HBO, relatively small. I thought the work was certainly good. I think we all really liked it, really were proud of the show. With the drug story resolving itself, we thought, *Hey, a clear victory, and then move on*, but David was convinced that he had more story to tell on it, that this was much more of a global look at a city rather than the one particular storyline that he had followed so far.

CAROLYN STRAUSS (PRESIDENT, HBO ENTERTAINMENT): I have always loved David. I've gotten along with David very well. He's very passionate. He can write and he likes to write, and he will. Opposed to somebody else, he'll pick up the phone and scream, but he puts it down on paper, and it's there for everybody to see. He cares about all the different parts of the show. As he did in the show, the way he sold it to us, the way he told his story, it's just part of it. He just is a master storyteller.

CHRIS ALBRECHT (CHAIRMAN AND CEO, HBO): He certainly would type these long, single-spaced letters and send them to me and then to Carolyn Strauss, to make his case as to why we should continue. It was David's letters. It was, almost literally. [And] the fact that I really appreciated the show. Carolyn Strauss really appreciated the show, and we liked David. Look, it was no denying the show was good. Certainly, *we* knew the show was good before America knew the show was good. The other thing that it had going for it was it wasn't very expensive. Shooting in Baltimore, great crew, guys that had done *Homicide*—these guys were very efficient producers. You had a lot of respect and admiration for the production itself. One of the things it had going for it was the show didn't cost a lot of money. Again, relatively speaking. It became, "All right, let's just do it. We don't want to hear from this guy anymore." He was overbearing, particularly about what he wanted to accomplish in the season.

DAVID SIMON (CREATOR): One of the reasons we stayed on the show also is we never went over budget. Every dollar we got was put on-screen. It was not a show that had big trailers and lobsters at the craft services table. We didn't put people up in the nicest hotels. We found the rates and we shot it in Baltimore, where things were cheaper. We tried to put it all on the screen, and we didn't have a lot. I know a guy who did three episodes on *The Sopranos*. They were shooting seventeen days an episode. We were shooting eleven.

NINA K. NOBLE (EXECUTIVE PRODUCER): We were just putting everything up on the screen, being very efficient in the way that we worked by evaluating and questioning every decision every day in terms of the value to the story. David and I, when we agree to do something, that's what we do.

DAVID SIMON (CREATOR): The one [storyline] that we missed, David Mills thought of it: immigration. It wasn't his fault, but it came to me after we were off the air for way too long, between Three and Four, because they were going to cancel the show after Season Three.

ED BURNS (CO-CREATOR): We could've done a story on police corruption, and we could've done a story on immigrants. That's two stories that we were thinking about. We were never going to get a sixth season. We were lucky to get the last two seasons, because we ended the third season, tied it up rather nicely.

DAVID SIMON (CREATOR): By the time I talked them back in—they'd given [us] Seasons Four and Five—by the time we were ready to go back on the air, we had to get all the actors back in contract and we got all of them back. That's to the great credit of all of those actors. Nobody held us up for money. They all came back, and we'd lost them all by contract. By the time we got them back, even to do the education story, to set that up and find those locations, we were going to be off the air for almost two years. To then pull up and have me go back to HBO and go, "Listen, I've got another one in between." We would have been off the air for two and a half, three years.

It would have pulled us out of the rotation completely. It could only go between Three and Four. Once you start the vacant row houses, that's Four and Five. By the time David [Mills] thought of it, I said, "You're right." Because what was happening in Southeast Baltimore, which David discovered by just sort of hanging out—not discovered; we all knew it, but it was hiding in plain sight—Baltimore didn't have any Latino population for years and years. It was the overlooked city on the East Coast when it came to Central Americans and Mexicans and Puerto Ricans. DC, yes. New York, yes. Philadelphia, yes. But Baltimore, no, for whatever reason. And Southeast Baltimore had become a magnet for Central Americans. It was changing so rapidly. David got into it when he was writing a pilot for CBS called *Mayor of Baltimore*. It didn't go. But then he put the immigration stuff in his pilot. He came to me and he said, "Man, my thing didn't go, but how are you not doing immigration as a theme?" As soon as he said it, I was like, "You're right, we missed that one."

ANDRE ROYO (REGINALD "BUBBLES" COUSINS): I remember going to David Simon and talking to him. I was that kind of guy. I liked people. I would always go to the writers' room, wondering about how these white boys is telling these stories with an all-black cast. David Simon was the dude. I'm like, "David, we never got nominated. *Boston Legal* got nominated. What we got to do, David?" He's like, "I'm not doing nothing. They're not going to catch on until we're gone. This is the type of show that they're going to pick up when we're off the show, like a book, and rewatch it over and over again." I remember my first response in my head was, *What an arrogant white boy. What the fuck is he talking about?*

He was right. He really understood that the audience was starting to change and the audience was starting to appreciate not being treated like they're stupid. Nothing has to be spelled out. They can stick with a story even though it's slow. They can stick with a story even though there's forty characters. They appreciate being treated like they're intelligent. All of a sudden, *The Wire* became that show where there was a hierarchy. If you say you like *The Wire*, that means you like reading books. That means you give a fuck about the human race. It made you feel like you bettered yourself in the crowd when you say, "My favorite show is *The Wire*." All of a sudden, people look at you differently. It became a badge of honor to tell somebody, "Did you hear about *The Wire*? You got to watch *The Wire*."

DAVID SIMON (CREATOR): There were moments where you would watch really strong performances by black actors and they would be utterly ignored. Khandi Alexander on *The Corner*. Do you know who won the Emmy for lead actress in a miniseries the year of *The Corner*? Halle Berry. Halle Berry played Dorothy Dandridge. Understand this. Beautiful Halle Berry played the beautiful Dorothy Dandridge and played it beautifully, but she was a beautiful actress playing a beautiful actress and was nominated and won the Emmy. Khandi Alexander, a beautiful actress, tore herself down to play a woman with a drug addiction, and it's not even noticed. They won for makeup for making Halle Berry [into] Dorothy Dandridge. Nobody was nominated for taking Khandi Alexander and tearing her apart.

What I am convinced of is if you show an exalted Hollywood view of anybody, black or white, it gets attention. It is regarded as exalted and it is regarded as artifices, and you are all a part of that. You have portrayed glamouring. You make a show about the inner city of Baltimore and anywhere else, and you put the camera on it, these motherfuckers in Hollywood think you're turning the camera on and it is just some weird documentary. It was like there was no sense that we were working to create, that that America that you left behind is deserving of as much attention and craft like that as the other America.

8

KIDS DON'T VOTE

Peruse Ed Burns's career path and you will find a man who has spent a lifetime trying to bring change to institutions where it's difficult to make a dent in the problems, let alone cure the ills wholesale.

Burns served in the infantry during the Vietnam War and worked as a policeman for two decades. He found teaching kids in Baltimore just as frustrating as those vocations, if not as harrowing. He taught at Hamilton Middle School and City College for seven years before departing for The Wire. "I never asked the question again, but I did ask one of my classes how many kids had been shot," Burns said. "It was eleven. One kid had been shot twice, and he was so proud. He's pulling up his shirt." For Burns, teaching became draining. Many of his students were stunted emotionally and mentally, and Burns could not rationalize the expectations that the school system placed on the students versus the realities of what they could handle. He estimated that among his eighth-graders, the students' reading levels ranged from first to sixth grade. "Opportunity is what these kids lack," Burns said. "The path is the corner or the stoop. We're talking about these kids here on the corner. They don't have advocates . . . Corner kids, there's nobody rooting for them. You have to change that world, and where you have to start is ages zero to three. That's the most formative years of your life, and you're not even in charge of it. You got to go back and you got to create institutions that give that child the dignity, the self-respect, the love that he or she needs to go out into the world."

For three seasons, Burns served as an integral architect in creating and outlining The Wire. *Nowhere is his imprint felt more than in Season 4, which critics universally hailed. "*The Wire *keeps getting better, and to my mind it has made the final jump from great TV to classic TV—put it right up there with* The Prisoner *and the first three seasons of* The Sopranos," *Stephen King wrote in a 2007 column for* Entertainment Weekly. *"It's the sort of dramatic cycle people will still be writing and thinking about twenty-five years from now, and given the current state of the world and the nation, that's a good thing. 'There,' our grandchildren will say. 'It wasn't all Simon Cowell.'"*

Each season marked the dysfunction of an institution and that dysfunction's impact on the city and the drug culture. In the political thread, newly minted mayor Tommy Carcetti (Aidan Gillen) decides that the governor's offer of a school bailout would be too damaging to his future political ambitions. The school system's breakdown results in kids being funneled onto the corner, where their real education takes place. The season focuses on the disparate, disheartening paths of four middle school children: Duquan "Dukie" Weems (Jermaine Crawford), Michael Lee (Tristan Mack Wilds), Namond Brice (Julito McCullum), and Randy Wagstaff (Maestro Harrell). They begin innocently enough, before most of the group is confronted with life's bleak realities amid a lack of opportunities and resources. The overwhelmed educators include two familiar faces from the police force, Roland Pryzbylewski (Jim True-Frost), who has turned to teaching after accidentally killing an officer, and Bunny Colvin (Robert Wisdom), who has become a field researcher, trying to offset his diminished pension after being reprimanded for creating Hamsterdam.

ED BURNS (CO-CREATOR): I knew how Season Four was going to be in an instant. I knew how Marlo would hide the bodies. It just comes to you. Once it comes to you, you have to unwrap it. It's like a gift. This is cool, now how do I get there? You have to unwrap it. That's the way I get stories. Once I have the idea, the essence of it, the gift, then you just start playing the characters in your head and you see them. They almost speak to you, and then you pick up bits and pieces and it unfolds. It's really cool sometimes to go out on the set and just watch guys like Andre Royo, those guys doing it, and it makes it like they're projections of my mind. You know what I mean? Strange relationship, but there's always an internal logic. The story has to have an internal logic that drives it, and that way you stay true to the characters.

DENNIS LEHANE (WRITER): On Season Four of *The Wire*, David nailed the thematic line that the entire season drove toward—"kids don't vote"—in the first week.

ED BURNS (CO-CREATOR): In high school, the game is already over. The dropout rate in Baltimore for the high schools in the inner city was approaching sixty, seventy percent. The kids that you want to tell the story about, if you put them in high school, they wouldn't be there. They had already dropped out. Middle school is where you see the biggest graduation ceremony. Kids get all dressed up and they arrive in limousines and all the family is there, because they all know that this is the last graduation they're attending. Middle school, that's where the heartbreak is. These kids don't go on. They just go off to the corner. That's what they're being trained for. It had to be middle school. High school would have felt wrong, real wrong. Today, you could probably do it in elementary, because the ravages of this holocaust has affected kids who are five and six years old in school. They would be too young to be actors. Middle school made all the sense in the world. Besides, I taught in middle school. You go with what you know.

JOE CHAPPELLE (DIRECTOR/CO-EXECUTIVE PRODUCER): Part of it goes back to the casting of the boys. We had to find four distinct character types. When you're following Dukie, you know exactly what he's like and what he looks like. You didn't want to have four kids who looked the same. We struck gold with all those guys. They were fantastic.

ALEXA L. FOGEL (CASTING DIRECTOR): I love those boys. It was a pretty massive undertaking for the amount of time we had. I think we only had about six weeks. So I hired people in different parts of the country. The one thing [that] is true of people in that age group is the cream rises to the top pretty quickly, which is what did happen, and so we were able to kind of narrow it down to about ten kids, then down to finally these four. We did do a big day of auditions in Baltimore with Robert [Chew] also there working with them and mixing and matching them, because so much of what they needed to do wasn't written yet, but it was in David's mind and the minds of all the writers. They knew what the story was going to be. So, we had to do work where we could see enough of what they were capable of, so when the stuff was written, they would be able to stand up to it.

TRISTAN MACK WILDS (MICHAEL LEE): My mom got me hooked on *The Wire.* It was one of the in-house rituals. Every Sunday, my mom would have to turn that on. My older brother would come in from outside, and my dad would watch it. It was one of the shows that kind of, in a weird way, it kept us all together.

I was a fan of Idris, first and foremost. He was the man. Idris and Wood Harris, the men. We didn't have very many shows that looked like what was going on outside of my door, right outside of my window. I grew up in the Stapleton projects, so a lot of stuff they were talking about and touching on, I was seeing and dealing with on a daily basis. To have a show that looks like us and feels like us and speaks in the same language as us, and you get to see both sides—you see [that] the cops aren't always good guys and the bad guys aren't necessarily quote-unquote bad guys. It was an amazing juxtaposition to always watch, and kept us on our toes just being able to see what was going on in the quote-unquote real life that *The Wire* was portraying.

JULITO MCCULLUM (NAMOND BRICE): A week or two weeks before my audition for *The Wire,* my mom, we went to another audition. At the audition, they wanted to get to know me, so they asked me a few questions, and one of the questions was, what's my favorite TV show? At that time, I was a young kid, really didn't watch much TV, so I asked my mom, like, "Mom, what do I put?" She said, "Put *The Wire.*" I was like, "What's *The Wire?*" She's like, "It's a really great show on HBO." She started telling me a little bit about it, and then she said, "If they ever got kids on the show, yo, it'll be great." Then, a week after, I went on the audition for *The Wire.*

MAESTRO HARRELL (RANDY WAGSTAFF): I knew a lot of people who loved it and watched it. At the time, I was thirteen, fourteen. Not only did it come on a little late because I had school and whatnot, also there was no HBOGo at the time or even Netflix. Was Netflix even around at the time?

JERMAINE CRAWFORD (DUQUAN "DUKIE" WEEMS): I wasn't old enough to even watch the show. I had no idea what I was getting into. I was just super excited to be cursing, and my mom was okay with it.

JULITO MCCULLUM (NAMOND BRICE): I was always Namond. I actually was the first kid to be casted, and when I went in for Namond, that was the day I booked the role. I think the first audition I went on, I was very calm and collected. Namond had just resonated for me, growing up in Brooklyn and in the projects, and my dad also being a drug dealer before he had his demise. It just resonated with me, the character.

TRISTAN MACK WILDS (MICHAEL LEE): Actually, my first audition was for [the part of] Randy [Wagstaff]. I went in for Randy and got pretty far, probably went through three or four auditions for Randy. It just got to the point where, after sitting in front of Ed Burns and David Simon and Robert Chew, God rest his soul, me at that age, I was too big for Randy. We ended all the auditions there, and I thought that was the end. Like, I thought, *Okay, it's a wrap. I'm not going to be on the show that me and my mom watch every Sunday. It's a wrap.* But, eventually, they called back, and when they called back, they were like, "We want to call you for another role. We don't know how it's going to go. Just come in. Just do the audition and we'll see from there."

JULITO MCCULLUM (NAMOND BRICE): I kind of lived the life like that where I was the kid in the class who liked to get the attention, who was probably the class clown. To see what had came from my life, personally, to know that I had the opportunity to portray a character like that and not live that life anymore, but I've got another success where I'm portraying a character like that, it was like, "Wow. I really came really far." I was like that as a kid. I was a Namond in the classroom.

JERMAINE CRAWFORD (DUQUAN "DUKIE" WEEMS): I auditioned for [the part of] Michael, and Michael took me all the way up to the end, and then it became Dukie. That was that. But I think that it worked out exactly the way that it was supposed to.

TRISTAN MACK WILDS (MICHAEL LEE): One of the conversations from Ed that I remember the absolute most, it was during my audition. We've had deep, intellectual conversations and we've had ones where he'll say a few words that will stick with you for the rest of your life. This is one of the joints that stick with you for the rest of your life. I was in the middle of the auditions, and it was kind of the last audition for the character of Michael, and it was me and one other kid that they had auditioning for Michael. Julito had already got the part for Namond. And I think Maestro was there, and Jermaine was there as well. I was in the audition room. I did the audition, and then they said, "We're going to give you a second and then we want you to come back and do the audition again."

Ed pulled me out. He's kind of sitting there, kind of just thinking. He said, "Less is more. Remember that for the rest of your life. Anything that you apply. With Michael, especially this character, less is always more. The less you do, the more everybody will feel it. Because we're so prone to seeing so much. With acting, with life, whatever. We're so prone to seeing so much more. But when there's less, the mystery behind it, it leaves people guessing. It feels so much more. So, just remember that when you're going back into this room and you're reading those lines. Less is more." We went back in and we nailed it. But just those words guided me through my entire career, through my life. It's just one of those things that I always keep in the back of my head. I always have him saying it in the back of my head, whenever I need it.

MAESTRO HARRELL (RANDY WAGSTAFF): Ed was like how almost like [Albus] Dumbledore does to Harry Potter. He would tell us things that I don't know if we were necessarily supposed to catch on to, but then they would probably really affect the decisions we made acting-wise. He's that guy. He's that intelligent where he can talk to you about something and then just plant an idea, but it's your idea. Like [in] *Inception.* He's a genius.

JERMAINE CRAWFORD (DUQUAN "DUKIE" WEEMS): Ed Burns, when we were filming some of the scenes, I remember he pulled me to the side and said, "Some of the kids in this room are real-life Dukies." It was that moment when it was just kind of like, *Wow. Oh, my gosh. These kids are like me. They are me.*

I would literally put myself in his shoes. I can remember it vividly, the eviction scene. The shit was out there. When you're younger, your imagination is so wild. They put me in the clothes. They put me in the hair and makeup. I was in hair and makeup for forty-five minutes every day, longer than everybody, because they had to make me look like shit each day, literally. It had an effect on me. My skin started breaking out. My hair was nappy all the time. I couldn't cut my hair. Everybody else could.

SEITH MANN (DIRECTOR): The thing about that scene [where the girl student slices the other girl's face] that really struck me, was Dukie and the fan. After this girl does this horrific thing, Dukie is reaching out with this fan in this sweet way. It was profound to me, seeing Dukie and the way he goes in the story. One of the things that makes everything so tragic about that season is that you get to know these kids and you fall in love with them, and we're not going to save them because it's a TV show. No, we're going to let things go south. We're going to show you life, because sometimes life doesn't save the kids, and they don't [get saved] in Baltimore all the time.

Seeing someone in the midst of all that chaos, for him to zero in on this girl and try to extend this gesture of kindness, of sweetness that can't really be articulated, was poetic. Even in the midst of all this madness, there's this sweet soul trying to touch somebody else and knowing the rest of the season and how he gets lost on his way, to a certain extent, is why I think that season is so powerful. Just having an inherently good heart does not help you when you're in certain circumstances. That's tragic.

GEORGE PELECANOS (WRITER/PRODUCER): Ed brought a lot of this stuff to the table. Ed, he's got all the experience in the world. He's a Vietnam veteran, a combat veteran, twenty-something years in the force, public school teacher in Baltimore right after that. I mean, you see where a lot of this stuff came from.

ED BURNS (CO-CREATOR): Here's the secret to teaching, [as] with anything else: If you blame yourself for the mistakes, you can only get better. If you blame the outside world, the kid, the person you're working with, if you blame them, you'll never get better. So, you're, *Why did I fuck that up? What can I do better?* If that's the driving energy, you come to the next day revved up and ready to go, *Let's see if this works.*

ERIC OVERMYER (WRITER): I was impressed by how much Ed Burns brought to the project. His experience in the Baltimore middle schools was really crucial. You can't touch David when it comes to city politics and issues of criminal justice and the drug war. He's very eloquent. He's very well versed. It wasn't that he didn't know about the middle schools, but Ed had hands-on experience. Many of the stories in Season Four really come out of Ed's experience. Oddly enough, Richard Price had some teaching experiences, too, and there was stuff from his experience that ended up in the show as well.

JIM TRUE-FROST (DET. ROLAND "PREZ" PRYZBYLEWSKI): His having played that role in real life and making that career switch was just like a constant resource available to me. I talked to Ed a lot. It's difficult to point to any particular tip he gave me. It's more just asking him for stories and observing how he talked about it and the emotional experience. It's like what comes through when you talk to Ed, and [what] comes through in the script, is his deep anger about the injustice of the situation, with kids in school who should have every opportunity that any kid gets, but who get so cheated and just happened to be born into the wrong zip code. I think it's the anger and also the sadness. He watched kids like Dukie. He watched kids like Michael, and he befriended them and helped them.

There's a sense of loss, and this isn't some sort of overleaning liberal pity party—it's just a human connection of being with those people, watching them grow, and watching most of them just cling to this track that they're in with no chance of getting out, no matter how much you give to them, no matter how much you pour into the job of being the teacher that they're with from nine a.m. to three p.m. I think from both Ed and my wife [a former high school teacher and now a law professor], that both anger and sadness is what I took away, both as a human and as an actor playing Prez, I was able to take away and process and use.

CHRIS COLLINS (STAFF WRITER): We were showing a failure at a very early stage in the lives of children that ultimately made them easy targets to recruit into the drug gang or to perpetuate a cycle of violence.

So, for me, Season Four really tried to get to the root of problems of why this is happening and to shine a light on how bad the schools are. It was a really great sort of accurate light into what some of the problems are in the inner city and how kids are being left behind at a very early age. People don't tend to talk about it a lot out in the real world. We used to talk about it in a way where people are paying attention.

For me, following in the tracks of those four kids and starting out as friends and then bifurcating their journeys was very interesting to me—how, like, for instance, Michael became sort of the next Marlo or Omar, the next guy that's going to run a crew and all that stuff. And seeing someone like Randy Wagstaff end up in social services, and Dukie unable to escape his situation at home, and then Namond, how his father was in prison and his mother, her version of love was getting him a pair of Nikes. It just offered all these various windows into these kids' lives. Kids that experience or grew up in that part of town or any urban area will be able to identify with those characters, whether they themselves have become those characters or if they knew someone. It just made them human. Despite the things that you were witnessing, let's say Michael with Snoop and Chris Partlow, being recruited by them for Marlo, how can you resist it if you're a kid growing up in that neighborhood and you have these larger-than-life figures paying attention to you when nobody else is?

SEITH MANN (DIRECTOR): When we were shooting the episode, there were parts that we had [where] kids come in and audition in the casting office. Then there were some of the smaller parts, just one line or two here or there. We were having a bunch of kids show up, so we figured, *We'll cast it in a day. Before we shoot, we'll have some of the kids come read and we'll pick the best ones. There's going to be two hundred, three hundred kids there.* Some of the kids would come in to read the sides, and some of the kids couldn't read the sides.

They're all seventh, eighth, ninth grade. They're students, but some of them didn't have basic reading fundamentals. It was so heartbreaking. I don't think I'm completely naïve about the world and how fucked up it is in the inner city. At the same time, I was being confronted with kids that are thirteen, fourteen years old who couldn't read language that was written basically like how they talked. It wasn't big words. It was like, "Pass me this," or something. I don't remember the dialogue, but it was sad. It was like, "Okay, I got to cast the kid that can read the lines." For me, it just really cemented how important it was for David and everybody to be telling this story.

Against betting odds, The Wire *had returned for a fourth season, but it would mark its reappearance largely without Dominic West, considered as much a star as any among the ensemble cast. West, who had a young daughter in England, was homesick and expressing increasing frustration at playing a character he felt he had taken to his full depths. He yearned to be a movie star, and his name had been thrown in as a possibility to be cast as the next James Bond. West's fellow cast members staged what amounted to an intervention. They pleaded that they needed West, needed McNulty, to finish a story that they had all striven and sacrificed for since the beginning. To placate West, Simon and Noble agreed that his role could be greatly diminished in Season 4—McNulty was reduced to a domesticated beat cop—but they needed him back and fully engaged for Season 5. West agreed, and signed a contract that included a stipulation that he could direct a Season 5 episode.*

DAVID SIMON (CREATOR): [Dominic West] had a life back home. He was having a kid. He was in exile in Baltimore. We had to make accommodations in Season Four to travel him and shoot him out a couple episodes at a time. The other people who were sort of disciplining of him, Andre and Sonja and Seth, are the people who'd be like, "Okay, Mr. Lead Actor Guy. You'll get work, but we're doing work here that matters to us. Strap on a helmet. Get on the team." They actually had a couple of moments of taking him out drinking, taking him by the shoulders and shaking him, which was actually great for morale, because he responded to that. When you're in the middle of doing something that long—it's five years—it's easy to think, *I'm not seeing it*. It's hard for anybody to see it, when you're getting one script at a time. He was being asked to go on faith. He doesn't know how it's going to end, whether or not we have a clue or a plan. We had to talk him back into the boat a couple years. I told him we had to finish the story, and he did. As we got toward the end, by the time he saw Season Four on the air, that came to an end. But at the end of three seasons, he just wanted to go home.

DOMINIC WEST (DET. JIMMY MCNULTY): I asked, stupidly—because I think it's the best season—but I did ask him in Three, I said, "You've got to give me a bit of a break," and he said, "Okay, we'll shoot you out in three weeks." I think I did it in three weeks. He said, "We'll do all your stuff in three weeks, and you can take a break as long as you come back for Season Five." Yes, I agreed to that—and managed to talk my way out of the best season of all, I think, like an idiot.

CLARKE PETERS (DET. LESTER FREAMON): Playing the same character for seven years of your life can take its toll, man. You're a family man. You're trying to get your life together. You've got to spend a lot of time away from your family. He had a young daughter who he loves. I do remember having one talk with him, basically that "this is our gig. This is what we signed up for. Let's get through it, and then it'll be all right on the other side of it. Sometimes it's the piece that makes you that also breaks you. You may not want to be McNulty. I may not want to be Lester, or it might get boring or tiring to answer the same questions and all of that, but you know what? If it wasn't for these characters, we wouldn't be where we are in our careers today. You at least give respect to that. At the beginning of this journey, you were very enthusiastic about it, so remember the days of thy youth. Just hold on to that."

I may have had a talk with most of the company. I seem to be the person everyone wants to talk their problems out with. Somewhere along the line, I think Clarke and Lester got mixed up.

ANDRE ROYO (REGINALD "BUBBLES" COUSINS): You just get burned out. You're just like, "I can't. I don't know what else to do. I can't do it anymore." He felt like he wanted to do movies. He was tired of being away. He's far away from London, from his family, being in Baltimore. We love Baltimore now, but sometimes you just want to go home. You want to work and, after work, go home, be a family. He was burned out. He was done. He had some movies that were coming out. I think it was *Mona Lisa Smile* or *The Forgotten* or some shit. He's like, "I'd rather do that world." He didn't want to come back. Again, we got canceled. HBO said the show was over. We're not like a network. We don't get to come back. Three years is a good run. It's a good run for the show. It did its course. HBO was like, "How are you going to tell a story without Stringer Bell?" David Simon was like, "If that's how you feel, listen, release everybody's contract. Let me send you a couple of scripts and see how you feel."

We all got released. I came out here in LA and I was like, "Hey wifey, let's go to LA. Let's figure it out." She was having it because I can always come back and do *Law & Order.* I moved to LA. I was testing for *My Name Is Earl.* I might have been Crabman. I got a call from David, like, "Yo, I sent them a couple of scripts. They want us back." I was like, "Oh, shit. Really?" I was about to test for this network show. David was like, "Listen, you're not under contract. If you don't want to come back, I understand. I get it. We had a good run, but our story's not over." I was like, "Shit." I didn't get the part for Crabman, because it might have been a harder decision. You're talking network for a different type of money, but it's also a pilot. Then I just got hit with a flashback at that point. We had lost Bob Colesberry. We had lost a great editor in Geraldine Peroni. She passed away. We had it mapped out for five seasons. We wanted to tell our story. We had to finish it. I went back. I know Dom didn't want to come back. Again, we felt like it was an obligation to the storytelling, to Baltimore, to the people that we played, and to ourselves to finish this journey for all the people, all [the] behind-the-scenes actors who gave us their time, that worked on it. It'd been selfish for us to not finish the story.

Each season of The Wire *carries a theme, and each season starts with a metaphor. Season 4's cold open highlights Felicia "Snoop" Pearson, who popped up intermittently the previous season. The show's creators urged Pearson to become serious with regard to acting. The open would test her dedication. It features the androgynous Pearson purchasing a nail gun that the fictional Snoop and Chris Partlow will use to lock up the vacant buildings where they detachedly stored dead bodies. She listens intently during the hardware store employee's detailed pitch in describing the power and recoil abilities of various nail guns—the moral being that one can be educated if the curriculum actually applies to his or her life. The employee describes a .27 caliber charge as "not large ballistically, but for driving nails, it's enough." His gleeful expression slowly transforms at Snoop's response: "Man, shit. I seen a tiny-ass .22 round-nose drop a nigga plenty of days, man. Motherfuckers get up in you like a pinball, rip your ass up. Big joints, though . . . Big joints, man, just break your bones, you say, 'Fuck it.' I'm gonna go with this right here, man. How much do I owe you?" In an* Entertainment Weekly *column, Stephen King crowned Snoop "perhaps the most terrifying female villain to ever appear in a television series. When you think of Chris and Snoop, think of John Allen Muhammad and Lee Boyd Malvo, only smart. And with a nail gun."*

DENNIS LEHANE (WRITER): The episode where Snoop shops for a cordless screwdriver at Home Depot. That made everyone's jaw drop.

DAVID SIMON (CREATOR): We'd let her be off book. We let her sort of get her own words. But that was a very specific metaphor about education. I wanted her to say the words of it. I remember going to her and saying, "Look. You're an incredible presence, and we hired you because you're an incredible presence and you're very real, but the question for you now is: Do you want to be a professional actor? Because this is the transition, because I have no doubt that you can be yourself in front of the camera. You've been doing it now for three or four episodes. You did well last year, but here's a moment where if I'm going to rely on you to carry a bigger burden on the story, then I need to know that when I send pages, the pages will prevail and that you'll find a way to say what's on the page and make it your own and make it real. That is acting. It's going to require work and it's going to require struggle. It's not going to come naturally. Nothing comes naturally that's this complicated. It doesn't mean you don't have talent. It means this is going to require work."

She looked at those three pages and she was like, "Damn. I got to know all this word by word?" I was like, "Look. Good news, it's not a stage play. We can get it in pieces, but we're going to get it." We had to run up. The first few takes were a struggle, but by the end, we had all of it. I was so proud of her. I was so proud of her. Little did I know she was getting glossies made and she was finding an agent and she was like, "What do I have to do to be professional?" She did not take that opportunity and piss it away. She really committed to it. That was her true test as an actor. Everything up to then was just her being herself on camera. That was her reading scenes and conveying somebody else's idea fully. I was nervous about it. Nina [Noble] was like, "We're going to be there all day." But we weren't. It took a little bit of time, but we were not there all day. She got it.

FELICIA "SNOOP" PEARSON: At first, I didn't get it, because that was my second season or whatever. But the writers and the producers was like, "Man, you the first face everybody gonna see. This a real big deal." So, I was like, "Word?" Then everybody was like, "Yeah, Snoop. It's a big deal." I still was humble, but I was excited. That scene right there, I think that only took us like two hours, and that's with them setting everything up, every angle or whatever. Took like, let's say three hours. It was a very fun scene.

JOE CHAPPELLE (DIRECTOR/CO-EXECUTIVE PRODUCER): We shot it, and the guy she played off against, the salesman, was really good, too. But she was so nervous that first day. She just kept rushing through her lines. You could tell she was very, very nervous. So, we did the scene, and then we looked at it and we decided to bring her back, and we reshot her coverage. The first pass at it didn't work. It was one of those rare times in television when you do get to go back, because it was the season premiere. *Let's make it work. We believe in her. We think she can do it. Let's get her to take another whack at it.*

We went back and we replicated the whole hardware store, and she nailed it because she was that much more comfortable with it. She was so nervous, which you just wouldn't expect from her. Her whole persona is very laid-back and very sort of in control. But then she got nervous and got a little flustered.

METHOD MAN (CALVIN "CHEESE" WAGSTAFF): That's what I want. I want a scene where it stands out like that where it's just a scene where people always talk about that shit. That was her meat and potatoes right there. That's what showed everybody, yeah, she's got some presence. Even before that, but that was like, "Here, this is for you. You're opening the show. This is like the cold open and it's all about you: one, two, three, go." And she nailed that shit.

TRAY CHANEY (MALIK "POOT" CARR): Snoop is still that reflection and that example. That's the real Baltimore when you think about Baltimore. Some of that stuff, Snoop wasn't faking. That was real. That was real life.

KWAME PATTERSON ("MONK" METCALF): Everything you see pretty much on *The Wire* is pretty much how I was on the streets. The same way. I was a different person then—not during *The Wire*, but when

I was younger. Now, I laugh and I joke around a lot. I play around, where, back then, I was real serious. I was mean. I was always paranoid, always keeping my head on a swivel type of thing. So, literally, I just brought all that to the character of Monk.

ANWAN GLOVER (SLIM CHARLES): Getting up every day with my older brother, he was in it, in the street life. In my neighborhood, getting up as a little kid, one day, going to school, saw a dead body by the trash can, get out of school and the dead body's still right there, with the yellow tape. I know how to adapt to those different situations, and then on *The Wire*, the last episodes, my little brother was murdered. And I had to shoot those scenes with me coping with my mom pulling her hair out, and producers and the writers are like, "Anwan, do you want to sit back for a minute?" I said, "Na, I've gotta keep pushing. I can't take no time back." Because I probably would have went crazy. But they were always in my corner with everything.

JULITO MCCULLUM (NAMOND BRICE): We were very intimidated by the adults and the returning cast. We were extremely intimidated. When I saw Chad [Coleman], I was like, "Oh, wow." I hadn't watched up until we started shooting. It was funny, after we did *Hack*, I would see Chad. We lived in the same neighborhood as well, so I would see Chad riding his bike sometimes, and we'd always stop and talk because he was like my first scene partner ever. *Hack* was one of my first jobs. When I saw him in *The Wire*, I was like, "Wow. This is home."

TRISTAN MACK WILDS (MICHAEL LEE): Chad, in one of my Off-Broadway plays, played my dad. So, there was already a dynamic there that we had. When I finally came around and we did *The Wire*, we kind of just kept it going. But it was crazy to play. This is two characters that are very reserved, very to themselves. They handle their own business. They go about their own way. But it was one of those things where I think you saw Chad's character trying to be more than that through Michael. He saw himself in Michael, the good and the bad.

He wanted to do what he could to try to keep him from the bad. But there are some things that are inevitable.

MICHAEL KOSTROFF (MAURICE "MAURY" LEVY): I once told Chad that he was playing this man of very few words, who kept everything inside, but it felt like there was an opera going on inside of his head. He said, "Oh yeah. There's a lot going on in there."

CHAD L. COLEMAN (DENNIS "CUTTY" WISE): I didn't have a choice. David wasn't writing monologues for me. Of course, that is the nature of the man, and that's partly what makes him incredibly compelling, is that he is not a master of language, but he has a lot going on inside. That was what Cutty was about: uplifting and not destroying. I think more than anything—we didn't explore it—but I think he had a prison experience that was what we would wish for anybody. Somewhere in there, he began to hear something different. That's not to jump to say he's Malcolm X. It's to say, in a very real way, that's one of the things that allows a person to change.

I think he met some knowledge and enlightenment that helped him really make a seismic change, and I think that's something we all can be proud of, and I know for a fact that the majority of the guys in our community come from his ilk as opposed to just rampantly saying, "I'm the gangbanger. Whoo-hoo, here we go." I was proud to take that on because so many people just have a difficult time seeing that these guys want to change. Some people don't, but many of them do. These guys who would normally be men of few words and who posture a lot, come out and be vulnerable and just want to come out and give you a pound and a hug and pound their chest and say, "Man, thank you. Thank you for representing me." That's a major experience for me.

JONNIE BROWN (OFF. EDDIE WALKER): Walker [a crooked African-American police officer who terrorizes black kids in the show], that was one of the hardest roles that I ever did, ever had. It's actually one of my most notorious roles on film and television. A lot of people remember me from that, but I gotta tell you, it started to get to me, around the third or fourth episode. I started to go to the writers. And I went to David and I just said, "Guys, what I'm doing in this character is completely outrageous. You got me in this completely dark *Twilight Zone*. Is there any redemption?" Because, from one episode to the other, they don't tell you what's going to happen. They themselves don't really know. They have an idea, but they change it at the last minute. It just started to mentally affect me. It really did. It was such a dark force, this character. And I went to them twice. I went to them twice, like, "Look guys. I mean, what is this guy doing? He's like the Terminator."

These are kids. I'm on set, literally having this debate. Like, these are kids. And they finally kind of opened up, and they said, "Jonnie, listen, the guy you're playing is actually based on a real officer, and right now we can't tell you too much, but he's on trial. Just know that you're doing everybody a service by going there, by taking these extremes." They were saying this stuff just to keep me going. "Don't let him blink. Don't let him say, 'You know, I've had enough of this.'" It was tough. I really can't stress enough how hard that role was, especially the scene where I had to do the car chase and I ultimately catch up with the kid [Donut, portrayed by Nathan Corbett] and create one of the most memorable moments on the show. That's what people tell me. They say that that scene was crazy, when I broke the kid's fingers. That was hard. That was pretty tough. I think, when we got done shooting that, we were all silent. There was no clapping. They watched it on playback, and they're like, "Holy crap."

JERMAINE CRAWFORD (DUQUAN "DUKIE" WEEMS): Because me and Julito are so cool now, I can say this, but we fucking hated each other. Oh my God, we hated each other. But it was so crazy because the dynamics of our characters was really our real dynamic. It was just kind of by circumstance. Like, me and Tristan were very close immediately, and he was kind of always like a caretaker. Julito was always talking shit. Maestro was just like, "Aw, whatever. I'm here."

We were literally our characters. You have no idea. But I think it was at the end of Season Four, Julito and I started to develop a really dope friendship, and to this day we keep in touch, got kids, speak, and we're really fond of each other.

JULITO MCCULLUM (NAMOND BRICE): I wouldn't say "hated." Just the dynamic: you were putting four kids together. Just me and Tristan had met, but we really didn't know one another. We were all new on the show. We didn't know each other. I was coming from New York, Jermaine from Maryland, Maestro all the way from Chicago. Maestro was the vet in a sense, because he had been working for many years before that. That dynamic was tricky. Then the long schedules and tutoring. We would have to mix in our long shooting schedules with trying to get work in with the tutor. That was extremely hard. We had our moments. We had our moments, and we were kids doing the main characters of a TV show that was one of the biggest shows in the world at the time. All that led us to have some moments.

SANDI MCCREE (DE'LONDA BRICE): When I was in Cleveland, I would go in the community and work with different social service agencies using drama-based activities to deal with some issues with kids. In this group of girls, we were talking subjects from sex to school to who they lived with.

This little girl came in and she had the word *bitch* in her nose ring. I said, "I'm not comfortable with that. Could you take it out?" She said, "No, my mother said not to take this out of my nose." I said, "Call your mother. I don't want you wearing this in here giving energy." She called her mother. Her mother came up right away to talk to me. I said, "My name is Sandi McCree, and I just want your daughter to take the earring out of her nose." She said, "Why? I bought it for her. She's a bitch. She ain't nothing but a bitch, and that's why she has it." I was like, "Well, I'm not comfortable, and we're trying to make smarter choices." She said, "Just take the damn thing out. Take it out. Take it out. Goddamn. Take it out. Give it to me before you lose it, because it's fourteen karats."

I was trembling on the inside because I could see why this girl inside my group was trying to act all tough, but when her mother came up, she was just broken down, nothing. She tries to be her mother when her mother was not around. I said, "Okay, thank you." And I told the mom what I was trying to do. I said, "We're trying to teach them about healthy choices, not getting involved so early with sex. These kids, they don't know about healthy relationships, you know, we've got to hug our kids more." She said, "I ain't hugging her. I ain't no lesbian."

This was the craziest, nastiest, ignorant—if I could have been De'Londa in real life, I would have smacked her ass. That's where De'Londa came from. This mother didn't have a clue about being a mother. She just carried that child in her womb, but she didn't know anything about love, and she wasn't passing on anything about love to that girl. My backstory for De'Londa was that hard bitterness. That's the only world that she knows. She goes at it hard, and she thinks she's being the best mother she knows how. I have made up that the reason Wee-Bey was loyal to her was that they met in foster care and they made their own little family. They created the strength, even though it was dysfunctional. They were trying to be a family because they never had a real one.

JULITO McCULLUM (NAMOND BRICE): The first time I met Sandi, I was like, *This is the nicest lady I probably ever met.* It was at either a table read or rehearsal, and when they said, "Action," and she turned into De'Londa, I was like, "What?" It was night and day. Sandi's the nicest person ever. Her talent is remarkable because she's able to turn it on and off.

ROBERT WISDOM (HOWARD "BUNNY" COLVIN): She is a sweetheart, and she played the hell out of that bitch.

In The Wire, *Proposition Joe serves as one of the final vestiges to the old way of doing things. As the drug kingpin of Baltimore's East Side, he is a chess master, always one or two moves ahead of his opponents until finally being cornered by Marlo. The character, played by Robert Chew, serves the storyline capably and provides memorable lines. In one such moment, he tells Omar that "a businessman such as myself does not believe in bad blood with a man such as yourself. It disturbs the sleep." Behind the scenes, Chew played a pivotal role in* The Wire. *He taught acting to children at Baltimore's Arena Players theater troupe, and many of his young protégées were cast in Season 4. "Whenever I had to dig deep and find kids who not only had the talent but the reality and the belief," Pat Moran, the Baltimore casting director, told* The Baltimore Sun, *"kids who didn't look like the ones in a Jell-O commercial, I called Robert." Chew also worked intimately, individually and collectively, with the four main kids cast for Season 4: Jermaine Crawford, Maestro Harrell, Julito McCullum, and Tristan Mack Wilds. Chew died of heart failure in 2013 at the age of fifty-two. "I don't think Robert Chew realized how good he was," said S. Robert Morgan, who played Butchie on the show. "I really don't. He was spectacular. What you have to understand is that what you saw in Prop Joe was so far from what Robert Chew really is. He is the most soft-spoken, understated person I have ever met."*

ERNEST DICKERSON (DIRECTOR): Season Four was when we worked with the kids. It was really amazing, because from the earlier episode and then going back later for the later episode, just seeing the growth in those kids, seeing how much they had learned. The person that was coaching them every day was Robert Chew. He was teaching them how to break down a script. He really taught those kids really, really well. By the time the last episode came around, they were like seasoned pros. Even Snoop, she was a seasoned pro by that time. She was helping new people on the set, helping them get acclimatized and getting used to being on set, giving them advice. It was a very fertile playground for the actors.

JERMAINE CRAWFORD (DUQUAN "DUKIE" WEEMS): I probably would not have gotten the role if it wasn't for Robert Chew. I remember it was down to the screen test, and we all were kind of battling for roles, and they were switching us in and out, and after I went in and did my first take, they had their notes, but he pulled me to the side. He said, "Look, Jermaine. You can really get this role. I need you to focus. I need you to lock in. I need you to pull from within. I need you to think about what you're saying." I went in and then, a week later, I got the call. And, of course, when we got every script, he would rehearse with us, so we would have our act together by the time it was ready to go up on camera.

JULITO MCCULLUM (NAMOND BRICE): Honestly, that first meeting we had, where we were all there and we met him, I came into this situation very nervous, very afraid that I wouldn't do the job correctly, even though I knew I was confident in Namond's character. I came in just wanting to do it right. I was a kid and I wasn't sure of myself. Robert was there. He was assigned, in a sense, to be with us throughout this journey and to make sure that we did these roles correctly and we brought the true Baltimore kids in. Because of his work with the children of Baltimore, he was the best guy for the job.

From the first day on, he was giving me advice and ideas on what the psyche of Namond is. That was just really a breath of fresh air to be with him and to be with him on the entire journey, because anytime I needed support, anytime I wasn't sure of myself, he was always there to say the right thing, to guide me in the right direction. I'm very grateful for Robert. I don't know if we could've done justice to the roles like we did without Robert, honestly.

JERMAINE CRAWFORD (DUQUAN "DUKIE" WEEMS): Tristan and me, Maestro, and Julito, we wanted to see the sex scene with Sonja Sohn, Kima, so we watched that. Other than that, that's the only thing I saw of the show before shooting.

JULITO MCCULLUM (NAMOND BRICE): We snuck and watched it, and we were like, "Oh . . . okay." It was cool. We had met Kima. We met pretty much all the cast members, but we didn't know who they were, so we didn't really know their characters. Then when we saw that. Yeah, it was a good time.

JERMAINE CRAWFORD (DUQUAN "DUKIE" WEEMS): There's film in the production office, and the production office wasn't too far from set. We would go to school in one of the office rooms. They had a room, and we got our hands on a DVD, because I believe one of them had seen it or heard about it. And lo and behold, we were all changed that day.

TRISTAN MACK WILDS (MICHAEL LEE): We all watched it and was like, "Holy shit." Now, of course, I had already seen it, but I'm young. So, that's one of the scenes that, when it comes up, my mom was covering my eyes. So, I really didn't get how deep or how graphic it was. It was always funny. My mom is more okay with me seeing somebody get shot on the show than actually letting me watch people have sex, which I still talk to her about today. "Mom, I can watch Stringer Bell get killed, but I couldn't watch Kima's sex scene? I couldn't do that? You wouldn't let me?"

MAESTRO HARRELL (RANDY WAGSTAFF): The one question that never gets old: "Oh man, so when you were shooting it, did you know?" That's one thing I can definitely say. We never got scripts early. I never get tired of answering that, because it's just like, "No, I did not know." I was thirteen. I was dealing with thirteen-year-old stuff, and I was a part of a show of that magnitude with some incredible actors, and no, I did not know it was going to be what it turned out to be. Even a lot of times people will say, "Oh, man. Season Four is my favorite." Even then, it's like, "Wow, that's amazing." Not just me. We all did something, all the kids, on a show that had already been running. We added something to it, and it already was an incredible show.

ROBERT WISDOM (HOWARD "BUNNY" COLVIN): That fourth season, when we were in the schools, there were three fields that spun into being. You had Jim True-Frost's world with the kids upstairs. You had our world with the kids downstairs, special needs kids. Then you had the world with the kids on the streets when they went home and what they went back to.

ED BURNS (CO-CREATOR): I was at Hamilton Middle School. After the first year, our test results hovered between one percent and three percent. I went to the principal. She was an open-minded woman. I said, "I had this idea between the stoop kid and the corner kid." She says, "First off, I don't like those terminologies. Can we think of something else?" I said, "I just have something here for you: acclimated and unacclimated." "How do we decide that?" I said, "It's very simple. The kid that can sit in the chair, he's acclimated, and if he can't sit in the chair, he's not acclimated."

And we divide the class up into acclimated and unacclimated. The unacclimated was about maybe ten percent to fifteen percent of the class of two hundred and something kids. We had the most experienced teachers working with them. My team, which was all young people, worked with the vast majority of the kids. Our classrooms were small, but we'd have like thirty-five to forty in a classroom. The other teachers had like five. We spent the whole summer preparing all sorts of ideas and getting small grants and stuff like that. The other team, they were experienced, so they didn't have to learn anything. In the two years that we went with these kids—we looped seventh through eighth—we got almost ninety percent of the kids in our group into special programs around the city that were for advanced kids. Our scores went up through the roof, and they shut the program down. They called it racist. All the kids were black and most of the teachers were black, but there was some white teachers, myself included, that were pioneering working with this, and the unacclimated kids ran riot over their teachers. That's the group I wanted to be with, because that's the kids I love, but I got the acclimated kids. The results were truly unbelievable, and when they shut the program down, that's when I left the school and I went over to the City College, which is a high school.

That's where I saw the greatest tragedy, because all the kids coming into City College and Poly, the two magnet schools in Baltimore city—Poly is the math/science, and City is the humanities—the kids coming into City College, from kindergarten all the way through eighth grade, were straight-A students. When they walked in my classroom, they couldn't write. They didn't comprehend what they were reading, but they were very, very quiet, and they went through eight years of middle school and elementary school being the good kids. We had lots of tears in the classroom, frustration. I went to the principal and said, "If we could do this, this, this, and this . . ." "We don't do it. We don't do that." Most of the kids that graduated from City went to bullshit colleges and were home after six months, five months, because they were homesick. They were insecure. They didn't have the skills. And that, to me, is a betrayal.

ROBERT WISDOM (HOWARD "BUNNY" COLVIN): In the restaurant scene, watching these kids who were larger than life back home, they just become tiny when they were in this room where they couldn't read the codes anymore.

JULITO MCCULLUM (NAMOND BRICE): Honestly, exactly how I played Namond was how I was in that scene. Myself, personally, I had no idea what the lady was saying. It was very real. They casted the extras perfectly. On the other side of the restaurant, it was the actual restaurant happening. The actual business was still going. When I looked at the menu, because I think they had asked us if we wanted to eat, I looked at the menu, I had no idea what was on the menu. It was very real. It was very real. Scenes like that—I didn't realize how important they were until I was older.

DAN ATTIAS (DIRECTOR): When Randy gets called to the principal's office and the principal is going to call his [foster mother] for the fact that he stood outside the bathroom while a girl inside was having sex and now she's saying it was rape, he's desperately trying to convince her not to call. She says, "I'm sorry. I'm going to call." He keeps offering up things. He says, "I can tell you about this and I can tell you about that." Then he says, "I can tell you about a murder."

I knew in that moment that that was kind of key to his whole downfall and the whole rest of the season, because he was going to be known as a snitch. That scene, by the way I was doing it with a child actor, which has always presented its own set of issues, but he was a really good kid and a really fine actor. As he offers up these sacrificial offerings, "I can tell you about this. I can tell you about that," just before he says, "I can tell you about a murder," I wanted him to have a catch in his voice, like some weird thing, way beyond his years, however old he is. He just knows that this is going to be a turning point. He catches himself for just an instant. But then his own need for survival and not to be sent back to the home requires him to blurt it out. I thought it was so great, because it just set up somewhere, this kid knew that this was going to turn everything, even before the audience knew that this was going to play such an important thing.

MAESTRO HARRELL (RANDY WAGSTAFF): I obviously knew that it was something he shouldn't be saying, just because Street Etiquette 101 is that you don't talk or snitch about anything. That being said, I still didn't know that things were going to turn out the way that they did post that episode. It was kind of funny, too, because I remember when I first even got the scripts, and I was like, "Oh wait. My house gets burned down. Whoa, whoa, whoa. This is all moving a little too fast. What the hell is going on right here?" It's kind of funny how that worked out, because I knew that it was something that he probably shouldn't have been doing, but I just thought it was going to be nothing more than some small repercussions, then he goes back to selling candy or whatever was popping at the time.

JAMIE HECTOR (MARLO STANFIELD): I created a backstory for [Marlo], and it was very similar with Michael's upbringing and his being an old soul and him being responsible and the trauma that he faced with his mother and everything that he has to see and visualize. For instance, Marlo's mother was very promiscuous, and she had relations with different men back to back every night. He would see this and walk in on it, which forced him to actually stay outside more as he had a chance to. In staying outside more, hanging around with the older folks, he developed that old soul, that old wisdom of the streets and power and leadership.

TRISTAN MACK WILDS (MICHAEL LEE): I personally think that's probably why him and Michael connected the way they did, or even why he ordered the hit for Michael's dad. These are the underlying stories of these kids that we see nowadays. These kingpins, or all of these kids that are growing up and being the killers that we see or the wild guys that we see, they all come from very similar circumstances. They all kind of grew up in very similar ways to where they feel like they have no other option, but they have to go out and get it, and this is the only option that they have.

ERNEST DICKERSON (DIRECTOR): In terms of Chris stomping Michael's stepfather, this was a guy who had been suspected of abusing Michael. That was the reason why Michael couldn't stand him. Him telling Chris that, it's such an illuminating moment for Chris, and it's such a horrifying moment that you really needed to see the damage that he was doing. I felt that if we never saw the damage that he was inflicting on this guy, it just wouldn't have had the right impact. It's one of those moments where you have to show the violence. You got to show the blood and guts. I felt that was a better way to tell that story to get the impact of what he was doing.

Without it, the audience would not have gotten the full feeling of what was going on. It was such an illuminating moment for Chris, who was pretty much an enigmatic person all the way through the series. He was always killing people very cool, very calm, very separated from what was going on. It was just like, "Okay, boom, boom. You're dead. Let's just put the body in the house." This was obviously something very, very personal to him, and it suggested [that] perhaps he, as a kid, had been abused. Maybe that's why he took it there. That moment of horror, we really needed to see it. The humor of Snoop just standing there, just looking at him, like, "Hmm." She played it beautifully. She's just looking at him. I think the line was, "Damn, you didn't even wait to get him in the house," which was really funny. It just underscored the horror of the situation.

GEORGE PELECANOS (WRITER/PRODUCER): Ed brought that storyline to the writers' room. Ed came up with the idea that Chris Partlow had been abused, which is why he was so blank, such a damaged guy, and it kind of explained him.

DEBI YOUNG (MAKEUP DEPARTMENT HEAD): Ernest, with his sweet, soft-spoken self. He was like, "Debi, this person is going to be beat to death. He's going to be beat so badly, we can't even use a stuntman." That's how graphic he wanted it to be. He said, "You're probably going to have to get a puppet." I sent this actor to a special effects artist on the West Coast who could replicate all of his features, and I remember telling him that I wanted him to look very contorted, so when the puppet is moved, it would have a look of agony on the face. When that wooden crate arrived to the makeup trailer and I opened up that crate in front of David Simon, I have never seen David smile so big.

NINA K. NOBLE (EXECUTIVE PRODUCER): Ernest loves horror. That's his thing. He and George Pelecanos used to do a lot of episodes together, with George as writer and Ernest as director. In some ways, George probably wrote to Ernest's strengths and the things he enjoyed doing. I don't think it was an accident that that was in on this episode. It was a storyline that was always planned, but when we assign the directors to episodes, we think about what's going to happen in the episode, and that definitely was planned for Ernest.

GBENGA AKINNAGBE (CHRIS PARTLOW): Ernest is going to make you look great on film. On top of that, he has such an understanding of story and depth that you feel comfortable just letting go with Ernest. So that, and then also it's Michael, Tristan, who's my boy. Because of the circumstances and the people I was working with, and obviously the writing, it was easier to go to that place, especially since it was the first time that you see Chris emote even in a small way, his first killing that wasn't strictly business. He started to care about Michael, and so someone had violated someone or something he cares about.

ERNEST DICKERSON (DIRECTOR): I found out later that the editorial staff freaked out when it saw the dailies because the camera was laying down on the ground beside him. First, we started off with the actor as he's down on the ground, and then, as Chris's foot starts to come down on him, we cut. Then we moved the real actor out and moved the dummy in. The editorial staff, they didn't see the change, because the dummy looked that much like the real actor. All of a sudden, the foot is stomping him in the face and the mouth, and the head is jerking. They were freaking out because it looked like we were actually stomping the poor guy. It was a beautiful special effect. That articulated dummy that we made of him, it worked.

Even they admitted that they had to cut down what I did. My cut was a little bit too much. I think it was longer with the stomping of the head. They shortened it. It was hard to watch.

GEORGE PELECANOS (WRITER/PRODUCER): You run the risk of [leaving the audience behind by not explicitly saying Michael or Chris was abused], but we are always just trying to make the best show that we can. We will take that risk, and we'll leave some people behind if we do something that we think is not too on the nose. You trust your actors. The way that Chris Partlow delivers that beating is different than all the other things that he does, that he carries out almost robotically.

We just hoped that people would know, and I think it's a good strategy. Executives, the people that are funding these shows, they always want you to be more on the nose and explain things. That's our most common battle with the execs, is let the audience figure it out. Trust them a little bit more, but you do, in the end, lose some people. But it's cool. It's fine.

TRISTAN MACK WILDS (MICHAEL LEE): Growing up into it, I didn't know what to expect at first. Of course, I didn't even know what a character arc was. I was kind of just doing what they were telling me to do. But as it progressed, and speaking to David and Ed and Robert Chew, and a lot more learning, just honestly learning about what he can do and the things that I should look out for, you started to see how they really built Michael to show you how these kids in these terrible areas, they could be great kids with great intentions, but with no options and with no opportunities to do anything else, they fall to the wayside, and the problem is that we don't even look at them. They fall to the wayside and they just become another statistic.

It's not even that people worry about it. But it's those kids that you should look out for, because you never know. They may turn out to be the next Omar.

JOE CHAPPELLE (DIRECTOR/CO-EXECUTIVE PRODUCER): The main part of the discussion [with Randy and Carver] is in a waiting room area. I wanted that to be very kind of subdued lighting, kind of dark. The hallway that Carver walks down was this kind of glaring fluorescent, ugly, white-bright light. The dialogue was fairly conventional in the sense that a lot of it plays in the two-shot of the kid and Seth [Gilliam]. They have their moment, and then Carver walks away.

But the kid, when he's talking to him at the end, the "You gonna look out for me?" I wanted him definitely in that dark shadow of the waiting room, and then Carver in that high-key white. I just felt that, for some reason, it would work right for that scene. On a very visceral level, I just thought it was really what it's about. He's literally leaving him in the dark and behind. That was a specific thing we talked to the cinematographer about. I wanted him to knock the lights down in the waiting room, but I wanted the hallway to be very vibrant, very bright.

MAESTRO HARRELL (RANDY WAGSTAFF): Sometimes you hear the actors going, "Don't break my character" and all that kind of stuff. Most of the time they just sound like assholes, but I got it. It was such a different mood on the set, because everyone knew [the] stakes were high and what it was. Carver was giving me so much back. I kind of got free rein to do, within the lines, what I wanted to do. I think it was more reaction and interaction. I worked through that as well, with Robert Chew. I'm just thankful that it reached people the way that it did. Even now, I'll be walking into a bar or doing something, and somebody will be like, "Oh, you gonna look out for me?"

It left that kind of impact on people who are twenty years my senior. All I remember about that day was, obviously, it was a great day. I think I even ended up going to ESPN Zone after that day, actually. I was glad I was able to get it right. I had the support of everybody on the set, from the people doing the makeup to the people doing the hair, everyone was just amazed and impressed that I was able to carry it out that way. That's really all I wanted, especially at that age. It's more of, *Man, I don't want to mess this up because I know that this is bigger than me.*

SETH GILLIAM (SGT. ELLIS CARVER): At that point, it started to dawn on me the strain and frustration that these officers must feel when you start to step a little bit outside of the zone and start having a positive impact, but then realize that you're kind of powerless. So, it was a pretty strong scene for me. And on that day, Maestro did a fantastic job with that scene. I had both being in the moment and being involved with the character and also kind of stepping outside and being proud as an actor. You know, rising to the challenge. The guys were so alive. It's not the way I think I would have done it, at that point, if I was acting when I was fourteen or fifteen.

ED BURNS (CO-CREATOR): In Season Four, they said we should kill somebody. David would throw out a bunch of names, but it didn't work. It's a process, and it turned out to be Bodie, his famous stand on the corner.

DARRELL BRITT-GIBSON (DARIUS "O-DOG" HILL): I'm walking and I get a phone call and I know the number because they're usually going to tell me this is where you need to be, because I knew I was supposed to be shooting. It's a girl, Megan. She's with casting. I get a call from her, and usually she's like, "Hey, so this is where you've got to be, Darrell. How are you doing?" This time, I hear something in her voice, and I'm sort of like, "Hey, Megan, what's up?" She was like, "I hate you." I was confused, and she was like, "I hate you." I'm like, "What are you talking about?" She says, "You're going to kill Bodie." I dropped everything, like the world stopped, and I was thinking to myself, *Wait, wait, hold on, back up. What? What?* She said, "Yep, you're going to kill Bodie. This is what you got." I'm shaking. *What?*

When I say everything stopped, it stopped, because I'm thinking, *Hold on, I'm new to this show and I'm being asked to do this? Is this a mistake?* I got told where I was supposed to go, and I hung up the phone and I had to sit down. I sat down and I had to regroup because, literally, like somebody had just hit me with a two-by-four, because I'm still thinking this is a mistake. I'm expecting another call to be like, "Oh, I'm sorry. We got that wrong." And I couldn't even tell anybody. Imagine sitting with this secret and all you want to do is tell somebody, but you can't. It's just like walking around with *The Da Vinci Code* and I can't share it with anybody.

I was thinking, *This is going to make me the most hated man in some circles.* It's incredible, because who doesn't love Bodie?

J. D. WILLIAMS (PRESTON "BODIE" BROADUS): It's kind of weird, because I saw it coming from the second episode. The show has its own reality and its own rules. From the very first episode of the fourth season and especially the second, you seen Bodie is outside by himself. Either he's going to get some help or he's going to get killed. I was on top of that from the first or the second episode.

I remember the sixth episode came around, and being that all of the young kids, that was my crew in the show—on set, we would be around each other so much—I basically adopted all those little kids. Keep them corralled, give them ideas and suggestions if they weren't doing something or if they needed help. I would tell them sometimes it's not looking so good for Bodie. The kids would come sit with me at lunch. It was like maybe six of them, seven of them. I was like the school mom. They would all sit around and we would talk, and David Simon came and sat next to us one day. He came and sat with us while we were talking. Somebody brought up "What do you think is going to happen?" I said, "I think Bodie is probably going to get killed." All of the kids looked at me like, *How could you say that in front of* The Wire? All of them almost threw up, had a heart attack, fell out their chair. It was ridiculous. David kind of looked at me, and David Simon is not like an overtly emotional person as far as I've known, but he just had this look on his face. It was kind of, not a surprised look, but he was intrigued, because he was like, "Go on." I explained why and everything, and David said, "Well, you never know. It's possible."

DAVID SIMON (CREATOR): He's right. He saw that. Once they guess it, it's sort of like there's nothing you can do. And he guessed it. So, I think a couple episodes after that, I came to him and said, "Well, you figured it out. Don't be doing that shit here, 'Oh my God, I'm dead in three episodes. This might be the last cup of coffee I ever have.' Performance has been perfectly fluid, perfectly paced, just keep doing what you're doing." You talk about a professional actor, J.D. is rock solid.

J. D. WILLIAMS (PRESTON "BODIE" BROADUS): They pulled me to the side and basically said, "J.D., we're going to take Bodie out, but we're going to make it great. We appreciate you and we're sorry that you're going." Like I said, I was very excited for it. I was fine with it. I think they were a little bit more depressed than I was at the time. So, they started handing me pages. I never got a whole script. It was very secretive, and they were sneaking me little pages and little scenes maybe the day before we would go do it. I really appreciated the way it was handled, the way they told me. I appreciated the secrecy and the respect they gave it as far as shooting it. It was shot lovely. It was acted lovely. I was really proud of it and very appreciative. I felt like they honored Bodie.

DAVID SIMON (CREATOR): We arranged that he was the keeper of the chess metaphor all the way through. He speaks about the pawns and everything, and then, on the corner, we killed him with a chess move, the knight coming up from behind.

The corner boys start the season as close-knit children. Those ties are methodically frayed throughout Season 4's thirteen episodes. By the end of the series, Michael (Tristan Mack Wilds) becomes a stickup artist on the run from Marlo's crew. He can no longer support Dukie (Jermaine Crawford), who dropped out of school without his friends and turned to heroin. Randy (Maestro Harrell) loses all his innocence. He is returned to a group home, forced to physically defend himself after being branded a snitch. Namond (Julito McCullum) represents the kid who lucks into an opportunity when Bunny Colvin and his wife adopt him, offering stability.

JOE CHAPPELLE (DIRECTOR/CO-EXECUTIVE PRODUCER): I wanted to get a sense of camaraderie [early in Season Four], so there's a lot of group shots of the guys, where maybe if it's a scene later down in the season, it's going to be more of a close-up. I remember in the exposition, in the early Episode One of that season, just trying to block scenes and shoot them, so it's like they're a group, they're a team, at the end of the season, knowing we were going to tear them all apart. It's a subtle visual, but that's what I was going for.

JULITO MCCULLUM (NAMOND BRICE): Very often, you don't get to see someone actually make it, in a sense, especially in film and television. It's not shown, but there are actually kids, like myself, who was able to break the stereotype and change their lives. They had the support of great people. I had my mom and also my agents and things like that. I'm extremely proud that I was able to give that to the world. I've got stopped in the street a million times, like, "Man, Namond shouldn't have made it, man." That just goes to show how great the series was that people are so invested that they're still thinking about it. I get stopped on the street every single day, still, because people are so invested in these characters and they feel like they were there. They watched them grow. They watched that transformation.

ED BURNS (CO-CREATOR): There's always one kid that has that break, and he's the one you didn't like at all hardly. We created him that way.

DOMENICK LOMBARDOZZI (DET. THOMAS "HERC" HAUK): What Ed Burns and David did that season, I think it's just some of the best writing I have ever seen and some of the proudest work I've ever done or been a part of.

CAROLYN STRAUSS (PRESIDENT, HBO ENTERTAINMENT): They were all really good, but if you put a gun to my head and said, "Pick your favorite season," that fourth season to me was just killer.

On a macro level, yeah, it was a big political statement, but on the micro level, watching those kids go through that, it was just killer. Not in a good way. It was a good way, but it was really so visceral watching that happen.

ERIC OVERMYER (WRITER): That summer, what I remember most is [Hurricane] Katrina, really, and being in Baltimore and wondering if my house was still there in New Orleans. Then, after Katrina, David and I started talking again about doing a show in New Orleans, which eventually became the seeds for *Treme*.

GEORGE PELECANOS (WRITER/PRODUCER): It wasn't really until Season Three that I felt like, *This is pretty extraordinary*, like we're really doing something. And that's where I think we hit our stride. I think Three and Four are our best seasons, in my opinion. Everybody's going to have a different opinion. This is what I think we did best: we showed people how things work, why things are the way they are. It's something that I've struggled with in my books, but I think we did it in the show. For example, if you take Season Four, if you came up the way I did, you've been hearing all your life, "Why can't these kids just pull themselves up by their bootstraps to get out of the ghetto?" Like it's easy. I think in that season, we showed America why it's very difficult for them to do that, because of everything they're up against. That's really what I'm proud of, is that we articulated on film the mechanics of why things are the way they are.

MAESTRO HARRELL (RANDY WAGSTAFF): It was pretty sad to see, "Man, this is what happened." I already knew that was the case. The second [that Randy] gets left in the group home, you see him get his ass beat, literally. That's the world. This kid went in and he got hardened, and that's what it is. He wasn't about to break. I think that's another thing about Randy. Randy didn't just break and fold. But he was like, *Wow, I did all this shit to not put myself in this position and then trying to do the right thing, I put myself in this position.* That's the world.

It's sad to think about. He's Mr. I Want to Sell Candy, Because I Don't Want to Sell Drugs. But if he would have just been doing that, he would have maybe gotten arrested, but past that, I don't think he would have ended up in that situation or if he would have started off in that situation, he would have just stayed in that situation, and then he would have been better adapted for it later. It would have been more of a "Yeah, I'm an orphan. Nobody puts up with me because I'm an asshole and I do *x, y, z.*" And then he would have turned eighteen, but he would have been prepared for it. Randy was really a good kid, bad situation. Since that's the case, when he got into trouble, he wasn't poised to deal with it.

ED BURNS (CO-CREATOR): You can rescue a child, but you can't rescue the children, and that's the difference. *Opportunity* is a much better word than *hope.* If a child sees the opportunity and you can direct the child toward the opportunity, then the kid's okay. Hope is like a dream. That's what I used to say to my kids. "Don't believe in hope. Believe in yourself. You got to put the energy in to get the energy out." Hope is just like something that the fairy godmother's going to come down and sprinkle on you. That's not the way it is for these kids. You got to work for it, then it'll come to you, because you open yourself up.

MAESTRO HARRELL (RANDY WAGSTAFF): That's life. I think that's really what it is. I know this might sound really bleak, but that's the way I kind of view life. Think of it this way: When we're kids, all we do is run around and play and smile all day. That's all we do. Then life happens, and you start thinking that way. Shit's just not that sweet.

That's really what it is, life constantly breaking [Randy] down, breaking him down, breaking him down. He's a light bulb that's shining a hundred watts. You can't keep doing that if your circumstances aren't getting better and there's no one there for you and there's no support system. Let's be real. We all know how awful the entire system is for orphans and kids without parents. It's not a fixed, great system, and especially not in West Baltimore. I think that's also an issue we have societally, which we're not here to talk about, but still it's like, what do you expect these kids to go do? Do you expect the kids from West Baltimore to just be like, "Oh yeah, no, no. I'm just going to apply to college and then go pay for it?"

I'm from Chicago, so it's the same thing on the South Side. It's like, are you serious? You really want to hold these kids to the same standard as some kids who grew up in Chicago on the North? No, you can't. They don't have the same experience. They don't have the same life. They have no support system. Most of these people don't know their father, and if they do know their mothers, let's hope they're clean. It's just a cycle, and that's the sad part about it. That's why I was so happy about what this show portrayed. Even look at Michael. He was taking care of his little brother. What was he supposed to do? Was he supposed to stay in school? That's not a real thing for him. He goes to school, and his little brother doesn't eat, and then they both come home sitting on their hands like, "Oh, well. This sucks and mom's on drugs." No, you've got to do something. It's sad, but that's the cycle.

The evolving ways that viewers were able to watch television revealed a sliver of The Wire's *future popularity. In 2004, HBO began releasing DVDs of the seasons, allowing the audience to absorb the show at their own pace. In the fourth season, the network allowed HBO subscribers access to episodes nearly a week before their airing, via On Demand. Also, HBO unfurled Season 4 in its entirety to critics months before its premiere, hoping to create elusive buzz and positive reviews. The ploy worked, with Stephen King among the legion of writers who showered glowing praise. Chris Albrecht announced his commitment to a final season shortly after Season 4's premiere. The early release also ignited a black market. The show became introduced to a fan base that typically could not or would not have subscribed to HBO.*

NEAL HUFF (CHIEF OF STAFF MICHAEL STEINTORF): The thing that happened that was so fascinating, that really altered the whole course of television history, is they were fighting for their lives for Season Four. They released the entire season to the press, which was a new thing to do. So, all of a sudden, they were getting Tony Kushner and Stephen King, these op-ed pieces about the greatest thing that's ever been on television. It also goes viral in the black market. So, it's already a huge, huge hit, and it just kind of created this conversation about the totality of the show before Season Four even aired.

KAREN THORSON (PRODUCER): In my travels back and forth to Baltimore, I would often look at dailies on the train. At this point, we're in the DVD world now. We went from VHS to DVD through the course of the show, and we remained film the whole time and we never went to widescreen. I would watch the dailies on the train, and by the last season, people would look over my shoulder and say, "Hey, are you watching *The Wire?*" I couldn't watch my dailies anymore.

DAVID SIMON (CREATOR): I did believe that if we finished it, it would be on the shelf. There were these things called DVDs, and I could now see them coming out. People would watch these shows on DVDs. It'll exist. They will find it. I did think that if we finished, people will find what we did and it would have merit, and that's how we'll be judged. I was trying to buck [Andre Royo] up. Andre was one of those guys whose heart broke after the Emmys came out. I was like, "That's not why we do the work. Think about why we do the work." He'd say, "Yeah, yeah, yeah, man. But this is my career. Without people noticing the work that we do, we die. It's all about the next role and the next role." He was right, too. It's easy for me to say, "Fuck the Emmys." It's a lot harder for a working actor to say that. I rooted for him, but I couldn't take it seriously.

RICHARD PRICE (WRITER): My personal story with the series DVD is that my girls were young-side teenagers when I started writing *The Wire*. It wasn't until after Season Three when the DVDs came out. All of a sudden, everybody can watch this maddeningly complex show. They can shoot up twelve episodes, and so the thing exploded. People discovered it on DVD because they could mainline it. All of a sudden, overnight, my girls are coming back from their schools, they're saying, "Dad, did you know you're really cool?" I say, "What?" At that point, I did three or four episodes of *The Wire* compared to—I have movies, eight novels. All of a sudden it's like, "My dad's a writer." That's the power of television. For everybody who reads a book, one hundred people go to the movies; for every one hundred people that go to the movies, ten thousand watch a TV show. It's a numbers game.

DOMINIC WEST (DET. JIMMY MCNULTY): I went into the local store, and this woman said, "Hey, you're on *The Wire*." And I went, *Oh, wow, how do you like that?* Then, a few days later, I was driving in London, and some guy probably cut me off or something. It was a hot, sunny day and I was in a bad mood, so I started shouting at him, or he shouted at me. Anyway, I was saying, "Fuck him," and swearing at him, and he suddenly stopped and he went, "Hey, you're McNulty." That was the first time anyone had recognized me for anything, certainly for calling me by my character name, but it was quite embarrassing because I wasn't behaving. I was swearing and cursing and angry, but that was really the first time I realized that there were lots of people watching it.

NEAL HUFF (CHIEF OF STAFF MICHAEL STEINTORF): I do think there was a racial component to why so many people did not watch the show when it was on. I think people saw a lot of black faces and [said], "That's kind of not my story." And it wasn't until it had been lauded to the point it was that people kind of came around to it. I remember being surprised when it was on that still people really weren't on board with it. They didn't know. They're like, "That's that really intense show. I can't watch something like that. I can't watch something about that type of crime on a Sunday night. I'm going back to work."

I was really disappointed in a lot of my friends. A lot of my friends in the business, to be honest with you, were completely unwilling to watch that show. It really took that whole thing with all the press that came after Four and Five that people came around to it. Friends were calling about having seen me on the show years afterward, which I do think is an interesting thing.

WENDELL PIERCE (DET. WILLIAM "BUNK" MORELAND): I remember I had a moment where I thought I was going to leave the show. It was after the fourth season, which I think was one of the most masterful seasons, because it really dealt with politics and the school system, the dysfunctional school system and where we actually lose our youth, displayed so perfectly. I met [Charmaine McPhee]. She said, "Hi, Mr. Pierce, I'm going to Brown. I'm sorry I didn't have any scenes with you, but I'd really like to work on some projects together soon. I look a little younger than I am, but I'm graduating this year and I'm looking forward to going to college and all."

I was just so impressed by this young lady, I'm like, "And you're on the show?" She said, "Yeah." "What character are you playing?" She told me "Laetitia." And I said, "That's the girl that slashes the girl's face, right? You're just totally out of control. There's no order to her life. We've lost her. Her conflict resolution is a razor to the face." And I said, "You played that?" "Yeah." I said, "Well, why aren't we telling your story?" This impressive young lady from Baltimore, or wherever she's from, going to school. "I'm sure you had challenges. Why aren't we telling that story? Shit, we're a part of the problem. We're a part of the problem. If we're going to take this time to tell a story that involves kids in our community, and these are the stories that we choose to tell and not her story, well, we have a problem."

I told myself, *I'm a part of the problem now.* Then the season came on, and by the end of the season, I realized that everything was not arbitrary, that there was a reason we depicted the dysfunction, to show how easy it is we can let our kids fall through the cracks and how you wail and cry for Dukie and Randy. And Randy's being beat up in the home, and Namond finally breaks the glass of dysfunction and finds a mother and father with Bunny. And then to see Michael, the most brilliant and most talented of them, turn into, ultimately, a murderer. We forget they're kids, and here we're challenging them to make good choices as if they're the adults, with no adults around them to lead them in the right direction to make sure that they're Namond, and he gets out, and you don't end up Dukie or Michael, or fall victim once again like Randy, when we're just trying to get another witness to take down another murder case and he falls victim with no protection. How can we make more Namonds? How can we save more kids? Look how we've lost these.

You never see a bunch of kids that you assume are just wilding out and never give them—hopefully, after looking at that fourth season—give them the benefit of the doubt that they need people in their lives who have their best interests at heart. If they don't have it at home, we have to give it to them somewhere. When we interface with kids, whether it's school, whether it's church, whether it's the playground, we have to make sure that they're getting every chance they can to have people who have their best interests at heart, to give them the best chance to make choices that will send them down the right road. Give them opportunity. I was in tears at the end of the fourth season. When I saw that, I said, "I can go back now." Fortunately enough, we would shoot and then it would come on the air. Because I had finished the fourth season when I met the young lady.

DAVID SIMON (CREATOR): I heard about that after the fact. He apparently didn't bring that to me. He resolved it in his own head or carried it as long as he could and somehow outlived it. I don't remember having to talk him back into the fold, but that doesn't mean it didn't happen. Not everybody went to the boss man with their angst.

WENDELL PIERCE (DET. WILLIAM "BUNK" MORELAND): My concerns were never, "Hey David, I've got to sit down and talk to you." He's right about that. I never brought my concerns to him. That was something that I harbored within me. Then the work showed itself to me. He may have heard a little bitching and complaining on the set from actors, like, "Why am I doing this?"

The only concerns I ever brought to David was, "Hey, man, trust the actors a little bit more." He doesn't like showing you the scripts ahead of time. Like, if you let them know what the arc is, there's some denouement that's going to happen in the barbershop, where you finally catch somebody. If you know that's happening in Episode Eight, in Episode Three, he thinks actors might go, "You know, something, I think I'm going to get myself a haircut at the barbershop. I hope everything works out."

He believed actors might tip their hand. I can embrace that to say, "Hey, I don't know what tomorrow brings, so if I'm living too fully in the character, I'm in the moment, so I don't need to know until I know." At the same time, the two can coexist. Actors know where the edge of the stage is on Broadway. They don't just walk off the stage. They live in that world conscious of the restraints of the physical world, of the stage being about two feet from the edge of it, and if you walk over there, your black ass is going to fall into the orchestra pit. They never wanted us to watch playbacks or anything like that. We're not that vain. Okay, maybe we are, but still. He trusts that to the directors to make sure we know where the edge of the stage is and he wants us to just be in the moment of the play.

CLARKE PETERS (DET. LESTER FREAMON): It was more like Four when it started to feel like more than just a show. That's when I think we all began to realize that we had been hired to be actors on a mission. The mission was to educate the public to connect the dots, between local government, the economic situation that a city might find itself in, what's happening with your children in school, and while you might be frustrated about that, the drug situation, the so-called war on drugs, which we know is a complete farce. These are things I was totally unaware of. I wasn't brought up here. I was brought up in Europe, so I was being educated to these issues myself, as time went on. I think that's the mission. It's that the American public, or American citizenry, rather than being sort of jerked around by sound bites of things, if they're better informed, like any citizenry, then you have a better chance of surviving and moving forward as a nation, as a country. When we start looking at people who are strung out on drugs as criminals rather than victims, it changes our attitude toward all of that. How can we possibly heal anything like that if we have the wrong idea about it?

9

TURN THE CAMERA BACK

David Simon occasionally countered critics of The Wire by saying
that the show's writers illustrated the world they themselves had
experienced and inhabited. Simon knew no landscape more intimately
than the media. A fictional version of The Baltimore Sun therefore
served as a focal point in the fifth and final season of The Wire. The
season arrived with some moments both condensed and hurried—for
good reason. Following Season 4, Simon had, again, barely stiff-armed
cancellation by HBO. He agreed to a shortened, ten-episode arc and
completed the season without some of his creative confidants. Ed Burns
had begun working on Generation Kill, an HBO miniseries about
the U.S. Marine Corps during the invasion of Iraq that Simon also
turned his attention to following The Wire, and George Pelecanos had
reverted to his day job of authoring first-class novels.

In the newsroom storyline, Dominic West's Jimmy McNulty concocts
a fake serial killer of homeless men to create the budget for meaningful
police work and the investigation into Marlo Stanfield's syndicate, which
McNulty eventually breaks up at the cost of his career. The Baltimore
Sun has been purchased by out-of-towners, and a shrinking newsroom
and dwindling resources decimate the paper. Scott Templeton (Tom
McCarthy), an ambitious and morally challenged reporter, claims to be
contacted by McNulty's fake killer. Gus Haynes (Clark Johnson), an editor

who becomes suspicious of Templeton, is cast aside by top editors who are eager to bring prestige to the paper through journalism prizes. The show's final montage features Templeton accepting a Pulitzer Prize. Honest attempts at journalism bookend Templeton's transgressions. Haynes links the workings of Councilwoman Nerese Campbell (Marlyne Barrett) to a drug dealer, and Mike Fletcher (Brandon Young), a young journalist, works hard to write a feature story that accurately reflects Bubbles's (Andre Royo) struggle for sobriety. With more episodes, Simon said the series would have explored the impact of absent fathers—Cheese Wagstaff, portrayed by Method Man, is the father of Season 4's Randy, played by Maestro Harrell, a nugget that the series did not have breadth to explore—and rounded out Templeton's character. "We'd have done a little more with Prez and the decline of Dukie, who's [Prez's] favorite," Simon added. "There would have been a little more anguish on the part of the reporter, Templeton's parts, in terms of the sins he was committing against journalism. He was a little bit more on the fence, have him do some worthy work somewhere that doesn't get quite noticed, but it's honest. So, it teaches two lessons, one of which is that the grunt work of real good journalism sometimes is not the straight path to glory. But you would have known he did good work somewhere, and that would have helped."

Some critics argued that Simon pushed a vendetta through the course of the newsroom thread. In interviews, Simon spoke negatively of two former top Baltimore Sun editors, William Marimow—the show even gave his surname to a lousy, unsympathetic lieutenant—and John Carroll. For Slate, Simon wrote that the pair "are notable journalists with impressive résumés. But in Baltimore, in their hunger for prizes, they tolerated and defended a reporter who was making it up wholesale." David Zurawik, a television critic for The Baltimore Sun who had authored glowing and appreciative reviews of The Wire's prior seasons, eviscerated the newsroom storyline. "In my preview of the season," Zurawik wrote, "I termed the newsroom scenes the 'Achilles' heel' of the series. Worse, they became a cancer that grew deeper and deeper into other parts of the drama as the season wore on."

Simon let most of the criticism pass. Earlier, Bill Zorzi had proposed

*that one of the characters come right out and state the season's theme—
what nearly everyone would miss. But* The Wire *was always a show of
exposition. It never told; it showed. The show's newspaper missed out on
every story of legitimate impact, such as the mayor who had promised
change and instead resorted to juking stats; or how the killing of an
appliance store owner actually signified a vicious turf war and the death
of the city's largest drug importer. "In Baltimore, where over the last
twenty years Times Mirror and the Tribune Company have combined to
reduce the newsroom by 40 percent, all of the above stories pretty much
happened," Simon wrote for* The Huffington Post. *"A mayor was
elected governor while his police commanders made aggravated assaults
and robberies disappear."*

DAVID SIMON (CREATOR): I was in Mozambique scouting or shooting
[for *Generation Kill*] when I got a call from Carolyn saying that they
were going to cancel after Season Four. I was shocked. I thought that
once they committed to the story of the vacants and Marlo, they
weren't going to stop. I remembered being utterly depressed traveling
in Mozambique. It was almost four in the morning when I got this
phone call, and I am thinking, *How can they cancel after Season Four?*
I can see them canceling after Season Three, when we had finished
the Barksdale story. As Chris said, don't seize defeat from the jaws of
victory. The show's going out with good reviews. It didn't get an audience. Lots of shows don't get an audience, but we got credit for a good
show. We can do better. We can take command of a scene.

GEORGE PELECANOS (WRITER/PRODUCER): At the end of Four, they
were definitely ready. They were like, "Congratulations, you just went
out on a high note. Let's not try again." David really was passionate
about getting that last season.

CHRIS ALBRECHT (CHAIRMAN AND CEO, HBO): Carolyn and I were always aligned about it. She's the best, and we had a lot of eye rolls and
behind-the-scenes laughs about David's passion for it all. If she and

I didn't both agree that the show deserved to continue, it wouldn't have continued. As much as David was an advocate, and as much as it certainly made a difference, ultimately the quality of the show was recognized by the two of us and by our colleagues at HBO, too. It was frustrating when you look at something that's good and say, "I don't understand why more people aren't getting this." But then, you almost become a little defiant. Your stance is, *I'll be damned if they're going to run me off my own property,* or whatever the analogy would be.

DAVID SIMON (CREATOR): To their great credit, they heard the story-lines [for Seasons] Four and Five, and they said, "We'll give you those." And then, they kind of wanted to get out of Five. I said, "You can't leave the bodies in the vacants. You've got to help me out, Chris, come on." And he helped me out again. I think I'm being fair with Chris, which is to say, it was a show that nobody was watching. It had already gotten all the good reviews it could by Season Three, and he wanted to get out and put the money in something else.

CAROLYN STRAUSS (PRESIDENT, HBO ENTERTAINMENT): We were able to take some big chances with that show and able to keep it on, even though it wasn't breaking the records in ratings. We were able to do things, I think, that may be harder these days.

DAVID SIMON (CREATOR): That year, they gave Ed and me seven hours of *Generation Kill* and they gave us time to finish *The Wire,* so we were taking seventeen hours of the programming pie. We were taking up a lot of pie. And I had the head of the network saying to me, "Can you do it in ten? If you can do it in ten, I can find the money." They were ready to cancel the show after Four. We were canceled twice. We were canceled after Three, effectively, and they gave me a chance to go back in there and argue. Then, we were canceled after Four, and they gave me a chance to go back in there and argue. But this time they said, "You've got to do it in ten. I don't have the money." And so, it's good faith. He's showing me good faith.

It's not my network. I'm a vendor. So, I went back in and had the ten, and we had to leave some stuff on the table we couldn't fit. Years later, after *The Wire* finished its run, people said, "Man, that show ended okay. That was a good ending." Chris was already gone by then, and he had held me to the ten. I got an email from him. It cracked me up. He basically goes, "Man, the only thing that could've made that ending better was two more episodes." I just emailed him back, "You motherfucker." It was affectionate, because that show had no audience after three seasons, and he heard the stories and he let us stretch for another two seasons. Yeah, I can't sit here and complain. It's unseemly.

CHRIS ALBRECHT (CHAIRMAN AND CEO, HBO): At some point, you got to just realize you run a business.

ED BURNS (CO-CREATOR): I've never seen Season Five, basically.

GEORGE PELECANOS (WRITER/PRODUCER): Ed had gone off to do *Generation Kill.* Honestly, I had sort of checked out, too. I was concentrating on my novels at that point. I had a contract, and it was a very good contract to write three books, and I wanted to honor that and do the best I could. So, Season Five, I would say, was quite a bit of David and Bill Zorzi, because Bill was a newspaper man, too.

DAVID SIMON (CREATOR): Whatever season it had been, if I had five, six, seven seasons, the capstone was going to be the media, because the last critique I wanted to send was, "If all this is true, if this is what the drug war is, if this is what the city government is about, if this is what public education is about, where were we? What was our attention drawn to? What were we jerking off to where we couldn't actually tend to our society?" That's the last thing to say: we turn the camera back to the audience and go, "You're complicit." That's the implied thing. "You're complicit. We're all complicit. We're not attending to any of this. We're so easily distracted. We're so easily entertained." That's the last thing to say. After that, there's nothing else to say. You can't swivel the camera back.

RICHARD PRICE (WRITER): Season Five—sometimes I thought David had a little too much of an ax to grind against the establishment.

GEORGE PELECANOS (WRITER/PRODUCER): I think there's a truth to that. I've written for newspapers, but I've never been in the newsroom. It's always been in freelance, the stuff that I've done, so I had no connection to that world. I didn't know who they were talking about when they were talking about their bosses at *The Baltimore Sun*. I had no idea what that was about. It was only later that I saw that some people responded in a negative way to the portrayal of some of the bosses in the newsroom, because they saw themselves in that. I think they actually used a couple names that were either close or right on the money.

These are all people that left *The Sun*. None of them were fired. They all left voluntarily, but very frustrated with how the newspaper business was going, the changing direction from hard reporting to going after prizes, which comes at a cost, because that's how [Stephen] Glass and all these people do it. They were fabricating things to win prizes.

They did have an ax to grind, in a way, but I feel like they were coming from an experiential position and they had a reason to feel that way. Having said all that, I think it's the most didactic of the seasons, where you see the people behind the show. It's the least successful of the seasons for that reason, in my opinion, but the least successful season of *The Wire* is still better than most anything you see on television. There's a lot of great moments in that season and, as a whole, I think it's less successful, especially coming after Season Four, which to me, is the best season of television that's ever been made.

WILLIAM F. ZORZI (STAFF WRITER): There was some bad shit that happened at *The Baltimore Sun*, but there was great journalism that went on at the same time. I think those guys who were down there every day doing the Lord's work, really, felt a little deceived by Season Five of *The Wire*, like somehow that tarred and tarnished them as well. That was definitely not the intent.

In the larger sense, we're speaking to the state of journalism. That was the state of journalism then. You have to remember, we beat it out and started writing it more than a year in advance of it going on HBO. In that period of time, journalism was in this downward sort of death spiral, overnight almost. It was pretty shocking.

That whole thing about Templeton making it up, that may have been based on some real people, a real person. He might have. David is a good talker, so I think David can probably take care of himself in explaining the circumstances under which he left. That became part of the battle in the aftermath of Season Five. "Oh, well, he's just pissed off because he didn't get a raise," or some shit. "What? David needs a fucking raise?" I don't know, it was a little much. I was like, "Let's just take a giant step backwards, just for a moment, and let's reexamine that statement."

ED BURNS (CO-CREATOR): I just don't watch television. I see enough of the takes of it on set, watching stuff like that. These characters are in my head, all right? Once I read the script to make sure that the characters are doing the right thing, then it's up to the producer, myself, or whoever's on set to make sure that the director or the actors don't fuck up the lines. That's all I need. Except for Season Five, I think that the first four seasons have a logic to them.

NINA K. NOBLE (EXECUTIVE PRODUCER): That's a true credit to our cast and to the family that we had created with cast and crew, because every single crew member, David wrote a letter to all of our cast and all the leads and asked everyone to come back and to not hold HBO up for money, which is normally what happens when somebody's contract lapses, then all of a sudden they want two million dollars an episode or whatever and David just said, "Look, we're still the underdogs. We still have the lower budget, but we really hope you'll come back, so that we can finish this story." He always had the five-year arc in his head.

ANDRE ROYO (REGINALD "BUBBLES" COUSINS): I got burned out and stressed out in four seasons. I just got frustrated. I was like, "I'm sick of it. I'm sick of these clothes." I was hitting bottom as an artist and as an actor. I was hitting my creative bottom. I was fed up. I don't want to be this no more. It was incredible that Season Five, that was probably the scariest season for me. After Season Four, I was like, "Wow. What a journey." This is the life that Bubbles was living. It was so fucking ugly, just so painful, that I was like, "I'm done." Then, Season Five, David called me and said, "We're going to pick up. It's a year later and you're clean." I was like, "What? I don't know how to play that. I don't know what that means."

I was playing this addict who's fiending, who wants to get high for four years. For four years, that means another two, three years in between, where I'm staying in character, staying in [Bubbles's] head-space. Now you're telling me that it's a year later and I'm clean? I was scared to death. I don't know what that looks like. I thought about me and Dom's conversation. I thought about how sick I was of being this character, which means Bubbles was sick of being high. I used that to just be organically, "Yeah, I'm clean. I'm going to fight to stay clean." That was wonderful, but it was also weird, because I remember in the fourth season, when I hung myself, I thought that was it. We're reading the script, and you see that [on] one page, [and] before you turn the page, I'm like, "It's time to go out. This has been crazy. This is my time." When I found out that I wasn't dying, there was a part of me that was a little weirded out, because I felt like, at this point, we were known as the show that's real. We're the realest show on television. I knew that the real Bubbles died. I was like, "We can't lie now. We got to be organic to what really happened."

David Simon and Ed Burns, they pretty much were like, "We just put this audience through a bleak, bleak look at the world and what it is and what's going on and the darkness of how this machine is so fucking broken. At the end of the day, with these people [getting] out of bed every day, with these people that at least wake up and hope, they got to believe that it can get better. It has the possibility of getting better. That's what Bubbles is." We decided that's what Bubbles is going to be. All the people on the show, the one guy you expect not to turn around or have that moment, we need to give that to the world.

ERNEST DICKERSON (DIRECTOR): Bubbles, he's a character that, whenever you see the show, you always worry about him. You just love him, but you always worry about him, and you're just so afraid that he's not going to last the full run of the show, and he actually did, which was one of the amazing things, which was pretty cool. He's the character that always kept me on the edge of my seat.

STEVE EARLE (WAYLON): I knew that Bubbles had to live. Part of that may be me—and I didn't have that inside information from anybody—but I would have bet money, and I do this with characters all the time. I almost once wrote a letter to J. K. Rowling and told her she was wrong about something once, but I always knew Bubbles was going to live. To me, he just sort of had to live. That's what he is. He's the hope that runs through the show. It's a heartbreaking story, but somebody has to come out okay.

ANDRE ROYO (REGINALD "BUBBLES" COUSINS): My mind was like, *That's it? Really? I can't have a job somewhere with a girlfriend, a couple of kids? This is how far the author's going to go?* David was like, "This isn't Disney. This is not Disney. Don't worry. The people that seen so much of your character, this is going to be enough." I'm like, "Okay." I trust the boss. I trust the genius that is David Simon and Ed Burns.

ED BURNS (CO-CREATOR): You don't know if he turned it around. That's the thing. Most guys do detox fifteen, twenty, thirty times before it might work. It's not like walk in, walk back out. No, sir. And remember that the quality of heroin that Bubbles was shooting, which would be heroin from the eighties and seventies, at the most, would be twelve percent heroin. Today, what they're shooting is ninety or one hundred percent. It's in that ballpark.

ANDRE ROYO (REGINALD "BUBBLES" COUSINS): He got an ending that suited him. This is what I love about the show and the conversations and just how magnificent the writing and the people were. Do I believe Bubbles had a happy ending? Yes. Bubbles, at that point, like life itself, he was happy. Yes, he had a happy ending. Did it stay that way? I couldn't tell you and I choose not to think about it, because it would probably make me sad because of the unknown, because of the headspace that Bubbles lives. I think the happiest idea of Bubbles is that no matter what, Bubbles was always going to try for that. He might have relapsed, but that's not what makes Bubbles happiest or sad. What made you so happy about Bubbles was that he was always trying. He didn't do that Hamsterdam shit. He just didn't give in and go, "I just want to be high." He would always try. I think that's the real beauty that you find in every human being that scares you. When a human being stops trying, when we don't give a fuck, when we say, "Ah, fuck it. I don't care," once that aspect comes into the human psyche, humanity is lost. You got to want to try. Whether you know you're pushing that rock up a hill or you're going to bang your head against a brick wall, the idea to not try cannot seep into our society. We got to try.

DOMINIC WEST (DET. JIMMY McNULTY): It must have been between about Season Four or Five or something, and Lance [Reddick] and Bubbles, Andre Royo, they had some time off and they'd gone up to audition for the same part. Andre didn't tell anyone about this part.

Lance didn't tell anyone, and they didn't realize they were going for the same part. They found out at the audition. It wasn't to play a woman, but it was to play a dude who dressed up as a woman. They both went full monty with it. Can you imagine these two, Lance and Andre, both in full makeup, wearing a dress or something, and they're sitting there?

Andre is sitting there in the audition hoping to fuck no one he knows turns up or sees him, and in walks Lance and he's wearing full makeup. They look at each other and go, "You fucking tell anyone about this, I'll kill you." Anyway, I don't think either of them got it, but it did make me laugh. He's so serious, Lance. The idea of him in eye shadow and lipstick was quite funny.

Clark Johnson (Gus Haynes), who directed the first two episodes of The Wire, *also directed the show's finale. Tom McCarthy (Scott Templeton) would go on to direct* Spotlight, *winner of the Best Picture Oscar in 2016. Michelle Paress, who is married to Lawrence Gilliard, accepted her first television role in Season 5 of* The Wire *as Alma Gutierrez, an ambitious, earnest reporter.*

TOM McCARTHY (SCOTT TEMPLETON): David remembered me and called me, and at that time, I was editing a movie up in New York. My second film, *The Visitor*. They made me an offer on this role, and I was really flattered and excited, but at the same time, I was in the middle of editing. I was like, "I don't know if I can do this." I didn't want to shortchange either job, the editing or my acting, so I was really hesitating on it, and a bit torn, and then David called me and said, "I just really think you should do it. I can't really show you much yet, but I think it's going to be a really interesting season and an interesting role." That was kind of enough for me.

MICHELLE PARESS (ALMA GUTIERREZ): Larry [Gilliard] was very happy for me. He was very proud of me. I think some cast members were actually a bit more sensitive about it than my husband, believe it or not. Some cast members were just a little weird at first, 'cause a lot of them didn't know I was an actor. They all knew me as Lawrence's wife, so when I show up to Baltimore to start shooting, some of the cast members felt a certain kind of way, because they were still recovering from the fact that he was no longer on the show, and then here I am coming on the show, and I think a lot of them just thought I was Larry's wife and maybe I was bored and decided, *Hey, I think I'll be an actor. Let me get this job on* The Wire. And that's not what happened at all. I've been acting since I was nine, and enjoying musical theater and community theater and talent shows since a very young age. So, I think because they didn't really know my background and that being an actor is what I've always wanted to do, I think they felt a certain kind of way about me being on the show.

LAWRENCE GILLIARD JR. (D'ANGELO BARKSDALE): Especially on a good show, it's hard for me to go and watch everybody else working and I'm sitting at home. It's like when you don't make it to the Super Bowl. When you're the team when you lost the one game and you didn't get to the championship because you missed the shot, do you really want to watch the finals? Everybody else is playing, and you're at home. She continued to watch the show, even when I wasn't watching the show. Then she got her opportunity to be on the show. She was really excited about it, and I was really happy for her and proud of her.

As I was watching the show, I was just rooting for her, just hoping she was having fun, having a good time. I know she was very nervous when she was doing it, because she's coming in the last season. The show's pretty well established. She sees the quality of the work, so she's sweating a little bit. She's like the new cat out of college and she's going to play with [Michael] Jordan.

TOM MCCARTHY (SCOTT TEMPLETON): David would constantly be inviting his reporter friends from *The Washington Post* and sometimes

The Baltimore Sun, and you'd be sitting there talking to an extra at your desk waiting for the shot to get set up, and you're like, *Man, this guy knows a lot about a lot.* Then he would ultimately introduce himself, and you'd be like, *Oh, yeah. You're not an extra. You're a wonderful investigative reporter for* The Washington Post.

CHRIS YAKAITIS (RESEARCHER): We needed newspapers created for that season that would show how the events of the show were being reported on by *The Sun*; what *The Sun* was doing was factoring into the police investigation. So, we needed these papers made, which was a pretty demanding task for a prop master. We were wondering how we're going to do this. We had some feature story we wanted the cameras to pick up that would help the story along, but you still needed everything else on the page. Traditionally, in television and filmmaking, they do what's called "Greeking." It's literally Greek. They'll pick some passage in Greek alphabet and print it on the page anywhere that's going to be slightly out of focus. Of course, that's not going to fly at *The Wire*, so we needed to do a whole front page, or internal pages, depending. There was a point early on in production where it was discussed actually getting an Associated Press subscription, so that we could reprint *The Wire* stories just to fill out these papers.

For each episode, I would basically write fake news stories that would populate front pages, inside pages. Then David and the other writers would do the headlines and the text for the main stories that we needed. So, we had our own little newspaper shop going while we're also producing a television show.

Dominic West directed the fifth season's seventh episode, "Took." "I was most anxious about how the other actors would feel about it," West said. "Why are you taking direction from a fellow actor who you've been with for five years, particularly people like Wendell and Seth Gilliam? And I thought they were going to kill me. I thought they were going to ignore everything I said or take the piss out of me. They were really amazing.

*They listened to the horseshit I was telling them. I remember saying
to Wendell, 'Play the silences,' which is the most ridiculous direction
anyone has ever given anyone. He would listen politely and nod and
then ignore me."*

NINA K. NOBLE (EXECUTIVE PRODUCER): Directing was part of what he
negotiated at first, and so it's sort of the price of having him continue
to be involved in the show, but he did a great job. He came in and did
his homework and was prepared and took it really seriously.

ANDRE ROYO (REGINALD "BUBBLES" COUSINS): If you want to direct
an episode, tell them you'll come back, but they got to let you direct
an episode. He had aspirations to do that. He didn't think they were
going to say yes, but they said, "Yeah, of course. Direct an episode."
That was one of the other things that got him back. He got to come
back and direct the episode. He was scared. He thought the show was
going to be whack. He didn't know that the whole world [had fallen]
in love with the kids. When we met the kids and it was going to be
from these young kids' point of view, we were like this: "You just
turned our show into *Fat Albert*? Is that what we just did? Did we just
turn our show into the *Fat Albert* fucking show?" I remember going to
a picnic with Dona, the costume [supervisor]. I met some of the kids.
"Don't fuck up. We got the ball rolling. Don't fuck it up, you fucking
kids." They were like, "Yes, sir. No, sir." They were really polite, really
cool, really awesome. We got caught watching these kids. When they
act, we were on the set like, "These kids are good."

DOMINIC WEST (DET. JIMMY MCNULTY): Nina Noble came up to me
afterward. She was never one full of compliments, and she said, "You
know what? You did really well." She said, "You do know that you
shot more footage of film than any other director we've had?" I said,
"Did I?" She said, "Yeah." She was in charge of the purse strings, so
I think she was being slightly critical about it, but the reason we did
is, we had this big court scene in Episode Seven, and we had this

brilliant, real-life lawyer [Billy Murphy], and he's a Baltimore attorney who had actually got Don King off a murder rap. He was a celebrity attorney. He was playing himself, and I said, "I better just see if he can act before we get him on the set." So, I went through the script with him, and he was brilliant. He was just playing himself, and he loved it, because he was a real showman and he's used to acting up in front of a jury, and he was perfect. I thought, *Oh, this is going to be great.* Then we get to the scene—and we have a lot of characters who were not actors, and they do great—we get to the scene, and he's brilliant and he has these pages and pages of speech that he's really good at, except that he has no idea about continuity.

I'd go, "Okay, cut. Okay, that was great, but you have to do that when you say that word, you have to have your . . ."—he was carrying a stick, and I should have not made him carry a stick—"Your stick is in the other hand." Continuity issues, which I hadn't really thought of. It completely threw him, completely fucked him up. We shot endless footage of him. It got pretty hard going because I'd constantly have to cut it and go back and say, "That works, but you've got to put your stick in the other hand." Anyway, all that technical stuff that you don't realize is part of the skill of screen acting, I suppose, and that was what Billy didn't have and therefore why I shot more footage than anybody else.

George Pelecanos often invited neighborhood kids inside his home to watch The Wire. *He wanted to see the show from their perspective, and he began noticing, like all the writers, that the character of Omar had taken on an unintended mythos. "But also," Pelecanos recalled, "things were being misunderstood by kids. Like when they burn Randy's house down and it's supposed to be a tragedy, the kids in my neighborhood were saying stuff like, 'Yeah, Randy's a bitch. He deserved it.'*

"I took that shit to heart. It got me thinking about the perception of this versus what we were trying to do, which is something that you always need to consider. You don't know what's in anybody's heart, but you also

don't know what the perception is of what you're doing, so the thing with Omar is, 'Let's make sure that people know he's not a hero.' He had a code and he was an honorable guy in his own way, but he's not a hero."

The conversation in the writers' room did not revolve around whether they should kill off Omar. That was a given. A debate centered on how Omar would meet his demise. They decided that he would not last until the finale, and ensured that his death would be sudden and unexpected.

GEORGE PELECANOS (WRITER/PRODUCER): Donnie [Andrews] was in the writers' room with us, and he was the model for Omar. The funny thing about that scene where Omar jumps out of the apartment balcony, breaks his leg: Donnie did that, and some of the stuff on the Internet was, "Now they've jumped the shark. That could never happen." We sort of laughed about that, because when Donnie jumped out of that balcony after a shootout, it was off of a floor higher than the one Omar jumps out of. Donnie broke his leg, but he walked on it to a waiting car, got in it, and sped away.

ED BURNS (CO-CREATOR): In the Nine Hundred building, he jumped out. When they're coming through the door with shotguns, it's not a bad move.

MICHAEL K. WILLIAMS (OMAR LITTLE): What we shared in conversations, I chose to keep that between [Donnie] and I, in his honor. I will tell you this, he's a good man. He lived with a lot of remorse for what he has done, a lot of pain, a lot of guilt, but he made good, I believe. He paid his debt to society and he made good to the community for all he had taken out. I'm proud to say that I've known him and he was a part of my life.

DENNIS LEHANE (WRITER): I liked the scene where Omar dies because I'd advanced the idea in the writers' room pretty passionately that he die randomly and without dignity, and that the killer be a child. Ed jumped right in to support the idea because Ed hated anything that smelled of wish fulfillment or romanticizing that world. And David agreed pretty quick, too. So, that was a win.

ED BURNS (CO-CREATOR): We were thinking about Omar dying, as he had to make room for Michael. Dennis Lehane says, "We should shoot him, not in the end, last cut. We should shoot him before that. Just have some kid walk in and kill him." And that sounded so appropriate, because that was the Jesse James story, with Robert Ford coming up.

DAVID SIMON (CREATOR): I knew we wouldn't write what everybody wanted to see, a big glorious gunfight, because they were watching *The Wire* for the wrong reasons. If they get the big, glorious gunfight and he kills Marlo, it's just going to add to his mythos. If Marlo kills him, there is an indignity to Omar's end in that the mythos is transferred to the guy who is the greatest sociopath in the story. That's too dark for even me: the drug dealer who is the most narcissistic and the most sociopathic character we had claims the one who began with maybe one of the more fundamental street ethics. So, there was no outcome of coming back to Marlo and vengeance.

There's no way to proceed other than to find a third path. We came up with the idea of the Errol Barnes [from *Clockers*] moment. I knew it was right. I had a lot of arguments in the room with other people. People wanted to see more out of the storyline, but it felt like, *No, this is right.*

MICHAEL K. WILLIAMS (OMAR LITTLE): I read the script like everybody else. You get a call from David never. It's business, man. It's a job. You just read the script. We in the field. No violins to play. We've got a job to do.

Omar ran the streets, so it's not like I didn't know what it was.

ANTHONY HEMINGWAY (DIRECTOR): The moment I found out I was directing Omar's death, there was a rush of emotions that ravaged my body. I cried like a baby. I high-fived everyone I encountered, whether I knew them or not. I screamed. I cried again. This was a huge deal to me and the show. It was, in an interesting way, the resolve to my debut. This was a pivotal episode in the grand scheme of the series, so the reality that I was being entrusted to handle it was an amazing feeling. Then it was time to get to work, and I began to do what I always do, which was: *Whatever it takes. No sacrifice is too great for me to give this my two hundred percent.* Once we found the perfect location to shoot the scene, I could then start to block the scene and break it down to figure out all that I needed to approach it and prepare to shoot this important and intense scene.

The funny part involving Thuliso [Dingwall, as Kenard], I didn't anticipate how the scene where he shoots Omar would impact him—or me, for that matter. At this point in the series, I had already prayed for forgiveness for damaging and corrupting this child. We had him cursing and completely going against everything that his mother and father taught him not to do. It was terrible. But by this point, I initially didn't think twice about him walking into the store carrying a gun and shooting Omar. And prior to shooting the scene, I had several conversations with him, which he, too, brushed it off, so there wasn't anything to be alarmed by.

The day we shot the scene, all our preconceived confidences had left the building. At the moment for Thuliso to do what he needed to do, there was something that washed over him, causing him to internalize and not say much. Thankfully, later, I discovered he was scared but didn't want to say anything and just wanted to do what he was needed to do.

THULISO DINGWALL (KENARD): I was in middle school, still around maybe eleven or twelve years old. I got the script a couple of days before, to see what was going on. I didn't quite understand it when I was first reading it, so my dad was telling me like, "Yeah, you're going to shoot Omar when you guys go on set tomorrow." I'm like, "Really?" He was like, "Yeah."

Me and my mom were going crazy. Just like, *What's going on?* We get on set. Initially, they're telling me how to hold the gun. They're telling me what's going to happen, breaking it down for me how the scene's going to go, because it's a very quick scene. I'm in the store, and there's a guy in the corner who had this machine on his back and it sprayed out, like, banana bits and like strawberry shit. I don't know what it was, but it was like strawberry. It really looked like brains. It was weird. They did really well on that, whoever's job that was. I think that's really what scared me as a child, honestly, was seeing all that stuff splatter on that Plexiglas. They gave me the gun and they said, "Look, don't shoot. Don't pull the trigger. Everything's going to be done by us. You just hold the gun, and then when we tell you to drop it, you drop it. Boom." That's what it was. Real simple.

When it happened, it just looked so real to me. I know I was young, but it just looked absolutely so real to me that I started to cry immediately after. Immediately after the scene was done, I ran out that store and down the block and cried because it looked so real, because I thought I really killed him.

MICHAEL K. WILLIAMS (OMAR LITTLE): He was traumatized is what it was. No, we should've been charged with child abuse that day, when you look back at it. I'll say it, because that was brutal. He was what? Ten, thirteen, twelve years old? No one prepped him. I think there was so much going on that day on the set. We had to hide me because, by that time, there were mobs of people. The people of Baltimore would come out. When they heard Omar was shooting in the hood, they would come out to see what Omar was going to do. They had to hide all that blood makeup because they did not want you to see I was indeed going to die that episode. That information was a hot topic back then.

THULISO DINGWALL (KENARD): I never held a gun in my hand before. This is new to me. The whole concept around kids and guns didn't really click to me until afterward, after watching it for the first time myself, when I was around maybe twelve, thirteen years old. I guess it made more sense to me then than it did initially, because to me it was just, "Oh, I'm gonna kill a guy on TV." It was nothing to me. I didn't really pay attention to the social problem of kids around guns.

MICHAEL K. WILLIAMS (OMAR LITTLE): No one wants to talk about the elephant in the room, which, in my opinion, was no one wanted to deal with the reality that it felt like mourning a fictitious television character. I don't think no one was able to go there that day. There was a job to do, and no one felt like no teary-eyed shit. I think no one just had mental capacity to go there. Everybody was supposed to act like it was just another day at the office. In my mind, it was an elephant in the room, a sadness that this shit was really coming to a fucking end. Nobody really wanted to really deal with that, in my mind.

I remember Dona, the wardrobe lady, she came in my dressing room, and I was sitting there listening to Young Jeezy, "Bury Me A G." I will never forget that, man. She walked in my trailer and she just looked at me and she said, "Uh-uh. We're not going there." She just snapped me back into a false reality, so I could get through the day. Then we got ready. We got the shot all together. Then the blood splattered, and then the woman's screaming behind the pane, and my body goes limp on the floor. This little kid looked at that shit, and it was too much for him. It was too much. The reality got blurred for him in that instant. It happens to us as actors, you know what I mean? Cross over and he was pulled into a place of shock and terror. That look on his face is so sincere. It's so sincere. He was like, "Oh my God. What have I done? What have I done?" We had to stop. We had to console him. I had to let him see it was just fake. I had to hold him, let him know he didn't kill me. I felt really bad that day that we didn't think about that shit.

DONA ADRIAN GIBSON (COSTUME SUPERVISOR): [Williams] was crying, because it had come full circle. I remember the day that we met, quite honestly, because he was a day player, and I don't think that anybody thought that he was really going to develop into such a cult character. It was great, because we were just kicking it. He's always just been lovely, and I guess it just really kind of rang true for him, right in that moment, that that whole legacy was over.

ANTHONY HEMINGWAY (DIRECTOR): My style of directing is akin to a lot of old-school training. I like to be as close to set as possible, if not right on set. Especially if the scene is intimate or requires me to be close. So, as I called, "Action," Kenard enters the store from outside, walks up to Omar, raises his gun, shoots Omar in the head—the blood squibs applied to Omar's head exploded, spraying blood everywhere, making this moment very visceral and real, then Kenard lowers the gun and runs out of the store. After I cut, I first checked on Michael, or Omar, then went outside to check on Thuliso, and he was in his mother's arms crying. And of course—I'm like a cup at the ready to run over on a dime—[I] started tearing up. But at that moment, I had a reality check, recognizing how this affected Thuliso in such a major way and that made me a little bit happy, happy that doing this act of violence would hopefully scare him from wanting to ever do anything like this again, especially in his personal life.

GBENGA AKINNAGBE (CHRIS PARTLOW): The first thing was like, "What?" It made sense because this thing is cyclical. To me, I'm surprised when people are like, "No, that can't be" or whatever. I'm like, "Oh, word? Have you not looked at any inner cities? Do you not see this thing, what our young people are?" These kids are feeding off of these things and learning. So, it totally makes sense. On top of that, with Kenard's character, if you track his character back, he's always been a little off and a little more aggressive than the other kids. He'd be the one.

I remember these conversations with Ed. I would have such long, lovely conversations with Ed. I remember just talking about people and life and demography and sociology, all kinds of things. He broke down to me a Baltimore classroom. He said the number of kids in Baltimore city schools, the number of kids who drop out and how many kids were left and how people become Marlo Stanfields and Chris Partlows and so on. The kid who something has happened to him and he's not socialized right, but they don't stay in school. School doesn't help. Then this one kid, something has happened to him, but he sees that he's got this kind of skill with people and so on. The different things that dictate the paths that these children take. In that story is a Kenard. In every school or classroom, there is somebody who can become Kenard.

The fascinating and great thing about *The Wire* is that it shows you how people become the people they're going to become, whether that's good or bad. We get to humanize these people, despite the horrific or great things they do. Because I'm into that type of story-telling, and it's most reflective of real life, I totally understood and bought how Kenard could be the person who takes out Omar, and how Kenard is the person that Omar doesn't see coming.

GEORGE PELECANOS (WRITER/PRODUCER): Marlo was cheated, but it was more a comment of how cheap life was and that [Omar] could be got. He had turned his back on someone in the market. He was buying a pack of smokes. He was depleted at that point, too. We didn't want to give him a big gun fight or anything like that or even what Stringer got, which is the satisfaction of Omar and Brother Mouzone hunting him down. We just didn't want to do that with him.

If you recall in that episode, after his death, you cut to the newsroom, and the paper comes across somebody's desk, and they look at it and they throw it in the basket. Outside of his world, he's nothing to anybody. In what we think of us as the proper society, and even in the newsroom, he's nothing. "Throw him in the basket. Put him with all the other guys." It's like in DC, in *The Washington Post*, they change the name of it quite frequently. It's been called "Around the Region" and "Crime," but buried in the Metro section are the murders of blacks in the city, and they get a paragraph or maybe two paragraphs, if they're lucky. But if a white person is killed on the other side of town, it makes the front page. What that does is subconsciously, it puts in the mind of people reading the newspaper, especially young people, is that black lives don't in fact matter. That was our way of saying Omar wasn't that big of a deal outside of his hood and the underworld that he ran with.

In true Wire *fashion, Omar's death would not be the final fatality of a significant character, especially with George Pelecanos's seasonal penultimate episode on deck. In it, the fictional Snoop meets her tender demise at the hands of a protégé. The series finale features the disclosing to superiors that Jimmy McNulty conjured the serial killer. Officials order a cover-up as McNulty and Lester Freamon retire from the police force and law enforcement breaks up Marlo Stanfield's drug ring. Marlo avoids jail but is wayward without his power—the irony being that he possesses the legitimacy Stringer Bell once desperately coveted, yet has no use for it. The series concludes with a lasting shot of Baltimore's skyline as cars whip past on the highway.*

The show managed to tie up a considerable number of storylines with fewer episodes than previous seasons. "Each main character had stepped off," Ed Burns explained. "Bubbles had stepped off, and another kid would come in, and Omar stepped off, someone would come in, this type of thing. We had one of the cops replace McNulty at the end, bringing in [Corey Parker Robinson's Leander] Sydnor. In the street, they call it a dandelion case. You pluck one dandelion up and turn around, and there's another one, and you pluck it and you pluck it, and they're endless."

FELICIA "SNOOP" PEARSON: [Tristan Mack Wilds], that's like my little brother. Even, me and Tristan, like the days on set, the times we wasn't working or whatever, he'd come to my neighborhood or we would just hang out, period. Just so he could get the feel of how we lived down here in Baltimore, not just that he's here to do a job, and that's what I love about him. I ain't put him in harm's way or nothing like that. But just for him not being on set, he wanted to see what Baltimore was all about and see how the kids interact with a lot of people. Just how they interact, period, so he could get his role down pat, and I think that's why he did an amazing job.

TRISTAN MACK WILDS (MICHAEL LEE): You build relationships with these people, like true, deep relationships. Snoop came to my crib in the projects. They ate food at my mom's crib. I came to her crib in Baltimore. I ate food there. I'm chilling in the hood in Baltimore. Ed Burns and David Simon had to tell me, "You can't go to the hood with Snoop. It's really, really bad out there. We're playing it, but it's really, really bad out there. You can't keep doing that." Snoop is like my big sister. Still, to this day, that's legit my big sister. Whenever I need anything, she needs anything, it's a phone call. I got the script, and it just seemed that everybody was weird that day. I remember everybody being on edge, just talking to me, and I'm going in there just to go to school. I'm going to the production offices. They hand me the new script. I read it. I'm running through the script, see how everything's going on. I finally get to that scene. Well, I'm getting to before that scene, and I'm like, "Damn. Y'all gonna kill me on the second-to-last episode?" Reading, reading like mad, nervous. Like, "Damn. They gonna kill me. They gonna kill me. They gonna kill me." Get to the last part. "You look good, girl. Boom." Like, *What the fuck?*

I closed the script, and I'm telling you, it was God or some sort of weird, uncanny timing. I walk outside the production office. I'm about to go talk to Nina Noble or something. And Snoop walks in the production office. I'm standing there, like, "Yooo . . ." She's like, "Yeah, I know. It's all good." I'm like, "Na. Yo, this is crazy." She comes over, gives me a big hug. She's like, "Na, it's all good. I knew it was going to happen. I'm glad it's with you." I'm like, "I can't do this. We're family. What? This doesn't make no sense." She's like, "It's good. We're good." And she carried that same mentality all the way through the whole thing. There were times when we were in the car and we were talking about it, and I was like, "Yo, Snoop, I don't think I can do this." She was like, "You got it. You good. Don't worry. You about to be a man." She kept on telling me that. "You about to be the man. Relax, you good."

FELICIA "SNOOP" PEARSON: Yeah, it was emotional for me, too. I'm from the street. This my first time shooting a movie. That felt like it was too real. That's why they don't do none of the blood scene or nothing like that. You just see a flash, because Tristan was young, and I felt a certain kind of way about it. It was just really emotional, and then we really felt emotional because we knew this was the last season. We were like, *Dang.* I didn't like that scene at all.

GEORGE PELECANOS (WRITER/PRODUCER): The famous scene where Michael kills Snoop in the car, I wrote, "How my hair look, Mike?" Right before he shoots her. It's the last thing she says to him. David called me up and he said, "I don't get it." So, I tried to articulate it and explain to it to him, but I'm not very articulate. I'm certainly not as articulate as David is. I can often not explain in detail why I've written something. I have an instinct for it. What I told him was that this is someone who's never commented on her looks, but she's pretty, and I think she cares about it, and I think it's the last thing that she would think about, knowing that she's going to die, is the way she looked and the way she's going to look when she's found.

David wasn't really convinced. They had the dialogue in the truck, and then I wrote it so that you're back in long shot, looking down in the alley at the truck, and all you see is the muzzle flash and you hear a little pop, and I said, "Let's shoot it the way I wrote it. You're going to cut back to that anyway, and in the editing room, if it doesn't work, you just cut out that last line, but at least we've got it." And he did that, and I know he liked it, because he wouldn't have kept it if he didn't.

FELICIA "SNOOP" PEARSON: I knew that I was going to get shot in my head because of that line. But when I had got my script and I seen the line or whatever, I told my hair stylist to put a design or something in my hair, because they're going to show my hair. I put a star in my head, but they didn't show it. They didn't show the squib. I thought they were going to show the bloody part, but they didn't do the squib.

TRISTAN MACK WILDS (MICHAEL LEE): It's so Snoop. It's so her. I just think it was a super dope, swag line to go out. She knew she was going to go out one way or another, whether it was here or somewhere else. It's one of those things that you carry with you if you're in that line of work, everywhere you go. She went out, in my opinion, as a G. It's like, "You know what? You got me. Go ahead." It's her way of saying, "Go ahead." But between us, it's just some last words to show how G she was. It's crazy.

FELICIA "SNOOP" PEARSON: I thank the writers and producers, the directors, everyone down to the craft people. I thank you all for just accepting me as a person. I know I wasn't the typical actress that they be around every day, but I thank everybody for just bringing me on as a family member, not just a cast member, as a family member, and I love each and every one of them, and I most definitely love Michael K. Williams for even just ice-grilling me.

TRISTAN MACK WILDS (MICHAEL LEE): To the genius of David Simon and Ed Burns, they purposely made the scene with me, Bug, and Dukie, me and Jermaine's last scene together. Because that was Episode Nine. We both had scenes in Episode Ten, but not together. And it was one of those things where he lives in Silver Springs and I'm living in Baltimore. I'm not driving and he's not driving, and I don't think his mom would drive him out to see me. It was one of those things where if we weren't working, we weren't going to see each other.

So, they purposely made those scenes our last scenes together, so that the emotion from it was immensely real. Me and Bug were walking up the house, and I'm patting him down, making sure he's right. "C'mon man. Men don't be shedding no tears." Because he's tearing up and stuff. Mind you, the kid is actually crying. His name is Keenon [Brice]. Keenon is actually tearing up, because he understands, "Damn. I'm not going to be here no more. I'm not even going to see my big brother no more. It's a wrap." And I'm feeling the same way. I think the last line is "Go on, Bug." I say it, and my voice cracks. I think it's probably one of those things that I notice only, but my voice cracks, because I was two seconds away from tears. If they wouldn't have cut away from me, I would have been bawling.

JIM TRUE-FROST (DET. ROLAND "PREZ" PRZYBYLEWSKI): The scenes with Dukie are so poignant and some are really heart-wrenching, but Jermaine, he's like a ray of sunshine. It's so funny, because he's a really sweet-natured and lighthearted guy.

JERMAINE CRAWFORD (DUQUAN "DUKIE" WEEMS): When people talk about acting and they be like, "Oh, this character, it became me," or they say, "Will Smith, he's like this when he's on set and you can't even address him, sometimes he's so zoned in," I thought it was really all bull. I thought it was all bull. But when I wrapped Season Five, this kind of thing stuck with me, just because I was so used to tapping into it, if that makes sense.

TRISTAN MACK WILDS (MICHAEL LEE): We never had a full conversation about [Michael becoming the next Omar], but it's always been an implied conversation. Understanding what Omar is to this entire show, to this series. He's Obama's favorite character. I'm like, "C'mon, man. What? That's crazy." It's crazy. I wish I had better words for it. First off, to play any character that's close to Omar or that can have the same effect that Omar has had for the series, is huge. And then to eventually, as time goes on, become that character. It's like playing a character named Bruce Wayne and then finding out you're going to be Batman.

JAMIE HECTOR (MARLO STANFIELD): Nina K. Noble is one of the producers of the show. She barely speaks, so you could be on set with her for a good two or three years, and you'd probably get like three words. She's the sweetest person and she barely speaks, and you barely really see her use facial expressions. That was the first direction that she even gave me, was for that ["My name is my name"] scene. She said any corporation that is being spoken about—let's just say Coca-Cola or whatever the case may be—there's something negative going on with it, and the workers know and it doesn't make it to the head, then the head will be very upset about it. As soon as she aligned Marlo Stanfield with a corporation and as soon as she associated the two, that right there triggered it for me. That was it. That did it. It was just like you could turn around and all of this is going on, and you're walking in a crowd and you don't even know what's going on with the business below you until it tumbles. That's what just took place. Once she said that to me and expressed it to me that way, then I realized how important it was.

KWAME PATTERSON ("MONK" METCALF): It was the first time you see Marlo lose his cool. That scene was powerful. It was a great scene for Jamie. That was the first time you see Marlo lose his cool, and then, for me, it was the first time where I kind of had to be vulnerable in a sense. That was something that Robert [Chew] helped me with.

GBENGA AKINNAGBE (CHRIS PARTLOW): We're there shooting. We also had a great crew that really took care of us. We're in these tight confines with doing this, plus we're getting toward the end. Our characters, we're being squeezed. As an actor, I had a great time doing that, but as Chris, he's trying to manage expectations. In many ways, he's kind of managing this thing. He's advising. He's his consigliere. He's trying to manage his boy. Chris is a sociopath, but he has to make sure Marlo is not the one who goes off and makes mistakes out of anger and emotion. It was a little frustrating because Chris hadn't told him that Omar was out there calling out his name. That was a strategic move not to do that, because there was a bigger picture. He finds out, and so he's got to tell him that this is happening, but he's trying to handle it. It was a little frustrating because he knows Marlo. To Marlo, that's more important than anything, his name on the streets. He gets a whiff that somebody is even trying to punk his name on the street, then it's, forget all the planning, forget all the strategy, forget the goals of what we're trying to do. He's like, "Go to war. Destroy all." His name is his name. For Chris, who does practice in the art of strategy and planning, it was frustrating to see that kind of blow up in his face.

JAMIE HECTOR (MARLO STANFIELD): That's a testament to the great writing that we had on the show, because people always strive for these things in life, right? When you get it, then you're just like, "Yeah, but I want something else. Yeah, this is cool, but okay. Next." Marlo was after power. I think what he really, really, really wanted was power. He had the money. He wanted the power. The thing about it with Avon is when you get locked up or you go away or you go on vacation for a while, wherever that vacation is, and you come back, people get older and things change. I think what Marlo really wanted is power, just pure, uncut, unstoppable power.

TRAY CHANEY (MALIK "POOT" CARR): Poot was definitely a follower. He wasn't one of those boss kind of characters where he was telling people what to do. He did have some moments like when he took over the pit and different things of that nature. But he was more so the kind of guy that kind of listened to everything from the older guys in the Barksdale organization. He was always told what to do, and he didn't mind being told what to do, but there did come a point where he had to kill his best friend, Wallace, or when he started seeing people die or hearing about people die around him, all the way up to the point where J. D. Williams, who played Bodie, was killed right there in front of him on his corner. That's when the character to me was like an American hero, by being able to turn the bad into good with ending up working in Foot Locker at the end.

That story couldn't have been ironed out no more perfect, because that's what society is about now. It's about choices. You just sat up there and watched all your friends get killed or locked up. You had a choice, whether you're just going to stay in the game or whether you were going to get out the game, and he chose to get out the game.

GEORGE PELECANOS (WRITER/PRODUCER): We had to choose somebody. We're not complete nihilists. We just thought he's a guy that could walk away. He wasn't a killer, really. He did the thing with Wallace, but he wasn't a guy who had bloodlust or anything. He didn't want to be the king. He was kind of going along with his friends, and when everything kind of fell apart and all his friends were gone, he just got a job. And it's possible. You don't have to be in it forever. That whole thing about "it's either jail or death is the only way it ends," actually it's not true. A lot of people get out. They just walk away from it.

DOMINIC WEST (DET. JIMMY MCNULTY): We were drunk for one scene. It was the last scene. My fake funeral. There was whiskey going around the bar. I remember I was lying on the pool table, and Wendell said, "Fuck it," because it was our last day. He said, "Come on, let's drink whiskey because we were supposed to be drinking whiskey." All I had to do was lie there and pretend to be a corpse, so I got hammered, and so did he.

Then, Clark Johnson, the director, said, "Okay, Dom, now we're going to do your close-up." I was like, "What do you mean by close-up? I'm a corpse." He goes, "No, no, no. No, we've got the camera starting really close in your face. Your eyes spring open, and we realize you're still alive, and then the camera is going to zoom away from your face." And I was like, "Oh, fuck it," because I opened my eyes and you could see it in the show. I opened my eyes and they were completely bloodshot, and I'm absolutely hammered, but I think that was the only time we got properly drunk doing a scene, but maybe my memory doesn't serve me quite as well.

DAVID INSLEY (DIRECTOR OF PHOTOGRAPHY): Every now and then, David would come in with rewrites and bring in new pages, and we'd be in the middle of a scene and he'd throw new pages at our actors. They'd have to do them right there. We'd have to redo the scene, because he wrote new pages. The last day, he brought in new pages, and it was [Wendell Pierce] and Dominic and they were in the police station, and it was like hour eighteen or something. It was really late. He said, "We have to do these pages. Just do them. Just read them and shoot it." It was Bunk and Dominic talking about Simon being a jerk and the director being a jerk, and they're being jerks and saying, "Why are we doing this stuff?" It was just such a big joke. It was really a great ending to the season. Simon could be really funny.

LANCE REDDICK (LT. CEDRIC DANIELS): The show wasn't trying to show a silver lining. I felt like the show was trying to show how the system works and what people have to sacrifice to be part of it and what they have to sacrifice to live up to who they really are. In some ways, what's cool for me about Daniels is he's one of the few people at the end of the show who's a truly heroic character.

BENJAMIN BUSCH (OFF. ANTHONY COLICCHIO): Its point is that this doesn't have closure. This is endless. Whatever perspective you have as a character, any of the characters there, your lot doesn't end with the final season.

MICHELLE PARESS (ALMA GUTIERREZ): Sometimes I say Season Five is the stepchild of *The Wire*. I don't know that we got as much love as all the other seasons, but it was a great storyline.

10

WE OPENED THE CONVERSATION

The 2015 death of Freddie Gray while in police custody brought
Baltimore's simmering unrest to the forefront of America's
consciousness. Gray was a twenty-five-year-old black man arrested in
West Baltimore. With pedestrians recording the disturbance on their
cell phones, the police officers immobilized Gray by pinning his feet and
dragging him into the back of a police van. Gray died from a severed
spine sustained while riding in the van. In Baltimore, police have for
years been accused of deliberately giving "rough rides," where the vehicle
is often stopped abruptly in order to jolt the detainee seated in the
rear. Famed attorney Billy Murphy, who had appeared in The Wire, *
represented Gray's family in court.

    In the wake of Gray's death, rioting and looting ensued on the same
streets that had filmed The Wire. *To some, the show predicted a death*
like Gray's in presenting the need for police reform. "If you watched The
Wire, *they did the same thing," said Anwan Glover, who portrayed Slim*
Charles. "Kids was put in the back of the wagon and they throw them
around and they'd let them out. Everything was true to a science." To
David Simon, the need for police reform is more a function of class than
racism. He will not stretch the show's foresight as far as Glover. "Given
that it was fifteen years ago, twenty years ago, and the drug war wasn't
even being critiqued in any serious way back then," Simon said. "It is now.

Was I wrong to suggest that there would not be activity? Did it anticipate that there would be a revolution in [cell phones]? That this would become the weapon of social change, in regard to [Black Lives Matter]? No. The power of these things, the smartphone and the camera, was yet to come."

Baltimore's uproar reflected The Wire's enduring impression on the city. Actors from the show again rallied around it. Some had never left. Simon had since moved on to several projects that did not feature Baltimore, but blogged a plea for the end of the looting. "There was real power and potential in the peaceful protests that spoke in Mr. Gray's name initially, and there was real unity at his homegoing today," he wrote. "But this, now, in the streets, is an affront to that man's memory and a diminution of the absolute moral lesson that underlies his unnecessary death." The next month, Simon met with Barack Obama inside the White House, at the president's request. Obama had repeatedly cited The Wire as his favorite television show, and Omar as his favorite character. The pair discussed the toll of the war on drugs on communities, mass incarceration, and the challenges encountered by law enforcement. "There is an increasing realization on the left, but also on the right politically, that what we're doing is counterproductive," Obama told Simon during the discussion. "Either from a libertarian perspective, the way we treat nonviolent drug crimes is problematic, and from a fiscal perspective, is breaking the bank. They end up spending so much more on prison than you would with these kids being in school or even going to college that it's counterproductive, and it means that everybody's taxes are going up, or at least services that everybody uses are being squeezed, or we can't hire cops to deal with violent crime, as you talked about. And as I said, the encouraging thing is, I think, awareness is increasing, in part because violent crime has gone down in a lot of big cities. People are more open to having a discussion about this." Obama ended the taped portion of the conversation by saying he was encouraged that the policing of communities was being discussed in smarter ways. "From your mouth to God's ear," Simon replied, delivering the same line that Idris Elba offered him discovering the impending death of Stringer Bell.

The Wire is now celebrated as one of the greatest television shows *ever made. The majority of the show's writers, crew, and actors couldn't care less about the accolades and especially the arguments concerning whether Omar or Stringer is the cooler character. David Simon never said he had answers to the world he searingly presented. But a solution will never be found if the problem is not at least presented honestly and discussed openly.*

MICHAEL K. WILLIAMS (OMAR LITTLE): [Obama saying Omar is his favorite character] made me cry. It also made me care about what he was doing. It made me believe that any president of the United States that can watch *The Wire* and say Omar was their favorite character, in my brain, is a man for the people, not just one, but for all. At least I matter to him and my community. I remember going to rooms early on, going to auditions, and one woman said, "That show is really good for people who want to let those types of stories into their life, into their home." It was a very strange remark. I'll never forget she had made it. But President Obama, we were good enough to be in his home. I was like, "Okay. Let me see what he's about, because he cares. He really cares. He gets it."

ANDRE ROYO (REGINALD "BUBBLES" COUSINS): It was amazing because, first of all, we were still stuck on stupid that there was a black man running for president. We still were like, *Can this really be happening? We're going to have a black president in our lifetime.* Then, I think it was *60 Minutes* or *Charlie Rose*, when they asked Hillary Clinton what she watched on her downtime, and she said *American Idol.* Then they asked Obama, and he goes, *The Wire.* "I watch *The Wire*." That was validation, and it blew our heads back. We all felt great. We also recognized that that's the type of show we were.

We were the type of show that when you said you watched *The Wire*, it made you a different person. It made you a highly intellectual motherfucker who cares, not just about the art, not to recognize the good storytelling, but cares about what's happening. You must read a lot of books. You must have compassion about community. When he said that, it just gave him a little extra swag. He's not just a black man, but he's a black man that's well rounded. He can play their games, but he knows our games, too. It was special.

When I did *Red Tails*, I'm out there in Prague, me and Anthony Hemingway. He was our script supervisor. Now he's a big-time director. He was shooting *Red Tails*. Me and a couple of the cast from *Red Tails*, we go to this area where Obama's doing his visit. He's doing a speech. I got my daughter on my shoulders. We're standing there looking at Obama speaking about the blah, blah, blah. He looks over, he sees me. He goes, "Is that my man Bubs? Does anybody know Bubs?" "Yes, Mr. Obama. How are you?" He's like, "What are you doing out here?" "Shooting *Red Tails*." "You keep up the good work." I was like, fucked up. My daughter was flipping out. "The president knows you? The president knows you." Everybody was laughing. It's wonderful to know that we impacted people who fell in love with the show. That's an amazing, amazing feeling.

CLARKE PETERS (DET. LESTER FREAMON): *The Wire* promoted a conversation that is still ongoing. It has become a reference point in universities, not only here, but in England as well. It's a topic to be studied. It was well studied, well researched in being put together. I think we accomplished the mission in that conversation. We opened the conversation, and it's still ongoing. It's not just in Baltimore. Not all the police are like all the policemen on our show, and that's eye-opening as well. There's a conversation that began with it and is still ongoing.

ANDRE ROYO (REGINALD "BUBBLES" COUSINS): Once you watch *The Wire*, once you finish and you get to that last episode, Season Five, you can't say "I don't know" anymore. You see what's happening. You know what's happening. Now this should be a collective conversation on "How do we fix it?" Instead of saying, "I didn't know that was happening. I didn't know that was going on." That's one of the blessings that will always stick with all of us. All of us that were involved in

The Wire, we'll always talk about how we were a part of educating and entertaining and inspiring people at the same time, which back then was rare for television to do all three, a scripted television show to do all three and not be over the top about it, but be as real as possible.

The Wire was the hidden understanding of how a city is destroyed. David Simon, he'll sit there and he'll talk about all the problems. He never came across like he had the answers on how to fix things. His whole thing was, "The first thing you got to know is you got to know the problem exists." A lot of people got their heads buried in the fucking sand.

ROBERT WISDOM (HOWARD "BUNNY" COLVIN): There are two kinds of people in the world. People who have seen *The Wire* and people who haven't seen *The Wire*. The people who haven't seen it, there's a large percentage of them who say they haven't seen it, because they go through that stuff in real life. They don't have to watch it on TV. They want to escape it. That's what our news industry, our newspapers, in particular, have become. It's the same thing with the local six p.m. news. What has that become? Nothing but car chases and fucking pie contests. But in terms of significant reporting, nobody bothers with that stuff. Why? Because they feel there's nothing they can do about it.

It happened. They feel sorry, but unless you're in an intimate relationship with somebody whose name is in that news, whether it's the obits or whatever, why do I care? But then, when it gets blown up into this show and articulated in the way that these people who were writers for the Metro section and the Crime pages, then we see, "Holy shit. This is us. This is who we are." The seeds and the vines of who we are right there in these pages daily. If we wanted to, we could change our cities if more people got involved, but that's a big stretch. *The Wire* was sitting right in our lives this whole time, and we prefer to have the more glamorous and the more literary analogy of [Charles] Dickens. That resonates with a different range of people. But, in fact, it's much more mundane than that. It's the Metro section.

ANDRE ROYO (REGINALD "BUBBLES" COUSINS): All of a sudden, that kind of character that you move away from in the subway platform, you walk on the other side of the street, or make a judgment about— now, all of a sudden that person is in your living room on your TV, and you're not looking away. You're actually looking at him and watching him go through what he goes through, and you're finding out about his life in such a well-written way that you start to care. You start to go, *I hope Bubbles makes it. Oh my God. Don't hurt him.* I just felt like that was happening for every character, these people that you have a preconceived judgment on. David Simon and Ed Burns, all of these writers were writing so well, and giving you the lay of the lands about who these characters are, that we really had to erase people's opinions, preconceived notions of who these characters are: A *drug dealer is a drug dealer. He's stupid for doing that.*

All of a sudden, you found out a drug dealer—he's not that stupid. If they make a mistake, they get shot. They better be a little smarter. You see cops. Back then, my idea of a cop—all you saw was the badge. All you saw was the gun. You didn't really see the person. You saw a cop and *Fuck a cop* or *I'm scared of a cop.* Now you're looking at cops, and some of them are good. They're trying very hard, but the system will make you not give a fuck anymore. You keep on arresting somebody, and they keep coming out. You just go, *Well, fuck them then.* You just start seeing things from a different perspective.

CHRIS BAUER (FRANK SOBOTKA): The show asked a lot of anyone who watched it. It was not easy viewing. It's hard to make a casserole and watch *The Wire* in the background à la *Law & Order.*

ANDRE ROYO (REGINALD "BUBBLES" COUSINS): Later on, all of a sudden, I'm going to get some doughnuts. I see in the paper, in 2009 or

2010, we're known as one of the greatest shows ever. I'm like, *Holy shit. When did that happen?*

ED BURNS (CO-CREATOR): I don't know what kind of life it's taken on. The day it was over, it was over for me. I'm an introvert. I feel uncomfortable when people say it's a great show and stuff like that, because that's their decision. That's their call. I never looked at all these *Wire* blogs and stuff like that. One of the main reasons I left Baltimore was because of *The Wire*. It didn't change anything.

NORMAN KNOERLEIN (RESEARCHER): Burns is the person who doesn't like a lot of big things. He doesn't live in Hollywood. He likes West Virginia. He likes his life.

PABLO SCHREIBER (NICK SOBOTKA): It was strange. There was a time there—I call it peak *The Wire*—where it felt like, it was maybe like two years after it was off the air, where it suddenly felt like everybody was watching it, and that was definitely the biggest time of getting stopped on the street for that particular show. Yeah, it was. It was like two years after it went off the air, which is odd. It was actually, I think, a big precursor to what's happening now, with all the streaming shows where people are watching content on their own time.

CHRIS ALBRECHT (CHAIRMAN AND CEO, HBO): It's a little bit ironic. I still have people literally telling me almost every few weeks, "Oh my God, we just saw *The Wire*. It's the greatest show ever." Then you go, *Okay. So, did the show change? Did people change?* The show was available on DVD at the end of every season. All of a sudden, what's changed?

I don't really know what's changed. If you are me, and you were someone who came up in programming, and you had people who worked for you that cared a lot about this, and you look at these shows and you look at *The Sopranos* and you look at *Deadwood* and you look at *The Wire*, and you go, *Wow, all three of these shows are really good. Hey, all three of these shows are really different and all three of these shows deserves to be on television.* I'm in a unique position to make that happen. These things don't grow on trees, although now it looks like they do. Let's back the quality of it all. We had the Davids there. There's David Milch, David Simon, David Chase. Even though each of the Davids had different experiences, I joke about how David [Simon] was a pain in the neck, but ultimately the decision was based on the same thing, which is, "This is good. Let's keep it going." Yes, *The Sopranos* was huge. *Deadwood* wasn't huge, and it ended in a weird way that there was a miscommunication with David Milch about what we had hoped to accomplish for a potential Season Four.

Certainly, on *The Wire*, all we had to do is look at this stuff, and we would look at the episodes of Season One, and we said, "I haven't seen this before." When you get to say that, and it's really good, then you want to know what happens in the next episode after you finish the one that's in your hands, it's a pretty good recommendation for continuing.

JAMES "P.J." RANSONE (CHESTER "ZIGGY" SOBOTKA): It was a bummer for a lot of reasons, because when that happens, the culture catches up to it, but the business has moved on. It's not a hot-button thing, where the industry is looking at me. So, I didn't really have any bounce. It was like a springboard that I could have bounced off of. The one person who I will say who was on top of it way before was Spike Lee, and I got my first big studio movie gig because Spike Lee was such a big fan of *The Wire*, and that was *Inside Man*. Because there was such a delay in the time from when it came out to when it became popular, it didn't give me a lot of business opportunities. And then I was also playing sort of like a really dislikable character for ninety percent of the time that you're watching them.

REG E. CATHEY (NORMAN WILSON): It's so funny now that it's known as the best thing ever on television. While we were shooting it, it was the best thing nobody watched. I remember going in for auditions; we would laugh about it. You'd go in for audition, and they say, "What are you doing now?" "I'm doing *The Wire*. "That's that thing in Baltimore, yeah?"

DOMENICK LOMBARDOZZI (DET. THOMAS "HERC" HAUK): I'm happy for everyone that was affiliated with that show. I'm happy when I see Andre on *Empire*, Jamie on *Bosch*, Lance on *Bosch*, Michael K. Anytime I see any of those guys doing something, it lightens my face up. I know what we went through. I know. We were the redheaded stepchild for a very long time. Nobody knew we were around. I remember auditioning the first couple of seasons, going into hiatus, and people would be like, "*The Wire*? What's *The Wire*?"

CHAD L. COLEMAN (DENNIS "CUTTY" WISE): If you're a trailblazer, you're ahead of your time. You're ahead of schedule. Where the people are is not forward-thinking. They're just in their day-to-day, whatever it is. When you're a trailblazer, you still have to be able to engage those people that say, "Well, it is what it is," and say, "Well, no, there is another way."

DEIRDRE "DEDE" LOVEJOY (ASST. STATE'S ATTY. RHONDA PEARLMAN): My favorite thing is that, years later, I ran into one of the DAs I had trailed, and he said, "You know, I read an article the other day that at ten every Sunday night in Baltimore, for three and a half years, the wiretaps would all go dead, and it is because all of the wiretapped people were watching *The Wire*." I thought that was pretty fucking fantastic, right?

DENNIS LEHANE (WRITER): I'd rather be part of something that was acknowledged in my time than in my moment. Moments pass.

MICHELLE PARESS (ALMA GUTIERREZ): It's true today as it was when it was shot, and unfortunately, it'll be true probably ten, twenty, thirty, forty, fifty years from now. It's the system. It's a revolving door, a cycle, a circle that just doesn't get broken. And I think *The Wire* was able to really show just life in the inner city, not just from the crooks' point of view, or the corner boys', but from the cops' point of view, from the news' point of view, from the kids' and how the school system is just so incredibly dysfunctional. It just shined a light on so many things that people just don't want to talk about, and I think that's why people are still talking about it and they're taking classes in it at Yale and Harvard, because [it] affected so many people on such a deep, deep level.

LAWRENCE GILLIARD JR. (D'ANGELO BARKSDALE): There's always going to be the clashes. There's always going to be the people who have more, the people who have less, and the people who have nothing. That's going to keep that show relevant forever, probably. There's always going to be corruption. That's just the way it is, man. That's just the way it is. I think it's going to be that show that just lasts forever and not just for entertainment value, not like *Friends* or *Seinfeld* or whatever. It's always going to have some kind of social impact and some kind of social relevance.

METHOD MAN (CALVIN "CHEESE" WAGSTAFF): It didn't just talk to one audience. It talked to a few different audiences. Each season was consistent with what Baltimore was about. That's why it always helps to have people that are in the communities, policing the communities, living in the communities, writing this stuff, because they understand it and they have their fingers on the pulse of what's going on in these neighborhoods. Mostly the hood gravitated to it because we love hood shit, especially when it's well made. And the other people, like critics and people of that nature, loved it because it didn't pull punches and it wasn't afraid to peel back that layer and show the real Baltimore.

DOMINIC WEST (DET. JIMMY MCNULTY): A show comes along every ten to twenty years which totally redefines the genre. *Hill Street Blues* redefined the cop drama. I think on the simplest level, so did *The Wire*. It completely refreshed our ideas of a cop show in so many ways. It showed you a deeper understanding of the world and of the world of both the gangsters and the cops. It's one of those shows that stand out as being revolutionary, iconoclastic in that way, and redefining the genre.

I think it's not too much to say it's spawned so many imitations and certainly in the UK, it's been considered, among other shows, a benchmark in how real and how intense and how broad and epic the television drama can be. I think the legacy of *The Wire* is it's made television drama everywhere much better. I used to constantly hear the BBC, they'd go, "We want to make something like *The Wire*." And it became a benchmark for writers and producers to make TV that was as profound an art form as cinema or writing novels. I think it was, in some ways, one of those first shows that became a novel on-screen. It had a deeper and broader scope than any two-hour film could have. It had the depth and scope of a great, epic novel.

MICHAEL B. JORDAN (WALLACE): One of the best shows to ever be on television. It's kind of crazy, and I said that with confidence, right? I said it like I meant it. Sometimes people say that and you're like, "He don't really mean that." I kind of mean that. I mean that. I'm very proud of being a part with that cast and that crew.

DENNIS LEHANE (WRITER): It's one of the most caustic, scabrous visions of America in decline that's ever been put on the screen. And it changed TV a bit, pushed its borders a little further than where they'd previously been positioned.

ERNEST DICKERSON (DIRECTOR): Movies used to be the place where the cool stuff got done. Now the cool stuff is happening on television. I think that all started with *The Wire*. It completely revolutionized the way stories are told on television.

MICHAEL KOSTROFF (MAURICE "MAURY" LEVY): Artistically, there's a hidden message, which is there's such a wealth of hugely talented black actors that we've never heard of. One after another, after another, after another. To me, the message is: write the parts, because the talent is there. There are so many, and these guys blew my mind.

LANCE REDDICK (LT. CEDRIC DANIELS): The subsequent success of the show has shown that, regardless of what the gatekeepers try to use as an excuse, mostly people don't care what color people are in their leads in shows that they watch. They just want to see great human stories. *The Wire* has become such a huge phenomenon in Great Britain, in Western Europe, in Scandinavia, truly by word of mouth. It's certainly not because of any awards, any promotion of HBO per se, compared to the way HBO promoted the other shows. I'd say that, for me, that's the legacy. So much of the great work that I've had the opportunity to do has come from young white guys between the ages of thirty and forty who grew up in the [world] of hip-hop and who were huge fans of *The Wire*, who just don't think about [race] because it's still their world. When they go into a room, most of the people in positions of power are white men. They just don't think about race the same way. You're not seen as a black actor as much. You're seen as an actor who happens to be black.

MICHAEL B. JORDAN (WALLACE): *The Wire* was one of the few shows ever, especially at that time, to have an eclectic group of characters being played by black actors. It was a calling card that it could be done. I think we just need to aspire for more stories like that. Once the characters are being written, we'll find the actors to play them and that's what we're going to do.

LANCE REDDICK (LT. CEDRIC DANIELS): Playing so many three-dimensional, highly intelligent characters, no matter what they were, that, for me, was the biggest part of what was so revolutionary and so cool about the show. When I was doing it, I didn't even realize how cool it was. I realized it in retrospect, partly because the industry changed so much with the beginning of the new millennium. I just felt like the industry started getting really white again. Given how much our show got snubbed, as predominantly black as the cast was, I never thought of our show as a black show or that it would be perceived as such, until then. To me, it was a human show. It's just most of the people happen to be black.

DOMINIC WEST (DET. JIMMY MCNULTY): The older it gets, the greater distance we have from it, the more cherished it seems to be and the more people realize that it's a classic.

It's been ten years now, I think. It's the gift that keeps on giving, really, and I'm really glad about that. Most shows, you finish and you're glad to see the back of them or the public's glad to see the back of you. I never really felt particularly that McNulty defined me or that I would never get anything else, because it wasn't really that sort of role. I've done roles since then, where I played serial killers and things like that, where there's much more danger of people not being able to separate you from the character and much more danger of not being able to move on to other parts. That was never the case with McNulty, partly because he was very different from me and sounded very different from me, so it's easy for me to move on and just enjoy the fact that, as the years go on, people are still watching it and still coming to it for the first time.

DAVID SIMON (CREATOR): I'm more interested in the arguments. I wish that were the legacy of the show.

RICHARD PRICE (WRITER): My theory about David is, because he's a police reporter, he likes adrenaline. He likes something happening, crisis after crisis. He didn't go back to books, because I think he would have to downgrade his metabolism to go back to being a turtle. He's a rabbit now. He even wrote me an email saying, because he owed [editor John] Sterling a book, years and years ago, and I'm paraphrasing, but something like, "Tell Sterling I'll get back to the book as soon as I finish sucking on the glass crack dick of HBO."

I think it really is crack for him. You sit in your office typing, all of a sudden you hear, "Six dead," or, "An explosion somewhere in Baltimore." Boom. You're out of there. Then you gotta compete with all the other dogs, and you're looking for angles nobody else has. He's got that. When I was going around with him, and he was hooking me up with cops, detectives in Baltimore, he saw police barriers and they wouldn't let him in, and he was very embarrassed. He scaled a backyard fence to get into the apartment where no one was looking where the fire took place. He's like an animal. Like any good reporter, he's an animal like that. His intellectual muscles, he can go from zero to sixty in an instant, and I think TV gave him that, because it's the same low-key sense of crisis every minute.

DAVID SIMON (CREATOR): Bad news: I'm the same guy who used to have his feet up and argue with other reporters on the Metro desk about what the news meant. That's infinitely more interesting to me than being political about entertainment that's already been off the air for five years. I just can't. I'm just not built that way. I'm not offended. I'm not personally invested in everything that was *The Wire*, but if you ask me whether I should give a fuck about, in a fair fight, who'd win, Omar or Stringer, or who's cooler, my initial reaction and my second reaction and my fourth reaction is, "Who gives a fuck?" That's who I am. I'm not saying I'm right and I'm not saying it's everybody's metric, but I know what I do.

ED BURNS (CO-CREATOR): With Freddie Gray, you can see that it's the same. I would like to see the confrontations continue. When the quote-unquote riots, when the disturbances, were happening in Baltimore, there was concern. Soon as they stopped happening, the concern disappeared.

The only cool thing that came out of it, as far as I know, is that when they hit the pharmacy and they got all the pills out, my daughter was working, at the time, at the VA. She's a clinical psychologist, and she had to walk up to her car, which was two blocks away from the VA in downtown Baltimore. The price of Oxycontin and all those things, which was, at one time, fifty dollars a pill after the riots, it was down to ten dollars a pill and slowly went back up to fifty dollars as the supply ran out. She was like, "Well, something happened. Something good happened out there." I love that story.

WILLA BICKHAM (CO-FOUNDER OF VIVA HOUSE): It's been more in the news because of the Freddie Gray incident, his death, but I have to say, there are days that we get really discouraged, especially living with all this vacant housing now. It is just disgusting. All the people that were in the soup kitchen today. They live in the cruddiest, crappiest—I've never seen such housing. I mean, it's never been quite this bad, but there's no money. Baltimore doesn't have any money.

KWAME PATTERSON ("MONK" METCALF): The marching was a very good thing. The marching needed to happen. It was good. I think it kind of helped bring the city together, especially with all the different gangs coming together at that moment and putting everything to the side and just protesting and being peaceful. I hate that it happened with Freddie Gray, but I think it was something that was way overdue with the marching and the protesting. The looting and stuff, that helps nothing. The first thing we do is we loot our own community. They marched down in Fells Point, but it wasn't looting in Fells Point. Police don't care about you looting in the hood. That's the hood. They don't care about that.

It's the same thing when the LA riots happened. It's like, "Y'all looting in the area where y'all live at. That's stupid. Go to Beverly Hills if you want to prove a point." Because they ain't going to let you come to Beverly Hills. They gonna shut you down quick. You looting in Inglewood, Compton, they just standing out there watching. They just making sure they don't get too crazy. They just stand out there. But come to Beverly Hills and start looting like that, they gonna shut it down quick, and that's just what it is. So, if you're going to do that, not that I'm condoning it, do it where it matters. That's why I've never been a big fan of the whole rioting stuff, because I think it's stupid. I feel like when they do that, they're not really about the cause. They're just trying to get some free shit. If you're really about the cause, you're going to go where it matters. If you're mad at white people, then go where white people live at. Don't loot where we live.

PABLO SCHREIBER (NICK SOBOTKA): It doesn't feel like we're doing much to change many of the issues that David was talking about. It doesn't really feel like it's had a huge impact in terms of changing things. I wish it had. I don't know necessarily where this country goes from here. But I think that was another point of view of the show as well, like, "Where the fuck can we go from here?" I don't know, man. I think it's probably a sad legacy. But at the same time, for people who want to think deeply about this country and our role in terms of trying to make it a better place to be, I think it's achieved more than any other show ever has.

BENJAMIN BUSCH (OFF. ANTHONY COLICCHIO): *The Wire* really lived in Baltimore. It knew the alleys and cellars. It knew the lingo and the night shifts. It knew the children. It remembered the dead. It was like [Joseph] Conrad's *Heart of Darkness,* like [Charles] Dickens writing about London, or [Herman] Melville about whales. Ed Burns and David Simon were not cosmetic surgeons. They studied terminal illness. They gave cancer a narrative for the first time. They kind of made it a character with sensibilities of its own, and I thought that was remarkable. I don't know that any of us knew, in the cast anyway, at first what *The Wire* was doing, that we would become delegates, but I think every one of us became its fiercest fans.

WENDELL PIERCE (DET. WILLIAM "BUNK" MORELAND): It challenged us to think about the material that we were dealing with. It challenged people who watched it. The reason we still are engaged with the show today is because it really expressed the most important role of art, which is the form where we reflect on what our values are, decide what they are and then act on them. It's where we have that debate of what we believe, where we failed, where we've triumphed. That's what the art is to the community as a whole: a place where you reflect on these issues and say, "This is what we value, and let's act accordingly."

S. ROBERT MORGAN (BUTCHIE): A million people interpret it as a commentary on Baltimore, and that's not what this show was about. That show could have been in New Jersey. It could have been in Arizona. It could have been somewhere in Florida or somewhere in Georgia. What it really was, if you think about the topical nature of the show, season after season, it was really about comparative institutions and the people within those institutions and what made them work and why they didn't work.

ED BURNS (CO-CREATOR): Baltimore's an interesting city. The majority's African American, and yet, there's been no programs coming out of Baltimore that would be cutting-edge, new ways of looking at things.

In fact, we adapt programs from Boston and Kansas City, towns that are totally unlike Baltimore. They come here and they fall flat on their face. The reason is because this is a very cheap little town, parochial. We don't think big. We don't think outside the box. Then, you got Johns Hopkins and the University of Maryland, which are the two big employers here, and nothing's coming out of them, so it's the same old crap over and over and over again, same old approach.

There's this wonderful line from a theologian named Dietrich Bonhoeffer, who got it in his head—he was a German—to leave England in 1944 to come back to confront Hitler. He was [executed] two weeks before the end of the war. He has this line, he says, "If you get on the wrong train, running down the aisle backward is not a solution. You have to get off the train." We created these programs, back in the sixties, seventies, eighties, nineties, that were the wrong programs. That's our train, and we tinker with them, but the problem's way back there and we're not getting off the train. There's this whole idea of the war on drugs. I mean, that is our longest war, and that war has more casualties than all other wars combined. We keep doing the same stupid things, and our great hope is that, now [that] white people are dying of heroin, [that] they might do something, which they won't. That's the thing. We're not willing to get off of that train because we're all experts on the train. We step off the train and now we have to open ourselves up to the problem and rediscover. Now we're no longer experts. If I had a PhD behind my name or two or three behind my name, I'm not getting off any fucking train. I'll ride that baby right into retirement.

ANDRE ROYO (REGINALD "BUBBLES" COUSINS): Sometimes you can't talk to [Ed Burns], because he truly believes the only way it's going to get better, the only way we're going to fix this planet, is they got to blow it up. The machine is too broken. You're trying to fix it from the inside, you're just wasting your time. It has to be burned down and rebuilt. That's how he feels. That shit is scary. I would call him every once in a while and talk to him about parenting. Parenting is rough, and I would want to hear from him what he thought about certain things. I would talk to him about politics. By the end of it, I'll have to take a shower. God damn, he would just jack me up. He's an awesome dude. I think a part of me, if I could work with anybody else again out of that whole cast, it'd be Ed Burns. I would love to do another show with him.

If you thought *The Wire* was slow, Ed Burns's show, if he had another show, it'd be even slower. He'll have a scene where somebody just walks. David Simon is cool, but he colorizes it up a little bit. I asked Ed, "What do you mean?" "Well, I would have that scene with McNulty just walking around the block." David Simon would be like, "I just need something to happen. I know that's what you want, but I need something to happen." Ed Burns was like, "Why? Something is happening. When he walks around the block and nothing happens, it shows that these two have nothing to do." He'll go into what he's trying to tell by the nothingness. You need somebody like David Simon to go, "Okay. That's fine. Instead of a whole hour of that, we'll do twenty minutes of that. How's that? Then something's got to happen." You need that extra something. Like comedians, you're trying to educate, but you got to do it with some sort of entertainment, otherwise people are going to turn it off. You need the balance. That was a powerful team between David Simon and Ed Burns.

While filming Frank Sobotka in Season 2, Chris Bauer stopped drinking, the longest he had gone without alcohol to that point in his adult life. "Forty days without booze made me think of how damn long Jesus was in the desert," Bauer said. "Now that I've gone without for over eight years, I realize what a grandiose and distorted association that was. I drank till I didn't. I'd love to play Frank Sobotka again with the part of my heart that has come back to life since I put down the drink. I would've been better, and they deserved better." A few other castmates battled addictions following the show. For some, the shadows their characters created followed them long after The Wire.

MICHAEL K. WILLIAMS (OMAR LITTLE): I was in a lot of darkness. I was in a lot of pain. I was in a lot of pain when I filmed Omar, a lot of excruciating, emotional, and mental pain. I tried to use that, [with] the character of Omar, as a way to exorcise that and to put it into that character, but instead, I allowed it to make it worse. My daily crisis, I was on my way to worrying about some things about my inner self. I got hemmed up by vanity. Motherfuckers calling me Omar on the street and "Oh, we love you." I was like, "Well, shit, this dude is more popular than me." When that Band-Aid came off, it was a really ugly bullet wound. I had to get real with all of that and grow up, basically. Just plain old-fashioned grow the fuck up.

JERMAINE CRAWFORD (DUQUAN "DUKIE" WEEMS): It really took me years. I think it was probably when I was twenty-one that I got my groove back, because I kind of went into a depression afterward. It was hard on me. It really was.

BRANDY BURRE (THERESA D'AGOSTINO): I just said, *I'm stepping back.* I still get really weird people writing things to me. They're like, "You were really great on the show." I said, "Oh, thank you." Then it's like, "Do you have any naked pictures that you can send me?" I'm like, "Really? Like, really?" I can't believe it. I shut all that down. Also, just seeing bad reviews. I wasn't ready for any of that. One bad review would knock me off my feet, even if there were one hundred good ones. I'd be like, "I don't want to see." This was right at the time in life when you could Google yourself. I'm on foot fetish websites, because there's weird people out there. My character isn't that crazy in the show or anything. I didn't like any of that. I didn't like any of that attention. I also didn't like the fact that the only roles I was being auditioned for were seminude, partly nude. I was just like, "I'm done. I did it. I did *The Wire.* What else do I need to do? It's not going to get any better than that."

GBENGA AKINNAGBE (CHRIS PARTLOW): That show changed my life, and I don't mean just because of what it did for my career, but who I am as a person. To this day, the people I go to and talk to when I have important matters have something to do with that show. Like Jamie [Hector]. I seek advice from George Pelecanos, Ed Burns. I freelance for *The New York Times.* I wrote a couple pieces. My first piece, the first email I got in the morning when my first piece was published, was from David Simon. These people are still very much a part of my life. They care.

One of my brothers on that show, Donnie [Andrews], before he passed, I went to the hospital to see him. I thank God that I was able to see him and be there for him while he was at the hospital. Donnie had affected so many people's lives. If there was ever somebody who had done a complete one-eighty with their life and show how beautiful we could be as human beings, it was Donnie. Donnie was the real Omar. Fran, his wife, I'm still in contact with Fran. These are just beautiful people that had gone through hell, some of them brought hell, then came out the other side just barely, and then affected so many people. What's great about my *Wire* family and what we were able to show and do is none of us are perfect. We've all been in it. We've all been good, bad. We've all been different sides of the story, the coin. But we're all on that journey of aspiring to just get to the next day and hopefully being a better person, making different decisions than the day before. That is perfect because that's what *The Wire* was, people just trying to get to the next day and aspire to make different choices than they did the day before.

ANDRE ROYO (REGINALD "BUBBLES" COUSINS): I can't shake him off. Bubbles will stay in me for the rest of my life because of the idea that I'm going to keep trying to be a better person. I'm going to keep trying to do the right thing. I think, for me, that's what I found to be the essence on how I played Bubbles, on what Bubbles was to me. Somebody that's going to keep trying to be his best self. I will never shake that. When people see me in other characters, they see that sense of, *He's so human. He's so real.* There's certain moments that I've been forced to question whether I want that in this business. For a couple of years, I couldn't work. They were telling me that they couldn't put me with another *Wire* actor because it was too iconic and people would start thinking about *The Wire.* This is back then. It's different now. Back then, I can't be seen with another *Wire* actor. There was a movie called *Snitch* that I wanted. They were like, "We want to give you this part. What part do you want?" I'm like, "I'll take that part." What happened to that movie? What happened was Michael K. Williams became the top dog and, "We can't have you two in the same movie." I was like, "Why?" "Because they'll start thinking about *The Wire.*" I'm like, "What are you talking about? You have two good actors." "No, you're Bubbles. You got to understand, you're Bubbles."

This is, again, how this business is sometimes. They would tell me, "People would rather believe that Bubbles is not acting. They would rather go, 'Wow, look at Bubbles's career now. Good for Bubs.'" They would rather believe that, than the actor played by Bubbles is now in other stuff. They don't want that. That's not a Hollywood narrative. A Hollywood narrative is, "Remember that junkie that they cast in *The Wire*? He's now working." I was like, "What's wrong with you people?" It's one of those backhanded compliments where people really thought, because David Simon was casting so many people from the neighborhood and giving people an opportunity, they just thought they found me. People were like, "Yo, I thought you were a real junkie they found and was now working." Mark Wahlberg was the first person. I saw him at an HBO party sometime. He's like, "You're doing a good job. Don't fuck up. Don't fall back on that shit." I'm like, "What are you talking about, man? I'm from the Bronx." "Shit, my bad." They meant it out of sincerity. They meant it out of you were like the real deal.

With that said, it's easier for somebody like Idris and Michael K., and Dom West. When you play a cop on TV, you got to understand, there's always going to be another cop show. Those people can stay working. Once you're known as a good cop, you play a good cop. You'll stay working because they'll always have cop shows. If Idris is playing this leader of this corner of a drug empire, he's playing a leader. He can be a president in a movie. There's always a dominant leading role for somebody to have that presence of power. Michael K. was the thug with the heart of gold. He played the thug so beautifully that he can always play a menacing type. There's always going to be other joints he can do. When you play a junkie, a downtrodden, hapless person, there's not that many characters on TV that they feel you can drop into. They don't like those type of characters to be series regulars on another show. It was hard for people to see or believe that I can portray another type, even though they said I portrayed a junkie so well.

It took a long time. That would start to affect me. The backhanded compliment is, I'm honored to have played that character that well because I'm honored to have brought people to not look at the downtrodden or the homeless or somebody down on their luck in a way of dismissal anymore. I can't help everybody, but they at least know that person right there, at least he's trying. He's a human being. For that, I will never shake off Bubs.

Now, I'm a man of fashion. I like clothes. My dad had a couple of stores in Harlem. I knew about clothes. In my own little sneaky way, every once in a while, I tried to make Bubbles have a little flair, a leather jacket. I think at one time I wore an Ed Hardy shirt with colors on it and dusted it up a little bit. People always get surprised in the beginning of the seasons when they saw me at parties and whatever. They were like, "Oh, my God." I know how to put on a suit. I like colors. That part of Bubbles, he's easy to shake off. Other than that, his essence will always be a part of my life forever.

DOMINIC WEST (DET. JIMMY MCNULTY): People haven't appreciated Andre as much as they should. No one's given him the role which would show the world how really great he is. He was great as Bubbles, but he's nothing like Bubbles. He's the funniest man I've ever met by far.

TRAY CHANEY (MALIK "POOT" CARR): I got pulled over a couple days ago by police for speeding. When he came to the window, I just looked at him, "Okay, officer, how can I help you?" He was like, "Yo, you're the guy from *The Wire*. You were speeding, but I'm going to give you a warning." I got that shit. I was like, "Yo, this is crazy." It's crazy man. The perks that come from such an awesome show.

J. D. WILLIAMS (PRESTON "BODIE" BROADUS): It's that strange, cock-your-head-sideways look. People are like, "You look so familiar." Police who don't get it right away always think they've arrested me. I have to convince police all the time that they have not arrested me.

GBENGA AKINNAGBE (CHRIS PARTLOW): Somebody brought [me and Jamie Hector] to meet Russell Simmons once at a party or something like that. The elevator doors opened, and there was Russell. I guess he was going someplace and we were going to meet him. It was like his breath stopped and he took a step back before he realized it was just us. I always forget the power of us being together because so many people have seen us together in certain circumstances, and it's usually not good.

By its final season, most television critics had belatedly come around to The Wire. *Emmy voters never did.* The Wire *is considered one of its biggest snubs. In its five seasons, the show received only two Emmy nominations for writing—for "Middle Ground," by David Simon and George Pelecanos, and the series finale's "–30–," by David Simon and Ed Burns. Neither episode claimed the award. The second season captured a Peabody Award, but the show would be comically overlooked by major award voters throughout its run. "It's like them never giving a Nobel Prize to Tolstoy," Slate's Jacob Weisberg described to the Associated Press. "It doesn't make Tolstoy look bad, it makes the Nobel Prize look bad." Simon never emphasized superficial accolades.* The Wire *had always been steeped in Baltimore, satisfied to tell the totality of its hometown story and unfazed by Hollywood's lure. But many who worked under him remain upset over the lack of recognition. "I'll be pissed off about it until the day I die," said Lance Reddick. "There's nothing to do about it. It's just what it is. Yeah, I'll always be angry about that." The disregard can be attributed to the dense plot and a story that voters could not relate to told by a cast that did not look like them.*

NINA K. NOBLE (EXECUTIVE PRODUCER): We got several [NAACP] Image Awards nominations and I attended the event several times and it was always so frustrating to me, because it wouldn't be our show. Take your pick of great minority actors and actresses. It was always the show that had the one Latina. The fact that we were so proud of the work that we were doing was always enough. It was never about the accolades from the outside.

CLAIRE COWPERTHWAITE (SCRIPT SUPERVISOR): How Hollywood treated the show, it was a metaphor for what I thought the country feels.

DENNIS LEHANE (WRITER): Look, we weren't unaware we were doing good work, don't get me wrong, but we weren't so egomaniacal to ever consider we were doing great work. But there seems to be the consensus in some quarters now that maybe we were. I have no idea if that consensus is correct, but, hell, I'll take it. I take no credit for it, mind you—it was David's and Ed's vision—but it was nice to be a platoon player on a championship team.

KWAME PATTERSON ("MONK" METCALF): You've just gotta chalk it up as maybe it was too black, in a sense. Yeah, that's pretty much it. There's no excuses. Numbers and every critic you can think of, that's all they can even talk about is how amazingly written that show was, how authentic the acting. It's just one of those things where, in our culture, we're used to it. Our projects don't get the critically acclaimed spotlight all the time like they should.

REG E. CATHEY (NORMAN WILSON): Life is funny. If I thought about that, I would lose my fucking mind. I would be in a home for the bewildered.

David Simon once equated why *The Wire* didn't get the kind of acclaim that it deserved was like if you have two neighborhoods and they're both the same socioeconomic levels. The houses are the same. The education and the people who live in the two neighborhoods are exactly the same. The only difference is seventy percent of one neighborhood is black and seventy percent of one neighborhood is white. The neighborhood with the seventy percent black is going to be thought to be inferior.

GEORGE PELECANOS (WRITER/PRODUCER): It doesn't really matter that we never won any awards or that not a lot of people watched us. What mattered was that over this period of almost twenty years now, is that it's still alive and that the best compliments we ever get is not, "I loved your show." It's happened to me several times, actually, when people have come up to me at book signings and stuff and said, "I became a teacher because of *The Wire*" or "I joined the Peace Corps because of *The Wire*." That, to me, is the highest compliment that you can get.

JIM TRUE-FROST (DET. ROLAND "PREZ" PRYZBYLEWSKI): You won't be surprised to hear that a lot of the people that take the time to stop me on the street and express their appreciation for the show and my character are people who are teachers now or were teachers or did Teach for America. To those people, I think that Season [Four], which a lot of people just enjoyed as really great television, they have a special appreciation for it, because it's such a rare example of their story being told in a truthful way.

DARRELL BRITT-GIBSON (DARIUS "O-DOG" HILL): I'm in LA, and this lady comes up to me. I'm in a conversation, and she sort of politely interrupts the conversation and she says, "You're on *The Wire*." Then, within five minutes, she's sobbing and she's telling me this story of how she is a schoolteacher and how Season Four ripped her apart because she said, "I teach those kids." She's sobbing, and everybody is kind of looking at the conversation, and I embraced her. In that moment, I said, "Oh my God, this is bigger than television."

Maria Broom grew up in Baltimore, exposed to the sum of its virtues, its warts. She depicted the drug-addicted Bunchie in The Corner *and* The Wire's *Marla Daniels, a councilwoman and the estranged wife to Lt. Cedric Daniels.* The Wire *had been off the air several years when unrest erupted over Freddie Gray's death. Broom reconvened with* several of her castmates at the behest of Sonja Sohn. They met with citizens in Baltimore and listened to their stories of injustices witnessed firsthand. "We wanted to know from them, 'What specifically were you doing?' What happened? What did you see?'" Broom said. The actors monologued the struggles onstage. "You got to see the actor from The Wire reading the words of the real person who gave us those words," Broom said. "It was very successful. People were impressed and kind of thrilled to see the actors in person, but also to have all the real people acknowledged. People were touched. People were moved by it."

The event continued the show's established spirit of philanthropy toward Baltimore during The Wire's run. "Coat drives, food drives, we did large fund-raisers to raise money for the Ella Thompson Fund," said Laura Schweigman. David Simon had featured Thompson in The Corner. A man raped and murdered her youngest daughter, Andrea Perry. Thompson tried transforming the tragedy into a positive by heading a recreation center that shielded youths from the often violent streets. She died in 1998 at the age of forty-seven, from a heart attack, while picking up donated computers. "We had a huge gala every year of The Wire, which, by the end of the show, had made five hundred thousand dollars for the Ella Thompson Fund," Nina Noble said. "We wanted to create an endowment through the Ella Thompson Fund, so that the recreation center could go on in perpetuity after The Wire was over. Every year, we'd give each actor a shoebox and we'd have them put items in it to auction off."

The altruism spread. A number of the actors volunteered campaigning for Barack Obama's presidential run. Sohn remained in Baltimore and became a pillar of the community. She created an initiative named ReWired for Change, which is devoted to rerouting the lives of at-risk Baltimore youths. In 2016, Wendell Pierce announced his plans to help restore Baltimore through an infusion of jobs and the development of a twenty-million-dollar apartment complex.

WENDELL PIERCE (DET. WILLIAM "BUNK" MORELAND): Baltimore is like a second home, and the thing I love about Baltimore is the fact that it reminded me of New Orleans so much—even though y'all don't know how to cook your crabs right. The people of Baltimore, I fell in love with. The city of Baltimore, I fell in love with. It became like a second home, and I can honestly tell you that some of the best days of my life, I look back on it, I was at my best, doing some of my best work, had so much joy in my life, being with the people doing that TV show. I would look forward to that six-month period every year.

That's why I wanted to stay connected. It felt like home. And with the images of the riots, it wasn't just some arbitrary streets that were burning. I knew exactly where people were. I felt like there but for the grace of God go I. I know those kids. I know the people that are involved. I know the police officers. It felt like that was my neighborhood. It felt like that was my city, just like New Orleans in the flood and Katrina. Twenty years from now somebody's going to say, "In Baltimore's darkest hours, what did you do, Mr. Pierce? In New Orleans's darkest hours, what did you do, Mr. Pierce?" I knew what I responded with in New Orleans. It was very clear. We had to rebuild our lives. We had to rebuild. I felt as though that was the same thing in Baltimore. The connection is the social justice movement of the twenty-first century is economic development. If we can look at China, if we can look at India as developing markets, we can look at the West Side, East Side, and see that these are developing markets, too.

Your greatest resource that you have in a democracy is its people. That's why I want to be a part of it. I have an idea. I really truly believe that the social justice movement of the twenty-first century is economic development. I can stop bullets with jobs. I met Ernst Valery, who is a young developer in Baltimore. As I was looking at different developers to help me in New Orleans, I built thirty houses in New Orleans to bring back my neighborhood, and I wanted to have a response to what I saw on television [during the riots]. I love the advocacy of the Black Lives Matter movement. To speak truths to power, make demands on power. To make the necessary institutionalized changes so that they will stop hurting and killing black folk, stop treating us as suspects. That is one front of it. The other front is: I believe that we need to make a monetary economic investment in our communities, because folks are dealing with the underground economy. We all know it. Some of the violence that comes along with dealing with the underground economy, that colloquialism is true, when people say, "I'm a street pharmacist." It's a silly joke now, but that's the truth. It's somebody just trying to say, "If I'm not going to get into one economy, I'm going to get in on another." A focus of that can be my contribution. What we're going to do is, first of all, let's create some jobs. The project that I'm doing, Station North, first of all, I wanted to do it in an artistic community, because I'm an artist. I don't want people to forget that about me. I hate when people say, "Oh, he's an activist." I'm not an activist. I'm an actor and an American that sees my communities [as] just as valuable as everybody else's communities and [who] has a belief that if we invest in our communities, we will have a great ROI, return on our investments.

With Ernst, I've discovered this project that I want to do. In Station North, we're building one hundred ten units. It's a twenty-five-million-dollar project now, one hundred eighty construction jobs that'll leave about thirty-five permanent jobs. Then we're going to have a developer's apprentice program. It's part of a thing called REDI, Real Estate Development Initiative. We're going to take folks and teach them how to be developers, pay them a stipend as we get properties, and go and develop the properties. As we complete the properties, they stay in our portfolio. That's one thing, but if they are refinanced or we sell them, then we take a portion of that profit and give it to one of the developer apprentices as an investment in their first project. That's how you create an economic engine.

Several years after finishing the show, Michael Kostroff was walking down a New York City street when a woman excitedly approached, having recognized him as the attorney from The Wire. *She wanted a lawyer, and her face fell when he responded that, no, he was just an actor. "She was excited by the possibility that I might actually be a lawyer, and she wanted to hire Levy, I guess," Kostroff said. Likewise, Steve Earle, a Grammy Award–winning artist, is often stopped by people who thank him for helping Bubbles combat his addiction. Many are unable to leave the show behind. Others are still being introduced to it. "People still think it's on, like, 'When is the next season coming out?'" said Melvin Jackson, who played Bernard. David Simon had achieved his objective (just not HBO's) of leaving the audience pining for more.*

TRAY CHANEY (MALIK "POOT" CARR): If David Simon said, "*The Wire* is coming back for Season Six," do you know what would happen to the world? Worldwide, it would be crazy.

BENJAMIN BUSCH (OFF. ANTHONY COLICCHIO): So many people want Season Six. They want to know what happens next. I think that both Ed and David have definitely said, "What happens next is what you imagine." That's the beauty of art that doesn't have a closure that television shows usually do. With *Law & Order*, you know within the first few minutes that you've got a criminal and you've got a half an hour to solve the crime, and they will. With *The Wire*, it's always the same question we all have when we finally become self-aware, which is, "How much time have I got?" That doesn't have an answer.

DAVID SIMON (CREATOR): Stories have a beginning, a middle, and an end, and there's other arguments to be had.

Works Cited

The interviews conducted for the oral history were all done firsthand. In some cases, I wanted to add quotes to the written passages from a particular moment in time. In those instances, the work is cited in the text. I also want to recognize a few books that proved instrumental in the creation of this one. Rafael Alvarez's *The Wire: Truth Be Told* contained David Simon's pitch letter to HBO and is home to a trove of insights concerning all things *The Wire*. Simon's *Homicide: A Year on the Killing Streets* and *The Corner: A Year in the Life of an Inner-City Neighborhood* (with Ed Burns) provided perspective on the creation of *The Wire* and are just damn good books. Lastly, Brett Martin's *Difficult Men: Behind the Scenes of a Creative Revolution: From* The Sopranos *and* The Wire *to* Mad Men *and* Breaking Bad, presented an intelligent dissection of not only *The Wire*, but also on the backgrounds of Simon and Burns.

Acknowledgments

Nearly every interview I conducted for this book included the subject vouching for the cast and crew of *The Wire*'s continued togetherness as a family. They remain a close-knit group today, another trait of the show's unique durability. I was a stranger hoping to gain enough trust to tell their intimate and important story. I needed a path, and I am eternally grateful that several key people provided a way in for me. My chief advocate became Alexa L. Fogel, the casting director with a discerning eye. To my extreme benefit, she saw value in this project. I'm not going to lie. Many of my initial emails and phone calls requesting interviews went unanswered or unreturned—to the point where I began doubting whether this book would be doable. People responded to Alexa. I leaned on her again and again and again. She helped facilitate interviews with Idris Elba, Wendell Pierce, Michael K. Williams, Dominic West, and many others. I was on the verge of wrapping up the book and had still not made much headway in interviewing Wood Harris. She took it on herself as a mission to get him for me and, of course, made it happen. Quite simply, this project would not have gotten off the ground without Alexa's unyielding assistance.

The same can be said of Reena Rexrode, the diligent assistant to David Simon, and Diego Aldana and Andrew Loane at HBO. They were always there to answer just one more email or phone call, expedite just one more interview request, or dig up one more old photo. Rexrode put me in touch with Simon's inner circle, including Nina Noble, George Pelecanos, and the elusive Ed Burns. At one point, she jokingly wrote that she felt as if she worked for Simon and me—except, in retrospect, she probably wasn't really joking. I am extremely thankful and indebted to them. Of course, this book would have been dead on arrival had David Simon declined to participate. He was giving with his time in entertaining my questions, many of which, I am sure, he has fielded countless times.

As much as I would like to take credit for it, this book was not my idea. The idea came from my wonderful literary agent, Daniel Greenberg, at Levine Greenberg Literary Agency. Daniel is the best out there. I would sign with him twice if I could. The same can be said for this book's editor, Nathan Roberson, at Crown Archetype, whom I did sign with, twice. Nathan was a wizard in wringing the excess out of *Boys Among Men*, a feat he capably duplicated in this book. And thank you to Tricia Boczkowski and Molly Stern for believing in this project.

I hoped to provide as many perspectives as possible from among those who experienced working on *The Wire*. A deep thanks to the many cast and crew members who participated in the interviews, many of whom also entertained follow-up questions. I'm mildly surprised that Burns, Pelecanos, Neal Huff, Andre Royo, and Bill Zorzi did not block my number after a while. Many of the talent's publicists, agents, and managers helped arrange the interviews, and I would like to thank all of them and in particular: Jake Attermann, David Belenky, Roger Charteris, Janet Dickerson, Raina Falcon, Shauna Garr, Alison Golanoski, Kenny Goodman, Michael Henderson, Mark Holder, Caitlin Hughes, Jessica Kovacevic, Matt Goldman, Shelby McElrath, Chris Schmidt, Scott Schulman, Maggie Schuster, Paul Alan Smith, Don Spradlin, and Nate Steadman. Michael B. Jordan agreed to be one of the first interviews for this book, an introduction made possible by my once boss and always mentor Bill Simmons. Knowing that I had an interview with Jordan already in the can with Bill's assistance sustained me through the early days of the unanswered interview requests, before Fogel descended like a superhero.

Another concession: I was one of the many shameful late converts among *The Wire*'s viewership. A journalism buddy, Stephen Clark, kept pestering me to watch this show. I was broke, fresh out of college, and did not have HBO at the time, but I finally gave in around the airing of Season 3. Thanks to Stephen for his persistence in introducing me to the show, and to Michael Becker, my roommate at the time, whom I would pester to watch just one more episode that evening after we had already consumed four or five in a row.

Long live *Grantland*, the home that allowed me to first experiment with oral histories, and a huge shout-out to Shea Serrano, the remarkably gifted writer and author who poured way more time and energy than I could ever have expected or hoped in marketing my first book. Some are just good people inside and out who help because it's what they do. Shea is one of those people.

In *Grantland*'s ashes, I was extremely fortunate to link up with an incredible unit at *Bleacher Report*. Thanks to Howard Beck, Rory Brown, Bill Eichenberger, Dave Finocchio, Shauntel Lowe, Dylan MacNamara, Matt Sullivan, Christina Tapper, and Joe Yanarella.

I deeply enjoyed my wife, Tanya, finally watching *The Wire* in full with me while I prepared to write this book. She quickly became a convert and proved more capable than me at catching on to the show's subtler parallels and themes. Thanks to her, as always, for her enduring love and support. She was pulled into this project as much as me, while being a mother, going through pregnancy, and working full time. I'm still amazed at all she accomplishes. Thanks to my family for your support: Mom, Michelle, Danielle, Matthew, Whitney, Dan, Dannen, Angela, George, Nicole, Jamaal, and Cadence. Danica and Jaxton, you guys are new to this world but already fill us with love and smiles. Lastly and certainly not least, thanks to my sons, Jayden and Aaron. Your laughs give me strength. Your joy brings me joy. All is for you.

Index